ANTHROPOLOGICAL PAPERS OF
THE UNIVERSITY OF ARIZONA
NUMBER 61

Ceramic Commodities and Common Containers

Production and Distribution of White Mountain Red Ware in the Grasshopper Region, Arizona

Daniela Triadan

THE UNIVERSITY OF ARIZONA PRESS
TUCSON
1997

About the Author

DANIELA TRIADAN, of Swiss nationality, was born in Bern and educated in Germany. She received her master's degree (1989) and her doctorate (summa cum laude, 1995) from the Freie Universität Berlin in American Archaeology and Anthropology, European Prehistory, and Ethnology. Dr. Triadan has conducted extensive research in the American Southwest and in Mesoamerica. From 1987 through 1992 she was a staff member of the University of Arizona Archaeological Field School at Grasshopper. She served as the assistant director of the San Estevan project in Belize and of various subprojects of the Petexbatún Regional Archaeological Project in Guatemala under the auspices of Vanderbilt University, and she is a co-principal investigator of the Aguateca Archaeological Project. In 1995 Dr. Triadan was appointed a material analysis postdoctoral fellow at the Conservation Analytical Laboratory of the Smithsonian Institution, where she continues chemical and petrographic analyses of ceramics.

Cover: Schematic drawings showing design characteristics of White Mountain Red Ware types (*see* Appendix A).

THE UNIVERSITY OF ARIZONA PRESS

Copyright © 1997

The Arizona Board of Regents
All Rights Reserved

This book was set in 10.7/12 CG Times.

∞ This book is printed on acid-free, archival-quality paper.
Manufactured in the United States of America

00 99 98 97   4 3 2 1

Library of Congress Cataloging-in-Publication Data

Triadan, Daniela.
Ceramic commodities and common containers : production and distribution of White Mountain red ware in the Grasshopper Region, Arizona / Daniela Triadan.
   p. cm. — (Anthropological papers of the University of Arizona; no. 61)
Includes bibliographic references and index.
ISBN 0-8165-1698-7 (pbk. : acid-free paper)
1. Pueblo pottery—Arizona. 2. Grasshopper Pueblo (Ariz.).
3. Pueblo Indians—Antiquities. 4. Pueblo Indians—Commerce.
5. Arizona—Antiquities. I. Title. II. Series.
E99.P9T74 1997
979.1'3--dc21   97-4567
                                                       CIP

To my father,

*Who, unfortunately, was not
given the time to take part
in this phase of my life*

Contents

PLATES

Following Page 16

FIGURES

TABLES

Foreword

Ronald L. Bishop

It can be argued that much of the archaeological "record" does not await discovery but rather is formed through archaeological activity that is influenced by the interests of the investigators, their backgrounds, questions, theories, and methodological approaches. And more often than not, a number of equally plausible alternative explanations can account for the patterns observed in materials that result from the behavior of past societies. Considering this potential for interpretative ambiguity, archaeologists have placed their theories and motivations under ever more explicit scrutiny; they also have evaluated the means by which information from the past is sought. Several techniques have come to archaeology from the natural and physical sciences that have the advantage of increasing the resolving power of the questions that are poised and often the complexity of the answers provided.

The use of natural and physical science techniques in archaeology stems not only from the strong ties to the natural historical and geological traditions of the nineteenth century out of which archaeology developed, but also from an appreciation of the role of empirical, objective data in archaeological interpretation. Determination of chronology, reconstruction of climatic conditions, determination of dietary regimens, and the characterization of archaeological materials are but a few areas of emphasis that benefit from scientific and technological developments and the specialists who apply them. Several of these analytical approaches developed out of the technological advances that followed World War II, and the practitioners of these techniques helped to contribute to the notion that a "more scientific" archaeology was possible. As interest grew in attempting a more behaviorally oriented understanding of past communities, there arose a greater appreciation for the evidence of variation in the study of cultural materials that could reflect changes or adjustments in social organization. New kinds of data could be used to explore such concepts as trade, exchange, specialization, social

interaction, and population movement. Among the different classes of archaeological materials, pottery has received the most analytical attention, with traditional considerations of chronology, context, typology, and style being supplemented by chemical analysis of ceramic pastes.

Ceramic materials have a long history of use in archaeology because of their durability and abundance and their ability to reflect spatial and temporal changes. Cultural practices involved in the preparation, use, and discard of pottery affect various measurable ceramic properties, and the objective characterization of these properties can contribute to the reconstruction of societal behavior involved in ceramic production and distribution. Although technological advances have resulted in both sensitive and precise analytical procedures for obtaining objective parameters that can be used to characterize archaeological pottery, investigations frequently provide little more than methodological description, failing to integrate the analytical data into archaeological interpretation. Even when viewed from a developmental perspective, many of the compositionally based ceramic investigations suffer from poor analytical protocols, insufficient (or absent) problem focus, and inadequate sample design. In the absence of sufficient understanding of the relationship of the pottery to existing archaeological knowledge, research is doomed to be carried out at a superficial level, no matter how detailed the analysis. Against the problems that plague the majority of previous compositional endeavors, Triadan's White Mountain Red Ware study stands in marked contrast.

The southwestern United States has extensive regional geological diversity, vast prehistoric riches, and a long history of archaeological exploration. It is a natural arena for the use of the analytical sciences to augment more traditional kinds of archaeological data. With decades of extensive ceramic recovery, questions pertaining to the ancient inhabitants tend to be at a much lower scale, permitting questions to be addressed at the intraregional as well as interregional level. Although this has increased the complexity of archaeological research, the findings can more realistically approximate the interactions of different social groups. It also means that the precision of the analytical techniques is sufficiently high to distinguish among subtle naturally or culturally induced patterns of compositional variation that occur in the archaeological pottery.

Focused on the Grasshopper region of central Arizona, Daniela Triadan's study of fourteenth-century White Mountain Red Ware makes a major contribution toward modeling aspects of prehistoric behavior in the southwestern United States at the time of Mogollon Pueblo aggregation. Through an intensive and systematic investigation of this pottery, she increases our understanding of this ceramic's compositional variation and leads us to conclusions regarding the sources of its production and subsequent circulation. Beyond such substantive contributions, however, this study is a striking example of interdisciplinary research and synthesis.

The differentiation of locally produced ceramics versus imported pottery is a basic objective of most sourcing projects. Commonly, as in the present study, a specific site or site cluster is the subject of attention. Yet all ceramic sourcing projects are, by their nature, regional in scope. Some threshold of compositional variation must be observed in the compositional data matrix that allows one to determine what is locally produced and what is not. While it is not always possible to identify firm boundaries for sources of resource procurement, compositional trends observed in the data can serve to differentiate among probable areas of production. This, however, is where many studies draw to a close, unfortunately just at the point when some of the most interesting questions can be probed. For example, if the pottery is determined not to be locally produced, where did it come from? Triadan's study addresses this question and draws on the techniques of materials analysis to place the ceramic compositional variation in the context of the compositional and technical variation of regional clays and sediments. A judicious use of petrographic examination of the nonplastic inclusions in the pottery assists in the interpretation of the observed chemical variation in the pottery. Through her analyses, Triadan places White Mountain Red Ware in a regional perspective.

This work clearly demonstrates the role of a well-formulated sample design as a prerequisite for robust interpretations of ceramic production and distribution. In designing her sampling strategy, Triadan has benefited tremendously from the many years of meticulous excavation at Grasshopper Pueblo and in the surrounding region carried out by Raymond H. Thompson, William A. Longacre, and J. Jefferson Reid. The extensive collections of well-provenienced and well-preserved pottery with good contextual information, combined with an abundance of whole and reconstructible vessels to inform on design variability, helped Triadan to focus the analytical effort. At the intrasite level, through her analysis of mortuary vessels, as well as at the regional level of Grasshopper Pueblo and neighboring sites, it can be clearly shown that archaeology must aid sourcing studies if the latter are to successfully address questions of archaeological interest. This is an interdisciplinary rather than multidisciplinary effort. This study also provides ample justification for the long-term and costly curation of excavated archaeological materials.

Triadan's White Mountain Red Ware study sets a new and demanding standard for the successful integration of ceramic compositional data within an archaeological context. It now joins the significant work of Suzanne De Atley, Veletta Canouts, Patricia Crown, Barbara Mills, and Nieves Zedeño, among others, who are proving that ceramic characterization studies are far more than demonstrations of "instrumental virtuosity." If pursued in a tightly integrated manner, they are, in fact, essential for the reconstruction of complex aspects of human behavior.

Preface

For more than a century, the study of ceramics has been a fundamental base for archaeological research and anthropological interpretation in the American Southwest. In this region sherds are well-preserved and abundant at prehistoric sites, and ceramics are perceived as being endowed with a host of behavioral information. Ceramics have been used to define cultural spheres (Anasazi, Mogollon, Hohokam), interaction, trade and exchange, and population movements, as well as sociopolitical and socioeconomic organization of prehistoric Southwestern peoples. A prerequisite to drawing meaningful anthropological inferences from the distribution of ceramics is to establish whether ceramics at a given site or within a given area were locally produced or whether they were intrusive. A thorough evaluation of the source or provenance of ceramics is therefore critical for any interpretation. Compositional analyses (chemical and petrographic) provide a systematic, analytical means to investigate the provenance of pottery.

The procurement of archaeometric data has almost become standard procedure in archaeological investigations, and during the last decade masses of compositional data have been compiled for the chemical and mineralogical characterization of ceramics. Rarely, however, have these analytical data taken center stage in archaeological publications. They are commonly relegated to appendices, if reported at all. In this monograph I present a systematic investigation of the production and circulation of a prominent Southwestern ceramic ware, White Mountain Red Ware, that was widely distributed throughout the northern Southwest in late prehistoric times. It is one of the few studies that integrate material analyses into archaeological research.

Among other decorated ceramics, archaeologists have frequently used the distribution of White Mountain Red Ware to develop models of late thirteenth- and fourteenth-century Western Pueblo sociopolitical and socioeconomic organization. Based primarily on stylistic analyses and the relative abundance of White Mountain Red Ware in site assemblages, researchers inferred that this pottery was manufactured within a relatively small, circumscribed area and that it was distributed from this area mainly via long-distance trade or exchange networks that may have involved controlled access to these ceramics. No systematic sourcing of White Mountain Red Ware had been undertaken in connection with these models.

The abundance of models of sociopolitical and socioeconomic organization that are based on ceramic distributions but the paucity of compositional research prompted me to carry out a large-scale compositional study on fourteenth-century White Mountain Red Ware to determine the sources of these ceramics and to investigate the mechanisms of their circulation. The research presented in this volume provides new data to assess prevailing models of late prehistoric puebloan social and economic organization.

The resolution of anthropological interpretations of compositional data is dependent on the sampling design and the quality of the archaeological information. Provenance studies are greatly enhanced if sampled artifacts are well-provenienced and have reliable context information. Extensive archaeological research in the Grasshopper region provided an exceptional data base for a large-scale ceramic sourcing study. During three decades of fieldwork, slightly more than one-fifth of Grasshopper Pueblo was excavated and numerous contemporary sites were recorded and surface collected. Excavations at Grasshopper Pueblo uncovered approximately 1,000 well-provenienced whole and reconstructible vessels, among them scores of White Mountain Red Ware and Grasshopper Polychrome, a late local copy of Fourmile Polychrome, the latest in the series of types within White Mountain Red Ware. Grasshopper Pueblo provided well-dated, large, in-situ assemblages, de facto refuse, and well-controlled site formation processes, and the long-term survey project in the area provided information on the regional distribution of decorated ceramics.

On the basis of these data, I implemented an encompassing research strategy. The whole vessel assemblage and ceramics from refuse contexts from Grasshopper

Pueblo provided the opportunity to determine if White Mountain Red Ware was locally produced at the settlement and to investigate the organization of ceramic production and consumption within a large, aggregated, late prehistoric community. In addition, I analyzed a large sample of ceramics from contemporary sites in the Grasshopper region and adjacent areas to define the source or sources of White Mountain Red Ware and to investigate its circulation. These analyses were augmented by a raw material survey and subsequent physical properties tests and compositional analyses of sampled source clays. As a result, the approach taken in this study provides new insights into the organization of ceramic production and distribution in the northern Southwest and into the processes of social reorganization that characterized the late thirteenth- and fourteenth-century Western Pueblo world.

The book begins with a discussion of the role White Mountain Red Ware played, and continues to play, in the reconstruction of Southwestern sociopolitical organization and a summary of the research objectives. Chapter 2 provides current environmental, geological, and archaeological information on Grasshopper Pueblo and the Grasshopper region. It includes a discussion of the occupational history of the pueblo and the regional settlement pattern, as well as a brief description of the ceramic assemblage at Grasshopper Pueblo.

In Chapter 3, I concentrate on the identification of the production source or sources of White Mountain Red Ware in east-central Arizona during the fourteenth century. After discussing briefly the principles of ceramic sourcing and the regional geology and evaluating the available natural resources, I describe the sampling procedures for the analyzed ceramics and the analytical methods used and then present the results of the compositional and petrographic analyses. I then investigate the role of White Mountain Red Ware at Grasshopper Pueblo in Chapter 4. In conjunction with the data obtained through the compositional and petrographic analyses, ceramics from household and mortuary contexts are analyzed to determine the production, distribution, temporal development, and function of this ware within the pueblo.

Next, I evaluate the production and distribution of local and imported White Mountain Red Ware in the Grasshopper region and adjacent areas in the mountains of east-central Arizona (Chapter 5). I discuss the organization of production and the circulation of the locally manufactured ceramics and present evidence that supports a differential regional distribution of imported White Mountain Red Ware. Lastly, Chapter 6 summa-

rizes the results of all analyses and discusses their broader implications with regard to traditional models of Southwestern sociopolitical and socioeconomic organization based on the distribution of White Mountain Red Ware.

Elemental concentrations for the analyzed ceramics are in Appendices C and D of Triadan 1995, available through University Microfilms, Ann Arbor. A copy of my doctoral dissertation, on which this volume is based, is on file in the Arizona State Museum Library and microfiches are filed at every university library in Germany. The data is also available on disk in the Arizona State Museum Archives.

Acknowledgments

I am greatly indebted to many persons who contributed their advice and skill to this research project, as well as to numerous institutions that provided essential financial support and research facilities. Foremost I would like to thank Prof. Dr. Berthold Riese and Dr. J. Jefferson Reid, who, through their enthusiasm and cooperation, made this German-American venture possible. I owe special thanks to Professor Reid for his exceptional support, guidance, and thorough advice during my stay at The University of Arizona. The faculty and staff of the Department of Anthropology welcomed me as a visiting scholar and provided invaluable help and needed facilities.

This research received funding through dissertation fellowships of the Deutscher Akademischer Austauschdienst (DAAD) and the State of Berlin (Nafög). Neutron activation analysis was provided through the University of Missouri Research Reactor (MURR) Predoctoral Internship Program in Archaeometry, funded by the National Science Foundation (DBS 9102016). A grant from the Agnese Nelms Lindley Foundation helped to initiate my research at Grasshopper Pueblo.

The University of Arizona Archaeological Field School at Grasshopper was located on land leased from the White Mountain Apache Tribe and the excavations proceeded under an agreement with the White Mountain Apache Tribal Council. I am grateful to the White Mountain Apache people for their interest in and encouragement of this program of scientific investigations and I deeply appreciate their hospitality. Apache crews were especially helpful in both the excavations at the site and the various archaeological survey projects undertaken in the Grasshopper region.

Support for the teaching program of the Archaeological Field School from the Advanced Science Seminar Program, Division of Graduate Education, National Science Foundation, began in 1964 and continued for eight years (GE–4601, GE–7781, GZ–22, GZ–397, GZ–745, GZ–113, GZ–1493, GZ–1924). In addition, several research grants for the study of prehistory at Grasshopper were awarded to the University of Arizona by the National Science Foundation (GS–2566, GS–33436, SOC–72–05334, SOC–74–23724).

During my stay in Missouri, Dr. Hector Neff and Dr. Michael Glascock showed extraordinary patience in teaching me the complexities of neutron activation analysis and multivariate statistics. The "meat" of this monograph is largely due to their efforts. I would also like to thank all the other staff members at MURR for their support during my four-month stay. Deb Bergfeld provided not only an, albeit sometimes leaky, roof over my head and became a good friend during this time, but also expertly analyzed my ceramic thin sections.

Dr. James H. Burton at the Laboratory for Archaeological Chemistry of the University of Wisconsin conducted the ICP analysis of a gruesomely large sample of sherds. Dr. Nieves Zedeño generously supplied her NAA data for comparisons, and our lively discussions of the implications of pottery production and circulation are ongoing. Charles Riggs did an outstanding job in computer-drafting the maps in my original manuscript. Dr. Michael Schiffer provided access to his Laboratory of Traditional Technology whenever the need arose. Dr. David Killick gave much appreciated advice concerning the petrography and let me use his laboratory to examine and photograph my thin sections. Discussions with Dr. Barbara Montgomery, Jeff Clark, Dr. Barbara Mills, and Dr. David Tuggle about the broader issues of the research helped to shape my final interpretations.

I thank Priv. Doz. Dr. Gerwulf Schneider and Prof. Dr. Ursula Thiemer-Sachse for their comments and frequent reviews of the original manuscript. Dr. Schneider provided advice concerning the material analyses throughout the course of this project. I am especially grateful to Prof. Thiemer-Sachse for her enthusiasm and support for a subject that is not very close to her own fields of interest.

I express appreciation to the expert staff of the University of Arizona Press, who helped to pull this volume together, and to Carol Gifford (Anthropology Department), whose tact, patience, and expertise as an editor cannot be praised enough. Most welcome has been the support for production costs kindly provided through the Grasshopper Publication Fund, Department of Anthropology, University of Arizona. Kathleen Hubenschmidt (Photo Archivist in the Arizona State Museum) assisted with the Grasshopper Field School photograph in Figure 2.4, which was printed by Museum photographer Ken Matesich. Dr. Nieves Zedeño skillfully translated the Abstract into Spanish. Dr. Ronald Bishop provided welcome comments and suggestions that helped to make the analytical part of the book more concise. Dr. Michelle Hegmon ably pointed out sections of the manuscript that needed clarification.

Michael Pfeiffer, dear friend and provider of the newest laser technology, patiently endured the biweekly forays into his home for yet another printout of sections of the original manuscript. In the dark hours, Laura Levi was always there with concern, encouragement, and advice. Takeshi Inomata not only donated considerable time to help revise the maps in this monograph, but suffered through all stages of the research, and without his patience, support, thoughtful comments, and love many of the "crises" would have been unbearable. Last but not least, I thank my family, who unwaveringly believed that this book could and would be done.

CHAPTER ONE

Ceramics in Modeling Prehistoric Behavior

The reconstruction of complex aspects of human behavior in prehistory, such as social and political organization and economics, is often based on the circulation of goods, artifacts in the archaeological record. Restricted access to and control of exotic and expensive trade goods, for instance, are interpreted as one factor in the emergence of social stratification in Mesoamerica (Pires-Ferreira and Flannery 1976: 288–289, 291–292; Rathje 1972; see also Drennan 1984 for a critical assessment). In turn, the distribution of locally produced, utilitarian artifacts may allow the reconstruction of the organization of production within prehistoric communities (Costin 1991). Obviously, different mechanisms were involved if raw materials or finished products were obtained over long distances (for example, obsidian from central Mexico that occurs in lowland Maya sites; Moholy-Nagy and others 1984) or if they came from a neighboring village or the next valley. Thus, to obtain behaviorally meaningful interpretations from the archaeological *provenience* of an artifact, its *provenance* needs to be considered. Early archaeological provenance studies (Damour 1865, 1866; Göbel 1842; Richards 1895; Shepard 1936, 1942) demonstrate that the sources of artifacts have long been an important concept of archaeological interpretation.

In areas of neolithic-level cultures, such as the American Southwest, pottery is the most abundant and best preserved class of artifacts. Consequently, the study of ceramics has long been a focus of archaeological research and anthropological interpretation. Southwestern archaeologists have used and continue to use ceramics to reconstruct prehistoric sociopolitical and socioeconomic organization. More specifically, analyses of Southwestern ceramics have provided inferences about cultural or ethnic affiliation (Colton 1953; Colton and Hargrave 1937; Gladwin and Gladwin 1934), political, cultural, and ideological boundaries (Adams 1991a; Adams and others 1993; Crown 1994; Graves 1994; W. Graves and Eckert, in press; Roney 1995; Upham 1982); demography (Haury 1958; Lindsay 1987; Zedeño 1994a), exchange and trade (Colton 1941; Deutchman 1980; Graves 1982; Hantman and Plog

1982), and community organization and interaction (Hill 1970; Kintigh 1985; Longacre 1970; Reid and Whittlesey 1982). All of these behavioral inferences are primarily dependent on the basic distinction of *local* from *nonlocal* (intrusive) ceramics in a given assemblage, in other words, an evaluation of their provenance.

MODELS OF WHITE MOUNTAIN RED WARE CIRCULATION

White Mountain Red Ware is a painted ware that presumably originated on the southern Colorado Plateau of the American Southwest. Carlson (1970: 1) describes White Mountain Red Ware as an arbitrary division of the Cibola painted pottery tradition. "This tradition is arbitrary in that types of black-on-white pottery which are as closely related historically to redware types as redware types are to each other are excluded by definition" (Carlson 1970: 1). The ware can be classified into stylistically different types that develop through time and occur from about A.D. 1000 to 1400. Vessels are generally characterized by a light paste, colors range from white to buff to light gray, and an orange-red, thick slip covers the whole vessel and is the hallmark of the ware. Designs are painted in black or black and white mineral paint on the red background (see Chapter 2, Plate 1, and Appendix A). White Mountain Red Ware vessels are predominantly hemispherical bowls.

During the thirteenth and fourteenth centuries A.D., White Mountain Red Ware was widely distributed in a large area of east-central Arizona (Carlson 1970: Figs. 14, 24, 28, 32, 38; Graves 1982: 319; Haury 1934: 129, Fig. 23). One of the most noticeable traits of White Mountain Red Ware vessels is the uniformity of vessel form and decoration throughout the area of occurrence during this time period. Because of its abundance in the assemblages of late Pueblo III and Pueblo IV period sites, its uniform appearance, and its wide range of distribution, various archaeologists have used White Mountain Red Ware for technological studies (Bronitsky 1986; De Atley 1986; Hawley 1938) and for modeling sociopolitical and socioeconomic organization of the northern Southwest (Carlson 1970; Lightfoot and Jewett 1984; Upham 1982; Upham and others 1981).

Carlson (1970) undertook a detailed study of stylistic and technological attributes such as design style and general paste characteristics of White Mountain Red Ware. He focused on its distribution and argued for the existence of an extensive long-distance trade network that spanned most of the Southwest during the thirteenth century (Carlson 1970: 103, 116). Carlson also suggested that population movements (linked to the abandonment of the Kayenta area) and "cultural interchange" between diverse peoples (migrants and resident populations in the destination areas) were factors in the development of late Pueblo III and Pueblo IV decorative styles on White Mountain Red Ware (Carlson 1970: 105, 109).

Graves (1982) concentrated on decorative design in his discussion of White Mountain Red Ware. Based on the relative abundance of the different White Mountain Red Ware types, he proposed that the production of White Mountain Red Ware was originally confined to a relatively small core zone (about 17,500 square kilometers or one-eighth the size of the distribution area) northeast of the Mogollon Rim and then shifted and expanded during the late thirteenth to early fourteenth century. Graves (1982: 335) also maintained that through time, White Mountain Red Ware spread out of the core area in increasing numbers and over greater distances in shorter periods of time. Yet, he saw no evidence to suggest that White Mountain Red Ware was locally produced at major Pueblo IV period settlements south of the Mogollon Rim, such as Grasshopper Pueblo, Point of Pines, or Kinishba. Graves (1982: 333) interpreted the distribution of this ware as evidence for an exchange network that signified social and economic relationships.

Upham (1982) and others (Upham and others 1981) used the distribution of White Mountain Red Ware, among other decorated ceramics, to develop a model of political alliances between settlement clusters on the southern Colorado Plateau during the fourteenth century. Upham (1982: 116, 119) postulated that exchange was a strategy for coping with the high-risk, high-diversity environment of the northern Southwest and suggested that "banking of nonlocal goods" (for instance, polychrome ceramics) was a means of risk management. In essence, White Mountain Red Ware ceramics were seen as valuable nonlocal trade goods that served as status markers (Upham and others 1981: 825, 828–829). Access to these vessels was controlled by managerial elites and they were distributed via formal exchange between polities or sets of polities (Cordell and Plog 1979: 420; Lightfoot and Jewett 1984; Upham 1982; Upham and others 1981).

Even though Shepard (1985: 336–341) had outlined as early as 1956 different factors that influenced the production and distribution of pottery (she approached this subject from the perspective of intrusive ceramics), for the last two decades trade and all forms of exchange have been the main explanatory framework for ceramic circulation (see, for example, Blinman and Wilson 1988; Douglass 1991; Doyel 1991; Earle and Ericson 1977; Fry 1980; Hegmon and others 1995; Toll 1991). It is thus not astounding that in the cited studies trade and exchange are viewed as the prime mechanisms in the circulation of White Mountain Red Ware. Very rarely, however, is any explanation offered of how this exchange worked and what was exchanged or traded for what. That exchange existed is an explicit assumption (Plog 1989: 131–132) and ceramic distribution and the presence of presumably nonlocal ceramics are interpreted as equivalent to exchange. Zedeño (1994a: 5–8, 14–21) has recently provided a detailed discussion of the different behavioral mechanisms that have to be considered in the investigation of ceramic circulation. She isolated three variables: the movement of pots, the movement of raw materials, and the movement of people.

Trade and exchange entail the concept that goods were produced at one place and then distributed to another, so the basic distinction between *local* and *nonlocal* is crucial. Accordingly, most archaeologists who used White Mountain Red Ware distribution for models of interaction and political organization explicitly inferred the locus of production of this ware and its subsequent distribution from this restricted production zone and then arrived at interpretations such as long-distance trade networks and political alliances. (The decorative uniformity of White Mountain Red Ware vessels established by stylistic analyses seemed to support the interpretation of a geographically restricted production zone.)

Whereas Carlson (1970) and Haury (1934: 131) saw the mountainous area south of the Mogollon Rim as the core area for White Mountain Red Ware (based on ceramic abundance), more recently archaeologists have argued that the ceramics were produced on the southern edge of the Colorado Plateau. Specifically, the Silver Creek area directly north of the Mogollon Rim, with its large fourteenth century pueblos such as Pinedale, Fourmile, and Showlow (type sites for White Mountain Red Ware) is an assumed source of production (Graves 1982: 322; Lightfoot and Jewett 1984: 61).

The determination of the production zone for White Mountain Red Ware is primarily based on abundance and stylistic and technological analyses rather than on compositional and mineralogical analyses of the ceramics. Upham (1982: 125–132) analyzed fewer than 45 White Mountain Red Ware sherds petrographically. Lightfoot and Jewett (1984: 41–44) submitted nine sherds to X-ray diffraction analysis. Using relative abundance, similarity in technology, and stylistic attributes to determine the locus of production and range of distribution is problematic, because they are not necessarily concordant with paste composition or resource procurement zones (Bishop and others 1982). Stylistic traits, for example, can occur on different ceramic wares and may have circulated much farther than pots. Pinedale style, which occurs on at least three different wares during the thirteenth century, is a case in point (Carlson 1982; Crown 1994). Zedeño (1991: 181–202, 1994a: 83–92) makes a detailed comparison of stylistic traits and the chemical composition of decorated wares.

Ceramic studies are often aimed at the reconstruction of complex mechanisms in prehistoric societies. Because the underlying principle involves the recognition of indigenous and intrusive ceramics, next to stylistic and technological assessments a thorough evaluation of the *sources* of the ceramics under investigation is crucial. Compositional analyses (chemical and petrographic) provide a systematic means to investigate the provenance of ceramics (Bishop 1994; Bishop and others 1988; Crown 1994; Zedeño 1994a). To evaluate the provenance of White Mountain Red Ware and the mechanisms involved in its circulation, I undertook large-scale chemical and petrographic analyses on White Mountain Red Ware ceramics from the Grasshopper region.

WHITE MOUNTAIN RED WARE IN THE GRASSHOPPER REGION

White Mountain Red Ware becomes a prominent decorated ware around A.D. 1300 at Grasshopper Pueblo (Fig. 1.1), a large fourteenth-century Mogollon settlement south of the Mogollon Rim in the mountains of east-central Arizona (Reid 1989). At the same time, this ware occurs in contemporary settlements throughout the Grasshopper region. Most abundant is the chronologically latest type of this ware, Fourmile Polychrome (Carlson 1970: 65–73).

In keeping with the assumption that White Mountain Red Ware was mainly a trade ware, researchers thought that this pottery was mostly imported into Grasshopper Pueblo and the surrounding region from north of the Mogollon Rim (Reid 1985: 171, 1989: 88–89; Whittlesey 1974: 105, 109). Zedeño (1991, 1994a) demonstrated that at nearby Chodistaas (AZ P:14:24 ASM), a small pueblo inhabited just prior to Grasshopper Pueblo, stylistically related decorated ceramics were predominantly imported.

Light-paste White Mountain Red Ware was probably manufactured from kaolinitic clays, and such deposits are located in cretaceous shales along the Mogollon Rim (Moore 1968: 72–73, Plates 1, 2). Clays south of the Rim are almost exclusively brown-firing or red-firing and no extensive kaolinitic deposits are known. The closest kaolinitic clay deposits occur about 34 km (21 miles) northeast of Grasshopper Pueblo (Moore 1968: 72–73, Plate 1). Also, Fourmile Polychrome vessels were portrayed as highly valued items and possibly social markers in the Grasshopper Pueblo mortuary context (Whittlesey 1978). From this perspective, Grasshopper Pueblo and the surrounding communities could be viewed as part of an extended trade network as proposed by Graves (1982) or an alliance system as outlined by Upham (1982) and others (Upham and others 1981).

However, research I conducted on the evidence of on-site ceramic production at Grasshopper Pueblo (Triadan 1989) challenged the inference that White Mountain Red Ware was primarily a trade item, imported into the mountains of east-central Arizona. Vessels with an atypical dark brown to dark gray paste, but with a perfect White Mountain Red Ware surface finish (Triadan 1989: 72), indicated that some White Mountain Red Ware may have been manufactured locally. Also, at Grasshopper Pueblo a decorated pottery type, Grasshopper Polychrome, occurs in considerable numbers. This type was traditionally interpreted as a (possibly late) local copy of White Mountain Red Ware (Whittlesey 1974: 105; Reid 1985: 171). A similar situation is reported for Point of Pines, where local copies of White Mountain Red Ware, named Point of Pines Polychrome, were found associated with the latest occupation of the site (Carlson 1970: 77–82; Wendorf 1950: 49).

RESEARCH OBJECTIVES

The primary goal of the research presented here was to investigate the production and circulation of White Mountain Red Ware in the east-central mountains of Arizona during the fourteenth century. More specifically, I sought to determine if the manufacture and dis-

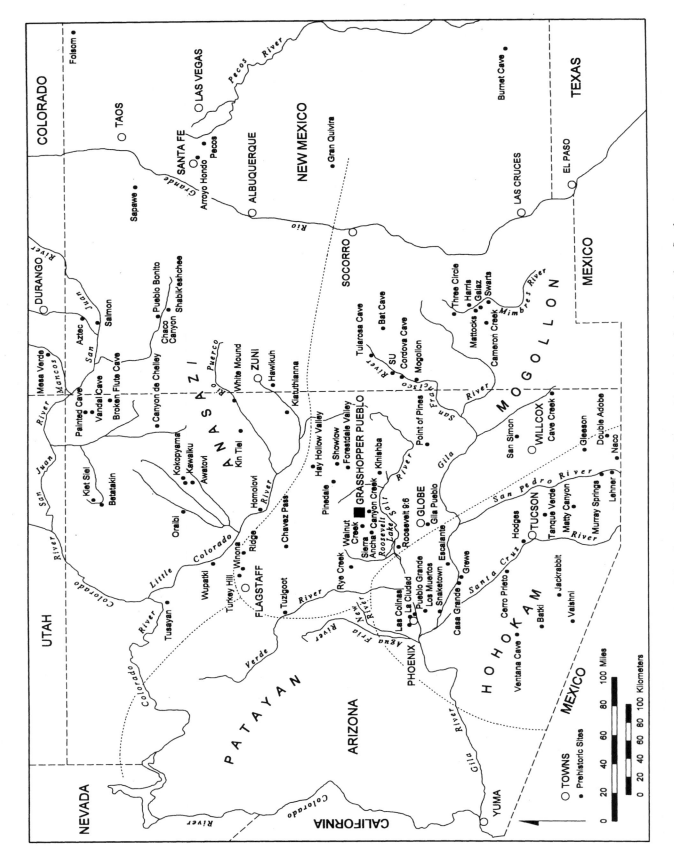

Figure 1.1. Location of Grasshopper Pueblo and other prehistoric sites in the American Southwest.

tribution of this ware was, as traditionally assumed, based in a restricted production zone and to assess consequent implications for social organization in the Pueblo IV period (A.D. 1300–1400). As mentioned above, some White Mountain Red Ware appeared to have been locally manufactured at Grasshopper Pueblo, suggesting that the production of these ceramics was much more localized during the fourteenth century than previously thought. This possibility leads to a re-evaluation of the sociopolitical and socioeconomic models based on the circulation of White Mountain Red Ware. Localized production in various regions stands in contrast to the idea that White Mountain Red Ware vessels were produced in a restricted area and were distributed through an extensive trade network, and it might contradict the notion of political alliances based on elite control of these ceramics. Instead, localized production may indicate that other factors, such as the movement of people, were involved in the wide distribution of White Mountain Red Ware during late Pueblo III and Pueblo IV times.

The fourteenth century or Pueblo IV period in the Grasshopper region is characterized by enormous aggregation and population increase. The number of habitation units grew tenfold, from about 200 rooms during Pueblo III times (A.D. 1150–1300) to about 2,000 rooms in Pueblo IV times (A.D. 1300–1400). Migration into the area, possibly prompted by a prolonged period of severe drought from A.D. 1276 to 1299, was certainly a major contributing factor to this aggregation (Fish and others 1994: 157–161; Reid 1989). Insights into the development of local production and distribution systems of White Mountain Red Ware in the Grasshopper region may lead to the reconstruction of patterns of migration into the area and thus partially explain the processes involved in the massive aggregation in this region during the early A.D. 1300s.

To understand the sociodemographic processes in the Grasshopper region, it is essential to establish if White Mountain Red Ware was locally produced at Grasshopper Pueblo, the largest settlement in the area. How is it spatially distributed within the site? Can it be associated with specific burial or residential groups? Was it a common household ware? If White Mountain Red Ware was locally produced at Grasshopper Pueblo, was it predominantly consumed at the pueblo or was it also distributed to the surrounding contemporary communities? If so, how far did Grasshopper-produced vessels circulate and can boundaries for their distribution be established? Also, was Grasshopper Pueblo the main supplier for these ceramics or did other pueblos in the Grasshopper region manufacture their own local versions of White Mountain Red Ware?

Resolving whether White Mountain Red Ware was produced at Grasshopper Pueblo opens new understandings of ceramic circulation in the east-central Arizona mountains. During the thirteenth century, Cibola White Ware, with pottery types stylistically similar to earlier types of White Mountain Red Ware, was almost exclusively imported into the Grasshopper region (Zedeño 1991, 1994a). Brown utilitarian wares, on the other hand, were produced locally within the late Pueblo III period settlements. Zedeño's results imply an exchange between local mountain people and people from the southern Colorado Plateau during the late A.D. 1200s or the movement of people between the plateau and the mountains, perhaps to exploit the montane resources on a seasonal basis (Zedeño 1991: 202–203, 1994a: 92-93, 1995). If during the fourteenth century White Mountain Red Ware was produced at Grasshopper Pueblo, then a change in the organization of production and distribution of decorated ceramics occurred during this time that may indicate a change in the mechanisms of pottery circulation in the region.

On an even larger scale, a reconstruction of the sociodemographic processes of the east-central Arizona mountains during the transition from Pueblo III to Pueblo IV times ties in with the dramatic reorganization of puebloan groups in the northern Southwest. From the early A.D. 1200s to the late 1400s, population dynamics of the northern Southwest were influenced by residential mobility, a series of migrations, aggregation, and abandonment that resulted ultimately in the configuration of the historical pueblos (Adler 1996; Cameron 1995; Cordell and others 1994; Dean 1969, 1970; Dean and others 1994; Euler 1988; Lipe 1995; McGuire and others 1994; Reid 1984, 1989; Rohn 1989; Spielmann, in press).

The aggregation in the Grasshopper region was part of the extensive population movements that occurred all over the Southwest in late prehistory, although Grasshopper was one of the last regions in east-central Arizona to experience the massive influx of people. In other areas of the mountains, such as the eastern part of the Fort Apache Indian Reservation and the Point of Pines region, and areas directly north of the Mogollon Rim, aggregation set in earlier, during late Pueblo III times (Haury and Hargrave 1931; Johnson 1965; Lowell 1991; Martin and others 1961; Mills, in press), when large, plaza-oriented pueblos with 100 rooms or more were built. By the early A.D. 1300s, most of the northern sites were abandoned and population aggregation culminated in an enormous increase in the numbers and size of settlements in the Grasshopper region and in the founding of very large pueblos like Grasshopper, Point of Pines, and Kinishba, with multiple plazas and more than 500 rooms. These large fourteenth-century pueblos seem to be the result of a series of movements of people from different areas in the Southwest (Haury 1958; Montgomery and Reid 1994). Increased contact of different groups starting in the late 1200s probably led to the mingling of cultural traits and ultimately to co-residence in large aggregated settlements such as Grasshopper Pueblo (Reid 1989; Reid and Whittlesey 1982). Thus, the sociodemographic developments in the Grasshopper region are an important part of a pan-Southwestern phenomenon, and a better understanding of these processes in this particular region contributes to the reconstruction of the population dynamics of the northern Southwest during the fourteenth century.

CHAPTER TWO

Grasshopper Pueblo and the Grasshopper Region

The Grasshopper region encompasses the research area of the University of Arizona Archaeological Field School on the western part of the Fort Apache Indian Reservation in east-central Arizona. In this context, "region" has no cultural meaning. The area is part of a geological transition zone between the Basin-and-Range province in the south and the Colorado Plateau in the north (Fig. 2.1; Peirce 1985). The northern boundary of this transitional zone is the Mogollon Rim.

Specifically, the Grasshopper region is the western part of a physiographic subprovince, the Carrizo Slope, which is described as a badlands topography incised into a south-southwest declining slope by generally south flowing streams (Moore 1968: 6–8). The streams drain into the Salt River and they have cut numerous canyons into the slope. Locally, the surface of the slope is modified by cliffs and benches that formed as a result of differential erosion determined by the varying hardness of the rock formations (Moore 1968: 6–8). Elevations range from about 915 m (3002 feet) at the Salt River to about 2257 m (7405 feet) above sea level (asl) along the Mogollon Rim.

The Grasshopper region itself is defined on the west by the steep canyons of the Oak Creek–Canyon Creek drainage and on the east by Cibecue Creek. The northern boundary is formed by the Mogollon Rim, the southern boundary by Salt River Canyon (Fig. 2.2). The area consists of varied and rugged terrain with large, flat, open areas between rolling hills and steep bluffs. The Grasshopper Plateau lies within this region, between Spring Creek and the Oak Creek–Canyon Creek drainage, and it extends north to Spring Ridge and south to the Salt River.

The modern environment of this area reflects the topographic diversity. The vegetation represents a continuum from the Upper Sonoran Desert of the Basin-and-Range province to the Evergreen Woodlands of the Colorado Plateau. Extensive grasslands and shrubs such as prickly pear and cholla cacti (*Opuntia* sp.), manzanita (*Arctostaphylos*), and juniper (*Juniperus*) are typical for the lower regions. Juniper and piñon (*Pinus edulis*)

woodlands mixed with open grasslands and stands of ponderosa pine (*Pinus ponderosa*) prevail in the intermediate elevations, with pines becoming denser and predominating the vegetation in the higher elevations.

The region is generally characterized by a biseasonal climate of cold winters and warm summers, with substantial fluctuations between the daily maximum and minimum temperatures. Precipitation follows this biseasonal pattern with rainstorms in late summer and early winter, succeeded by intermediate dry periods. Cibecue, about 17.4 km (10.8 miles) southeast of the Grasshopper Plateau and at an elevation of 1554 m (5098 feet), has a mean annual rainfall of 4727 mm (184 inches), often in the form of substantial snowfall during

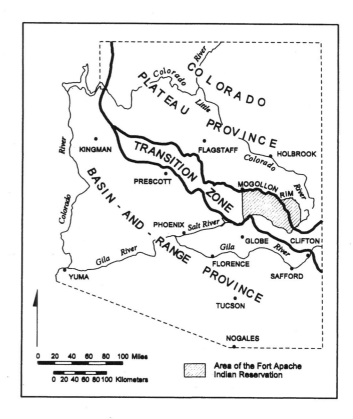

Figure 2.1. Physiographic provinces of Arizona.

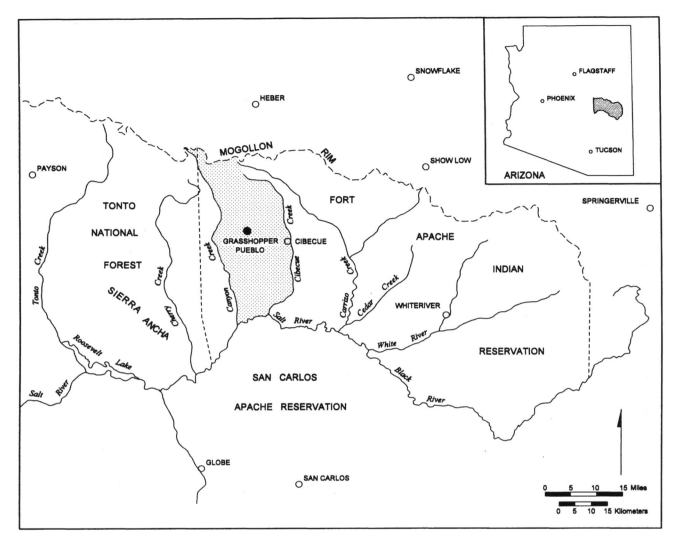

Figure 2.2. Grasshopper Pueblo and the Grasshopper region.

the winter. The mean average temperatures range from 2.3° to 23.3°C (36°–74°F) with normal extremes of –6.7° and 35°C (about 20°–95°F). The average length of the growing season (frost free days) is 140 days (Holbrook and Graves 1982: 5). Reconstruction of the prehistoric environment through dendroclimatology (Dean and Robinson 1982: 53–59), faunal analysis (Holbrook 1982b: 82; J. Olsen 1982: 63), and analysis of plant remains (Bohrer 1982: 102–105) suggests that slightly more favorable climatic conditions existed during the fourteenth century A.D. than exist today. Precipitation was probably somewhat higher, which would have resulted in perennially running streams and slightly higher summer temperatures, which in turn may have supported a longer growing season.

GRASSHOPPER PUEBLO

Grasshopper Pueblo (AZ P:14:1, Arizona State Museum Site Survey) is a large fourteenth-century Mogollon site (Reid 1989) located about 17.4 km (10.8 miles) northwest of Cibecue on the Grasshopper Plateau. The pueblo was built along the seasonally flowing Salt River Draw at an elevation of about 1829 m (6000 feet) asl (110°40'E, 34°5'N). The area around the site is fairly flat with mainly open grassland on an aggregation of alluvial soil. The terrain slopes up gently to the north, giving room to juniper-piñon parkland with scattered ponderosa pines (Holbrook and Graves 1982: 5, Fig. 2.3), and is dissected by Salt River Draw. The site covers an area of roughly 9.45 hectares (23.34 acres).

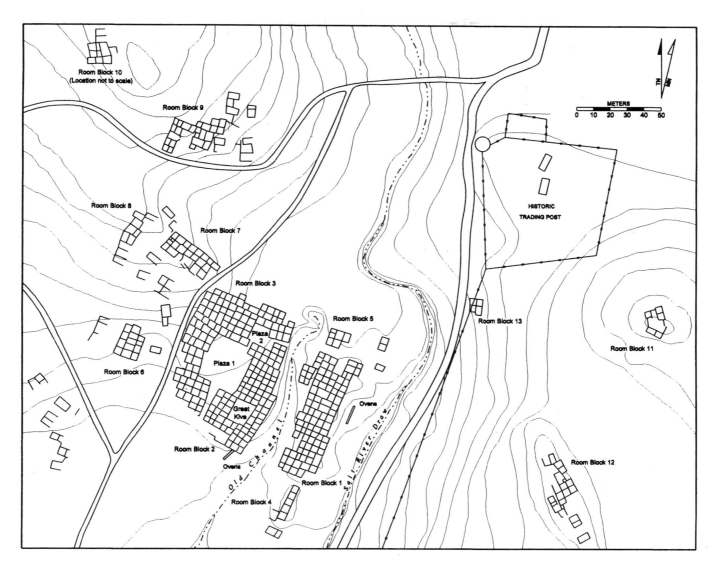

Figure 2.3. Plan of Grasshopper Pueblo.

The masonry pueblo consists of at least 500 rooms organized in three major room blocks, 10 small room blocks, and 15 small groups of rooms or single construction units (Fig. 2.3). Parts of the pueblo were two stories high. The three major room blocks are located along the old channel of Salt River Draw, with Room Block 1 on the east side and Room Blocks 2 and 3 on the west side of the stream bed. Room Blocks 2 and 3 enclose three plazas, one of which was converted into a Great Kiva (Plaza 3). These two room blocks are separated by two narrow corridors, the southern entryway to Plaza 1 and the eastern entryway to Plaza 2, which provided the only access to the interior of the complex.

The small room blocks are located either adjacent to the main settlement or are outliers on the surrounding slopes to the west, northwest, and east. These outliers are architecturally different from the main pueblo. They consist principally of low, stone-walled structures with an insubstantial ramada-style roof. Large U-shaped or three-walled enclosures are common.

ARCHAEOLOGICAL RESEARCH IN THE GRASSHOPPER REGION

The ruins of Grasshopper Pueblo were first visited by Walter Hough of the U.S. National Museum in 1918 (Hough 1930: 1). In 1919 Hough returned and con-

Figure 2.4. Room 97 at Grasshopper Pueblo, with numerous vessels on the floor.

ducted limited excavations at the site (Hough 1920, 1930: 1–6, 10–20). During this time the site was also briefly visited by Leslie Spier (Spier 1918: 384). The visits of Spier and Hough and Hough's excavations were the only archaeological investigations carried out at Grasshopper until 1963, when the Archaeological Field School of the University of Arizona moved to Grasshopper under the direction of Raymond H. Thompson. William A. Longacre became director in 1965, who was succeeded by J. Jefferson Reid in 1979. From 1963 until 1992, 30 consecutive field seasons were carried out by the University of Arizona Archaeological Field School in the Grasshopper region. Intensive excavations focused essentially on Grasshopper Pueblo; 107 rooms (Fig. 2.4) and Plaza 3 were completely excavated, and 665 burials containing 674 individuals were unearthed. Additionally, numerous test excavations were conducted in Plazas 1 and 2 and in extramural areas (Fig. 2.5). To reconstruct the devel-

opment of regional settlement, a long-term intensive and extensive survey program within the Grasshopper region was implemented (Reid and others 1996; Tuggle 1970) and the numerous Pueblo III period (A.D. 1150–1300) and Pueblo IV period (A.D. 1300–1400) sites of the region were recorded and mapped.

Extensive excavations also took place at Chodistaas Pueblo (AZ P:14:24 ASM) and at Grasshopper Springs (AZ P:14:8), and limited excavations were undertaken at AZ P:14:197, AZ P:14:12, and AZ V:2:12. The first three sites date to the late Pueblo III period, about A.D. 1250–1300, and directly precede occupation at Grasshopper Pueblo; the last two sites are contemporaneous with it. In addition, one room of a highly defensive Pueblo IV period hilltop site, AZ P:14:188, was partially excavated. Thirty years of multidisciplinary research produced a wealth of well-provenienced artifacts and a multitude of dissertations and publications on various aspects of Grasshopper prehistory (Table 2.1).

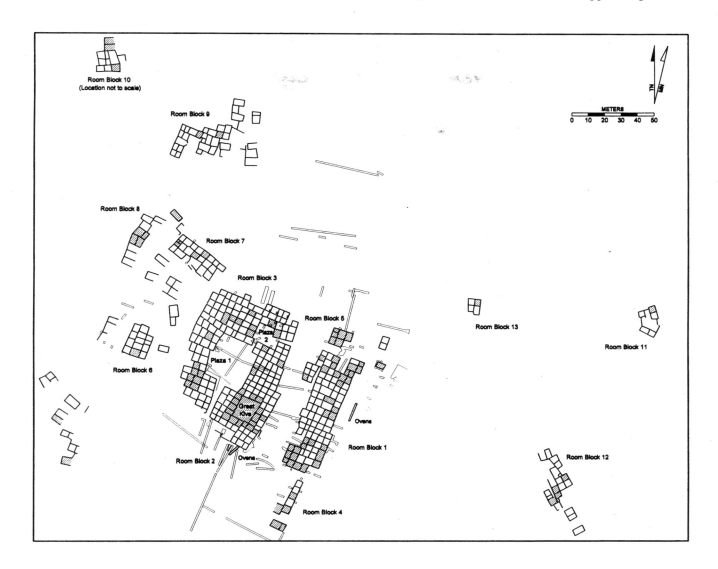

Figure 2.5. Areas of excavation at Grasshopper Pueblo.

OCCUPATIONAL HISTORY OF GRASSHOPPER PUEBLO

To establish the occupational history and construction sequence of Grasshopper Pueblo, more than 2,000 tree-ring samples were recovered during the ongoing fieldwork and submitted to dendrochronological analysis. Despite this large sample, only 164 specimens were datable and only one specimen provided a cutting date, A.D. 1263. Unfortunately, this sample came from one of a series of extramural, contiguous pit ovens east of Room Block 1 (Figs. 2.3, 2.5), and it probably represents stockpiling of wood. The rest of the dates have to be treated as date clusters (Dean and Robinson 1982: 46; Graves 1991), which makes exact dating of different construction phases of the pueblo difficult. However, analogous to a cyclical model developed by Reid (1973, 1989: 83–85; Reid and Shimada 1982: 15–18) that was based on Fortes' (1971: 1–14) model of the developmental cycle of domestic groups, settlement development at the pueblo can be described in four stages.

1. Establishment Phase
    (A.D. 1275–1300)
2. Expansion Phase
    (A.D. 1300–1330)
3. Dispersion Phase
    (A.D. 1330–1355)
4. Abandonment Phase
    (A.D. 1355–1400)

**Table 2.1. Multidisciplinary Research in the
Grasshopper Region**
(Partial listing)

Research	Sources
Formation of the archaeological record	Montgomery 1992, 1993
Prehistoric:	
Climate	Dean and Robinson 1982
Environment	Holbrook 1982a, 1982b, 1983
	J. Olsen 1982
Paleobotany	Bohrer 1982; Kelso 1982
Fauna	McKusick 1982
	J. Olsen 1980, 1982, 1990
	S. Olsen 1968, 1982
	Olsen and Olsen 1970, 1974
Migration, Population movement	Longacre 1975, 1976
	Reid 1973, 1989
	Zedeño 1994a, 1995
Settlement pattern	Reid 1984, 1989
	Riggs 1994
	Sullivan 1980
	Tuggle 1970
Interregional exchange	Graves 1982
	Whittlesey 1974
Regional exchange	Tuggle 1970
Ceramic production and circulation	Crown 1981
	Montgomery and Reid 1990
	Triadan 1989, 1994
	Van Keuren 1994
	Whittlesey 1974
	Zedeño 1991, 1994a
Craft specialization	Triadan 1989
	Whittaker 1984, 1986, 1987
Room function and household organization	Ciolek-Torrello 1978, 1984, 1985, 1986
	Ciolek-Torrello and Reid 1974
	Reid and Whittlesey 1982
	Rock 1974
Ethnicity and sociopolitical organization	Reid and Whittlesey 1982
	Whittlesey 1978
Human adaptation	Ezzo 1993
	Lorentzen 1993
	Reid 1973
Diet	Ezzo 1991, 1992, 1993, 1994
Health and disease	Berry 1985
	Hinkes 1983
Osteology	Birkby 1973, 1982
	Fulginiti 1993
	Shipman 1982
	Sumner 1984

NOTE: Additional bibliographic overviews are given in Longacre and Reid 1974; Longacre and others 1982; Reid 1974, 1989; and Thompson and Longacre 1966.

Riggs (1994) recently undertook an architectural study to determine expansion episodes at Grasshopper Pueblo. He was able to refine the chronology for individual construction events within the pueblo and his results supported Reid's community growth model (Riggs 1994: 87–88). Riggs divides settlement growth into three periods: Growth Period 1 is equivalent with Reid's Expansion Phase and dates from about A.D. 1278 to 1325–1330. Growth Period 2 equals Reid's Dispersion Phase and dates from about 1325–1330 to 1345–1355. Growth Period 3 in general parallels Reid's Abandonment Phase and dates from about 1340–1350 to 1375–1400 (Riggs 1994: 65–88).

Establishment Phase

Reid (1973: 124–126, 1989) states that the main pueblo at Grasshopper developed from seven separate core construction units in the three major room blocks, each ranging in size from 5 to 21 rooms (Reid and Shimada 1982: 16; Riggs 1994: 44). A review of the date clusters for the early rooms suggests that construction in all three room blocks started around A.D. 1300 (Dean and Robinson 1982: 46; Graves 1991: 106–107). Walls that underlie some of the masonry and some late Pueblo III period pottery indicate an earlier occupation of the site. However, because this earlier settlement was almost obliterated by the fourteenth-century construction, it is not well documented.

Expansion Phase

From about A.D. 1300 to 1330, Grasshopper Pueblo expanded rapidly into its basic configuration of three major room blocks enclosing three plazas (Fig. 2.3; see also Riggs 1994: 44–48). Available dates suggest that the roofed southern corridor was built around 1320 and that during this time Plazas 1 and 3 were in use. Additions of rooms to Room Blocks 2 and 3 joined isolated earlier construction units toward the north and started to delineate Plaza 2, probably after 1320. Room Block 1 expanded mainly west during this phase (Riggs 1994: 44–48). Toward the end of this period, possibly as late as 1347 to 1360, Plaza 3 was roofed and converted into a Great Kiva. Reid (1973: 126–129, 1989: 83; Reid and Shimada 1982: 17) estimates that the conversion of Plaza 3 into a Great Kiva took place around A.D. 1330. Dean and Robinson (1982: 47–48) interpret the construction of the Great Kiva as the latest dated event in the life of Grasshopper Pueblo. The latest dates from the Great Kiva range from 1321vv–1347vv (Dean and

Robinson 1982: 48). Graves (1991: 108) argues for construction between 1347 and 1360 based on the estimated loss of outer rings for these timbers.

Dispersion and Abandonment Phases

Settlement dispersion is difficult to trace at Grasshopper Pueblo. However, Reid thinks that the establishment of other large settlements in the Grasshopper region during this time, such as Canyon Creek (AZ V:2:1 ASM), resulted from the dispersion of the population at Grasshopper Pueblo, possibly shifting toward a more seasonal use of canyon environments (Reid 1973: 129–131; Reid 1989: 85; Reid and Shimada 1982: 17–18). Most of the outlying low-walled room blocks at Grasshopper Pueblo were probably constructed after A.D. 1340. The much more ephemeral construction of the habitation units in the outliers may indicate both a dispersion of offspring from the population residing at the main pueblo and a more seasonal use of the environment around the pueblo. Riggs (1994: 50–53) demonstrates that construction in the main pueblo during the Dispersion phase decreased considerably.

During the Abandonment Phase only a few, mostly single room, units were added to the main pueblo (Riggs 1994: 52–57). The process of abandonment was probably gradual over a period of some 40 years, culminating in the total abandonment of the community and, indeed, the whole region around A.D. 1400 (Reid 1973: 132–133, 1989).

SETTLEMENT PATTERN IN THE GRASSHOPPER REGION

As mentioned above, the fourteenth century in the Grasshopper region is characterized by enormous settlement aggregation, a trend that is observed in other parts of the mountainous region of east-central Arizona as well (Kintigh 1985, 1996). During late Pueblo III times, only a relatively few, small, dispersed settlements were present in the area, the largest containing 20 rooms (Reid and others 1996; Tuggle 1970). For the whole area, habitation units numbered around 200, but this number increased ten-fold to about 2,000 rooms in the Pueblo IV period. Next to Grasshopper Pueblo, which was the largest community in the region, 7 pueblos with more than 50 rooms each were established, the nearest 4.6 km (2.8 miles) and the farthest 16.2 km (10 miles) from Grasshopper (Fig. 2.6). Additionally, numerous small settlements with 20 to 40 rooms were built. Though changes in subsistence strategies (Welch 1991)

may have caused some population growth, an increase of living space of this magnitude over such a short time span cannot be explained by population growth alone (Longacre 1975, 1976). Migration into the area was most likely a major contributing factor (Ezzo 1991: 122–125, 1993; Price and others 1994; Reid 1973, 1989: 80-81). Longacre (1976: 182) and Graves (1991: 110) argue for migration from settlements *within* the region, but the population throughout the Grasshopper region was sparse during late Pueblo III times (Reid and others 1996; Tuggle 1970). Migration from *outside* the region must have been an important factor for this massive settlement aggregation and population increase.

By the end of the fourteenth century, Grasshopper Pueblo and the surrounding region were completely abandoned, as were the other areas of the east-central mountains of Arizona. Rapid aggregation, a phase of relatively short consolidation, and subsequent total abandonment within a large geographic region happened in a surprisingly short interval of about 100 years. This is by no means an isolated phenomenon. Similar events of rapid population aggregation, short-lived occupation of substantial villages, and subsequent abandonment have periodically taken place elsewhere in the Southwest (Dean 1969, 1970). In the east-central mountains of Arizona, the fourteenth century A.D. is characterized by a high mobility of people that may be linked to the abandonment of some of the Anasazi homelands to the north around A.D. 1300 (Dean 1970: 158-161).

THE CERAMIC ASSEMBLAGE AT GRASSHOPPER PUEBLO

Parallel to settlement aggregation in the Grasshopper region, a rapid replacement of predominantly black-on-white pottery with black-on-red pottery and polychrome vessels is documented for the late Pueblo III to early Pueblo IV transitional period (Montgomery and Reid 1990). This ceramic trend occurred more or less simultaneously all across the northern Southwest (Carlson 1982; Crown 1994; Hays 1991; Kintigh 1985; McGuire and others 1994; Smith 1971). Although the utilitarian wares stayed the same (essentially brown corrugated and small amounts of brown plain), the preference in decorated ceramics changed substantially, and the diversity and variability of decorated ceramics increased considerably (Zedeño and Triadan, in press). The decorated ceramic assemblage at Grasshopper Pueblo consists primarily of White Mountain Red Ware (Carlson 1970), Roosevelt Red Ware or Salado Polychrome (Gladwin and Gladwin 1930; for Grasshopper Pueblo, see Mayro

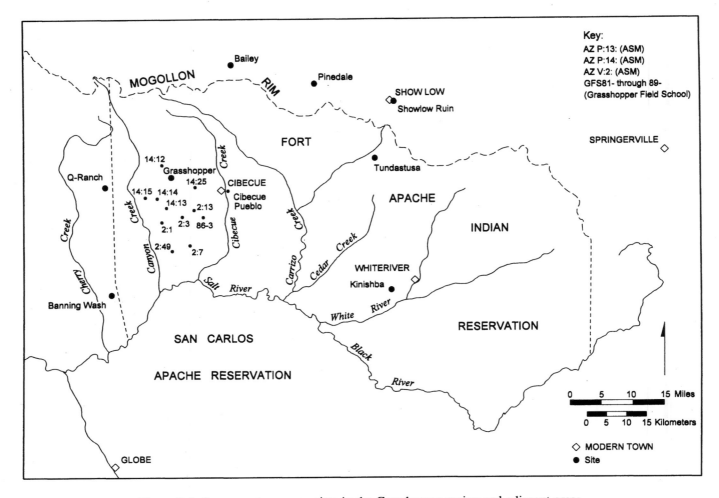

Figure 2.6. Large contemporary sites in the Grasshopper region and adjacent areas.

and others 1976), and Grasshopper Polychrome (Whittlesey 1974). Cibola White Ware (mostly as water jars; Colton 1956; Colton and Hargrave 1937), Cibicue Polychrome (Haury 1934; Mauer 1970), some Kinishba Polychrome (Baldwin 1938a), Salado Painted Corrugated and Salado Painted Plain, and a red-slipped ware make up the rest of the assemblage. Because both White Mountain Red Ware and Grasshopper Polychrome are the focus of this research, they are described here in more detail.

White Mountain Red Ware

White Mountain Red Ware is characterized by a light, relatively fine tempered paste, and its hard, orange-red fine slip is its most distinctive feature. Vessels are completely coated with the slip. Paste color ranges from white to light buff to light gray (Munsell Color 7.5 YR 7/, 2.5 YR 5/, 2.5Y 7/, 5YR 3/2, 10 YR 8/1). The red background of the vessels is primarily decorated with geometric designs executed in black or in black with fine white outlines. Both the black and white paint are derived from mineral pigments. The black paint is usually composed of manganese or copper carbonates (for example, malachite or azurite; De Atley 1986; Haury and Hargrave 1931: 65; Hawley and Hawley 1938: 16, 20, 26; Shepard 1939: 220, 222, 1942: 220) and an organic base. Kaolinite is used as pigment in the white paint. Hemispherical bowls (Plate 1) constitute the predominant vessel form (87.2% of the whole and reconstructible White Mountain Red Ware vessels recovered from Grasshopper Pueblo), but jars occur in small numbers.

White Mountain Red Ware is differentiated into a sequence of chronologically distinct ceramic types that date from about A.D. 1000 to 1400. The two earliest types, Puerco Black-on-red (1000–1200) and Wingate Black-on-red (1050–1200) have bowl interiors that are decorated in black-on-red in Holbrook, Puerco, Wingate, and Tularosa styles. The decoration extends to the rim of the bowl. Bowl exteriors are undecorated (Carlson 1970: 7–17). Wingate Polychrome (about A.D. 1125–1200) is characterized by either an overall white exterior slip with broad red designs, contrasting red and white areas on the exterior, or broad red designs .that are directly applied onto the unslipped exterior (Carlson 1970: 27).

St. Johns Black-on-red and St. Johns Polychrome (A.D. 1175–1280) are most abundant during the early A.D. 1200s. Both have black-on-red interior designs, predominantly in Tularosa style (Carlson 1970: 29–41). Whereas the exterior of St. Johns Black-on-red is undecorated, St. Johns Polychrome has isolated motifs in broad white lines on the red-slipped exterior.

Pinedale Black-on-red and Pinedale Polychrome are the most common types during late Pueblo III period times (Carlson 1970: 47–57). Bowl interiors are decorated in Pinedale style, in black-on-red or black-on-red with white framing lines; the decoration extends to the rim. Polychrome bowl exteriors exhibit isolated black motifs with white framing lines.

During the fourteenth century or Pueblo IV period, White Mountain Red Ware vessels were mainly polychrome, classified as Cedar Creek Polychrome and Fourmile Polychrome (Carlson 1970: 57–73). Cedar Creek Polychrome is a transitional type between Pinedale Polychrome and Fourmile Polychrome. Bowl interiors of this type are still decorated in Pinedale style, whereas bowl exteriors are decorated in typical Fourmile fashion, with one or two black bands framed by thin white lines and parallel thin white filler lines between them (Carlson 1970: 57–65). Cedar Creek Polychrome was relatively short-lived and produced in limited quantities. Only a small amount of it occurs at Grasshopper Pueblo, which suggests that vessels of this type were not used beyond about A.D. 1320 in the Grasshopper region. Carlson (1970: 61–63, 65) originally suggested an interval from 1300 to 1375 for this type.

Fourmile Polychrome (Carlson 1970: 65–73) is decorated in Fourmile style and represents a radical departure from earlier White Mountain Red Ware design concepts. Designs on bowl interiors are asymmetrical, often figurative, and focus on the center of the bowl. They are executed in black-on-red, partially outlined in white. The center design is usually separated from a black rim band by a broad band of red background. As described for Cedar Creek Polychrome, the exterior is most often decorated with a series of parallel fine white lines be-

tween two black bands below the rim. Fourmile Polychrome was the predominant type of White Mountain Red Ware at Grasshopper Pueblo and in the Grasshopper region. Thus, I suggest a time frame from about A.D. 1300 to 1400 for Fourmile Polychrome in this area. Carlson (1970: 69–71, 73) proposed a slightly more restricted interval from 1325 to 1400 for Fourmile Polychrome.

Showlow Polychrome (Carlson 1970: 73–77) is basically a variant or subtype of Fourmile Polychrome. Most Fourmile jars are classified as Showlow Polychrome. Bowls have an all or partially white-slipped interior. Showlow Polychrome spans the same time interval as Fourmile Polychrome. Appendix A provides a schematic overview of the White Mountain Red Ware types that occur at Grasshopper Pueblo. (A detailed description of the different types and the technological and design characteristics of White Mountain Red Ware are presented in Carlson 1970.)

Grasshopper Polychrome

Grasshopper Polychrome is interpreted as a locally made imitation of Fourmile Polychrome (Whittlesey 1974: 105). It is easily identified by a very dark gray to black, coarsely tempered paste and a chalky, pinkish red slip. Designs are painted in black carbon paint with yellowish white outlines; the white paint was probably derived from burned limestone (Hodges 1981: 157; Triadan 1989: 55). Vessel surfaces are usually heavily abraded and eroded, sometimes even spalled. Because carbon paint was used for decoration, original firing temperatures for Grasshopper Polychrome had to be fairly low, below 750°C (1382°F; Rice 1987: 88), causing the poor preservation of the vessels. Refiring experiments on Grasshopper Polychrome ceramics suggested an original firing temperature below 700°C (Triadan 1989: 69). Hemispherical bowls are the predominant vessel form (Plate 1) and represent 89.44 percent of the whole or reconstructible Grasshopper Polychrome vessels recovered from Grasshopper Pueblo. Jars occur infrequently (Plate 1).

Although most Grasshopper Polychrome vessels are copies of Fourmile Polychrome, some are imitations of another type, Kinishba Polychrome (Baldwin 1937: 4, 1938a; Cummings 1940: 87, Plates 26, 27). The decorative color scheme on Kinishba Polychrome is almost an inversion of Fourmile Polychrome; vessels have a light buff slip with black designs outlined in red (Plate 1). Paints are based on mineral pigments, and the design motifs are similar to Fourmile Polychrome. As Baldwin (1937: 4) noted: "The form and structure of the designs are much like those on Four-Mile Polychrome, and this type probably represents an outgrowth of it" (Baldwin 1938a: 24, Plate 1). The Grasshopper Polychrome vessels that are copies of Kinishba Polychrome have a chalky buff slip with black designs outlined in red. The black paint is also carbon, and the slip and paint of these vessels are normally as eroded as are the surfaces of vessels that are copies of Fourmile Polychrome. The distribution of Grasshopper Polychrome seems to be restricted mainly to the Grasshopper region.

Ceramic Analyses

The three decades of archaeological research in the Grasshopper region resulted in an extraordinary wealth of artifacts and archaeological data. Besides tens of thousands of sherds, more than 1,000 well-provenienced, whole and reconstructible vessels were recovered at Grasshopper Pueblo. Furthermore, during the long-term survey large quantities of ceramics were collected systematically and under controlled conditions at sites in the surrounding region. These ceramic assemblages provided not only the material for large-scale compositional analyses but also the opportunity to evaluate the behavioral mechanism involved in ceramic production and distribution.

I submitted a representative sample of White Mountain Red Ware and Grasshopper Polychrome vessels and some additional sherd samples from Grasshopper Pueblo to petrographic and compositional analyses to establish if White Mountain Red Ware was locally produced at the settlement. The whole vessel assemblage was also used for intrasite temporal seriation. Ceramics in household debris and floor assemblages of late abandoned rooms (Ciolek-Torrello 1978; Reid 1973: 114–118) were analyzed to investigate the frequency and function of White Mountain Red Ware and Grasshopper Polychrome in domestic contexts. The spatial distribution of these ceramics within the site, including burials and households, was analyzed to examine if they were associated with specific burial or residential groups. Surface material from controlled surface collections at Grasshopper Pueblo was analyzed to establish the distribution and variability of decorated ceramics, to establish discard patterns, and to allow comparisons with surface material from surrounding contemporary sites. Ceramics from contemporary sites within, and from large contemporary pueblos adjacent to, the Grasshopper region were included in the compositional analyses to investigate the organization of production and distribution of White Mountain Red Ware in areas south of the Colorado Plateau. Most of these samples came from controlled surface collections. These analyses and their behavioral implications are described in detail in the following chapters.

CHAPTER THREE

Sourcing Fourteenth-century White Mountain Red Ware

Archaeologists are able to determine the geographical source or provenance of pottery through chemical and mineralogical characterizations of the raw materials used in its production, predominantly natural clays. The mineralogical and chemical compositions of clays are determined by the geological formations from which the clays weather and, depending on the presence or absence of certain geological strata, they may differ from region to region. Clays, then, reflect both their geologic and geographic origin. Primary or residual clays tend to mirror the parent rock and may contain significant amounts of rock inclusions. Because they have been transported, secondary or sedimentary clays are normally much finer and better sorted than primary clays; often sedimentary clays consist of a mixture of materials from different origins.

The chemical composition of clays does not change significantly through firing. Theoretically, chemical profiles of pottery can be related to chemical profiles of source clays. However, the process is complex because potters often alter raw materials by adding nonplastics (temper) or by mixing different clays together (Arnold 1985; Rye 1981). Therefore, the ceramic pastes used to form vessels rarely reflect a "pure" source clay, as the addition of nonplastics alters the concentrations of certain elements within the pastes (Bishop 1980: 50–55; Bishop and others 1982: 295; see also Elam and others 1992; Neff and others 1988, 1989).

The mineralogical and chemical compositions of ceramics can be determined through physical and physico-chemical analyses. Mineralogical analysis in the form of petrography concentrates on the identification of the nonplastic inclusions, because clay minerals themselves are too small to be identified by petrographic microscope. Individual clay minerals, such as kaolinite, are only visible through a scanning electron microscope (SEM). Although clay minerals can be determined non-optically by X-ray diffraction analysis, the crystalline structure of clays is destroyed by firing, unless the firing temperatures are low. Because most pottery is fired

above these temperatures, identification of clay minerals in fired ceramics by X-ray diffraction is difficult (Rice 1987: 385; Shepard 1965: 82, 1985: 19–20, 147–148). However, above about 900°C (1652°F) clay minerals form new silicates, called high temperature minerals, if the high temperatures are held long enough (Rice 1987: 90). Clay minerals can be identified through these high temperature minerals and X-ray diffraction analysis may be useful for the characterization of clays used in pottery fired at high temperatures (Rice 1987: 385–386). Through petrography, the nature and quantity of temper can be discerned.

The chemical composition of ceramics can be qualitatively and quantitatively determined by physico-chemical analyses such as X-ray fluorescence, atomic absorption, inductively-coupled plasma emission spectroscopy, or instrumental neutron activation. Varying amounts and concentrations of elements can be determined, depending on the techniques used. All of these techniques are bulk chemical analyses, meaning everything in the pottery is analyzed, the natural clay as well as the temper that may have been added. Through elemental analyses, chemical profiles of analyzed ceramics are established.

Ceramics with similar chemical profiles form a compositional group. According to the so called "provenience postulate," the compositional difference *between* sources is greater than variation *within* a source (Bishop and others 1982: 301; Weigand and others 1977: 24). Thus, distinct compositional groups are commonly interpreted as being derived from different sources. Under this postulate, different compositional groups may reflect the use of different source materials or indicate different production loci. (The potential problems of temper and other paste preparation effects are not considered in this assumption.)

To move beyond the mere compositional or material distinction of ceramics, two comparative approaches are normally used to investigate the actual provenance of pottery: (1) comparison to the chemical composition of *raw materials* from geological resource procurement zones (Bishop and others 1982: 276; Rands and Bishop 1980) and (2) comparison to the chemical composition of *ceramic reference groups.*

Because of cultural behavior involved in paste preparation, matching ceramics to source materials is often difficult. However, if ceramic compositional groups can be correlated with the elemental composition of raw materials, a strong case for ceramic production within a specific resource procurement zone is established. The scale of interpretation is dependent on the geological diversity of a region, the sampling strategy used to obtain the raw materials, and the strength of the clay signature in the ceramics. In an area of geological homogeneity, interpretation beyond the regional scale may not be possible. To determine a specific production locus, the geological conditions have to be favorable and sensitive analytical methods must be used. The determination of individual production loci may be possible through trace-element analysis when the material comes from a geological zone that is sufficiently diverse. If a specific clay associated with a prehistoric site can be linked with some probability to a ceramic compositional group, the manufacture of those ceramics at that site can be argued convincingly.

A ceramic reference group consists of a group of ceramics with identical or similar chemical composition from a context securely associated with ceramic production (Schneider and others 1979), such as unfired pottery or wasters of a specific ware associated with a kiln. Obviously, the higher the number of samples with similar composition from a known context, the better the argument for a specific reference group. Unknown individual samples or compositional groups can be compared with established reference groups, and if they match compositionally, their provenance is thus determined.

Unfortunately, favorable circumstances for establishing compositional reference groups are rare or nonexistent in the American Southwest (Sullivan 1988; Triadan 1989: 5–6), and pottery provenance studies predominantly depend on matching ceramics to raw materials. However, if the pottery of a region is systematically analyzed and compositional groups can be identified, and if they can be correlated with local sources, then those compositional groups can be used as ceramic reference groups in the future.

REGIONAL GEOLOGY

Geological diversity is one factor to consider when evaluating research aimed at the sourcing of ceramics.

Clays are formed by weathering from geological formations. The type of parent rock determines the formation of specific clays. The more diversity in the geology of a region, the more variety can be expected in source clays. Moreover, nonplastics in the form of crushed igneous rock are frequently used as tempering agents. These igneous formations can be highly localized and unique for a specific area.

Ceramic sourcing often entails the identification of the locale of ceramic production. However, in an area of broad geological uniformity, it is extremely difficult to determine loci of ceramic manufacture other than on a regional scale. With this in mind, the following discussion of the geology of Grasshopper and the surrounding regions provides important background information for the interpretation of the mineralogical and chemical data of analyzed ceramics from these areas.

The mountainous area encompassed by the Fort Apache Indian Reservation is roughly divided into four physiographic subprovinces: the Canyon Creek–Salt River Canyon area, the Carrizo Slope, the White Mountain area, and the Bonito Prairie area (Fig. 3.1; Moore 1968: 6–8). These subprovinces are not only topographically different, but also notably distinct in their geology.

Canyon Creek–Salt River Area

The Canyon Creek–Salt River area includes the deep canyons of the Canyon Creek–Oak Creek drainage and the Salt River and the lower portions of their tributaries at the western and southwestern edge of the reservation (Fig. 3.1). Outcrops of the oldest geological formations of the reservation are present, consisting of Older Precambrian granitic and related intrusive, igneous rocks and a greenstone-metadiorite complex. Although only exposed in this area, similar rocks presumably form the basement of the entire reservation (Moore 1968: 19). Immediately overlying these Older Precambrian igneous rocks are Younger Precambrian sedimentary rocks. Extensive faulting occurred during Younger Precambrian times, preceding or accompanying an intrusion of diabase that occupies portions of the fault planes. The diabase is the youngest Precambrian unit, intrusive into all preexisting rocks. The volume of injected material is substantial and about equivalent to the volume of the Younger Precambrian sedimentary rocks deposited in the area.

The major structural feature of the Canyon Creek–Salt River area is a roughly north-south striking fault extending more than 64 km (40 miles). Two major move-

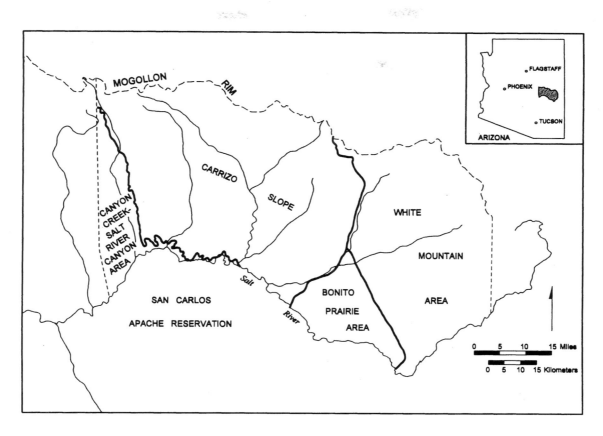

Figure 3.1. Physiographic subprovinces of the Fort Apache Indian Reservation.

ments seem to be associated with this fault. The first movement raised Pennsylvanian beds in the west block as much as 549 m (1800 feet). The second movement raised Cenozoic rocks in the east block almost 396 m (1299 feet), which led to a net displacement of Pennsylvanian rock of about 153 m to 244 m (500 to 800 feet). The early episode of movement was post-Pennsylvanian and possibly younger, but definitely older than the Cenozoic rocks disrupted during the later movement. The second episode of movement occurred later than the Cenozoic formations (Moore 1968: 26). Topographically, a steep escarpment resulted that runs along the east side of the Oak Creek–Canyon Creek drainage. In the southwestern part of the area, some Quaternary or Tertiary conglomerates were deposited on top of Older Precambrian basement rocks (Plate 2).

Carrizo Slope

The Carrizo Slope extends east from the Canyon Creek escarpment to the White River and south from the Mogollon Rim to the Salt River (Fig. 3.1). It is characterized by mostly Paleozoic sediments. Precambrian rocks cropping out in the Canyon Creek–Salt River Canyon area extend under the Carrizo Slope and, as stated above, probably form the basement of the entire area of the reservation. To the north, near the Mogollon Rim, the Upper Paleozoic formations are overlain by unnamed Cretaceous sandstones and shales. Cenozoic "Rim Gravels" consisting of consolidated gravel and conglomerate rest on top of Cretaceous and Permian formations along the Rim. To the south, the Rim Gravels cap Pennsylvanian sediments on mountains and ridges such as Spotted Mountain, Blue House Mountain, Bear Butte, and Cibecue Ridge. Some small andesitic to basaltic flows and basaltic plugs and dikes, mostly overlying the Rim Gravels, form the tops of these prominent mountains and ridges in the southern part of the Carrizo Slope (Plate 2).

The area around Grasshopper consists of Pennsylvanian and Pennsylvanian–Permian marine sediments (Plate 2), mostly sandstone and limestone mixed with some softer shales and siltstones. Grasshopper Pueblo is located on the contact of the Pennsylvanian Naco Formation and the Pennsylvanian–Permian Supai Formation. The upper part of the Naco Formation is a zone

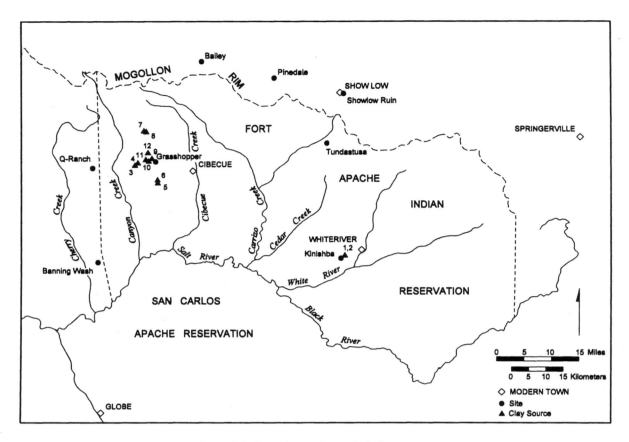

Figure 3.2. Locations of sampled clay sources.

of gray limestone and shales that weather light brown. The change from Naco to Supai is gradual, and the contact with the Supai Formation is arbitrarily drawn at the top of the gray limestone. The lower member of the Supai Formation consists predominantly of red sandstone and reddish brown mudstone and siltstone. The Naco Formation covers a large part of the Grasshopper region. The Supai Formation is extensively exposed throughout the reservation and forms much of the surface of the Carrizo Slope (Plate 2).

White Mountain and Bonito Prairie Areas

The White Mountain and Bonito Prairie subprovinces form the eastern part of the reservation (Fig. 3.1). This part of the reservation is basically monolithic. Clastic sediments and volcanic rocks were deposited on Paleozoic and Mesozoic sediments. Basaltic andesite flows, agglomerate, aggregates of pyroclastic materials, and some tuffs cover the Tertiary sediments, outcrops of which are visible only along the western edge of the volcanic field. Locally, dikes and plugs, filling the orig-

inal vents or orifices through which volcanic materials extruded, form ridges and buttes (Moore 1968: 79–80). Younger Tertiary basaltic flows and cinder cones are present in the northern part of the White Mountains, and in places they overlie the andesitic rocks (Plate 2).

In sum, the geology of the reservation is heterogeneous and can be divided clearly into three major, distinct geological areas (Plate 2). This geological variability facilitates pottery provenance studies, because localized sources of different tempering materials and a variety of locally distinct clays can be expected in such a diverse geological environment.

RESOURCE EVALUATION

To evaluate pottery production in the Grasshopper region, raw materials were sampled and submitted to physical properties tests, petrographic analysis, and chemical characterization. The locations of the clay sources I sampled are indicated in Figure 3.2. Earlier, as part of her doctoral dissertation project, Nieves Zedeño conducted a raw materials survey around Cho-

Table 3.1. Source Clays, Tempering Materials, and Pigment from the Grasshopper Region
(1991 Raw Material Survey)

Survey No.	Sample No.	Provenience	Material	Description
91-1	1	Kinishba Ruin	Clay	Light orange-beige
91-2	2	Kinishba Ruin	Clay	Light orange-beige
91-3		Kinishba Ruin	Sand	
91-4		NW of 3 Way Tank	Sand	
91-5	3	NW of 3 Way Tank, Road 011	Clay	Red
91-6	4	3 Way Tank, Road 011	Clay	Dark gray-brown
91-7		Schoolhouse Point, Roosevelt	Sand	
91-8	5	South peak of Spotted Mountain	Clay	Dark brown
91-9	6	North peak of Spotted Mountain	Clay	Dark brown
91-10		Oak Creek	Sand	Specular hematite
91-11		Oak Creek	Sand	Quartzite
91-12	7	North Spring Creek	Clay	Yellow-brown
91-13	8	North Spring Creek	Clay	Yellow-brown
91-14	9	Grasshopper Pueblo	Clay	Brown
91-15	10	Grasshopper Tank No. 2	Clay	Dark olive-brown
91-16	11	South of Mud Tank	Clay	Gray
91-17	12	1 Mile Tank	Clay	Dark olive-brown
91-18		Limestone Canyon	Limonite	
91-19		Oak Creek Ranch	Diabase	Yellowish-gray
91-20		Oak Creek Ranch	Diabase	Dark gray

NOTE: Sample numbers indicate clays on which physical property tests were performed and identify the clays on the distribution map (Fig. 3.2).

distaas Pueblo (AZ P:14:24 ASM), a small, late Pueblo III period site located about 1.6 km (1 mile) northeast of Grasshopper Pueblo. During the 1988 through 1990 field seasons, she surveyed an immediate catchment area of about 7 km (4.3 miles), mostly along stream beds. Furthermore, she located clay-bearing deposits outside the immediate vicinity of the site (Zedeño 1991: 99–100, 1994a: 43–44).

As Zedeño's research was concerned with light-paste Cibola White Ware, the emphasis of her survey was directed toward the availability of gray-firing or white-firing clays. However, she did not find suitable light-firing clay sources in the area. The locally available source clays fire red or brown. In contrast, my study investigated whether decorated pottery was produced at Grasshopper Pueblo with these dark-firing clays, and if so, to what extent.

Raw Material Survey and Sample Collection

To assess the availability of suitable pottery resources, I undertook an additional clay survey in 1991. Clay samples of approximately 2 kg were obtained from various locales within a radius of about 7 km (4.3 miles) around the site (Fig. 3.2), following Arnold's (1985: 50) definition of resource procurement zones.

For the survey, I walked the area intensively, especially along stream beds. I obtained a few samples, such as the specimens from Spotted Mountain and upper Spring Creek, by intentionally targeting clay-bearing deposits. One sample from Grasshopper Pueblo came from a clay-bearing alluvial stratum directly underlying the site. Additionally, I collected five samples of sands from stream beds, two samples of weathered diabase, and one sample of limonite that possibly represent prehistoric tempering agents and a pigment respectively. All clay samples consisted of secondary, sedimentary clays, predominantly from stream banks and road cuts. In addition to the samples collected from 1988 to 1990 by Zedeño, I obtained 20 samples of clays and tempering materials (Table 3.1).

These source clays and tempering materials were subsequently subjected to physical property experiments, petrography, and chemical characterization. Zedeño conducted neutron activation analysis and weak-acid inductively-coupled plasma spectroscopy (ICP) on her source clays and on a representative sample of archaeological clays (Zedeño 1991: 112; 1994a: 52–53, 115–125). I submitted an additional 16 clays, including one yellow-slip clay from a room at Grasshopper Pueblo, to petrography and to neutron activation analysis.

Physical Property Tests on Clays

To evaluate the workability and firing performance of the sampled clays, I conducted a variety of physical property tests. These tests provided a simple but systematic means to assess if the clays could have been used for making pottery.

In 1989, Nieves Zedeño and I performed an original series of tests with a representative sample of Zedeño's source clays and clays from Room 113 at Grasshopper Pueblo (Triadan 1989: 57, Table 4; Zedeño 1991: 101–103, Table 5, 1994a: 45–50, Tables 6.1, 6.2). Subsequently, I conducted physical property tests on the clays obtained through the 1991 survey, including some clays from recent excavations at Chodistaas Pueblo (AZ P:14:24) and Grasshopper Pueblo respectively (Table 3.2 lists clays analyzed in 1989 and 1993).

Table 3.2. Analyzed Clays

Sample No.	Provenience
Archaeological clays analyzed in 1989	
FN 621	AZ P:14:1, Grasshopper Pueblo, Room 113
FN 802	AZ P:14:1, Grasshopper Pueblo, Room 113
FN 854	AZ P:14:1, Grasshopper Pueblo, Room 113
FN 907	AZ P:14:1, Grasshopper Pueblo, Room 113
FN 1223	AZ P:14:1, Grasshopper Pueblo, Room 113
Source clays analyzed in 1989	
89-1	AZ P:14:24, Chodistaas Pueblo, Room 10
89-2	AZ P:14:24, Test Pit 88-12
89-3	About 3 miles south of Grasshopper
89-4	Spring Creek
89-5	Chediski Farms
89-6	Carrizo Creek
89-7	Canyon Butte
89-8	Hop Canyon
89-9	Forestdale Valley
Source clays analyzed in 1993	
1	Kinishba Ruin
2	Kinishba Ruin
3	NW of 3 Way Tank, Road 011
4	3 Way Tank, Road 011
5	South peak of Spotted Mountain
6	North peak of Spotted Mountain
7	North Spring Creek
8	North Spring Creek .
9	Grasshopper Pueblo
10	Grasshopper Tank No. 2
11	South of Mud Tank
12	1 Mile Tank
13	FN 154, P:14:1, Grasshopper Pueblo, Room 414
14	FN 206, P:14:1, Grasshopper Pueblo, Room 420
15	AZ P:14:24, Chodistaas Pueblo, Room 18

NOTE: FN = Field number.

Workability

Two physical characteristics of unfired clays were measured to obtain information on the workability of the clays: *plasticity* and *drying shrinkage*. Clays are composed of minerals that are ordered in layers or sheets. Because of this structure, clays are able to adsorb water between the layers and they become plastic and malleable. Upon loss of this noncrystalline water through drying, the clay body shrinks, becomes hard, and retains its latest shape.

One of the most common assessments used to obtain comparable data on the working range and plastic limits of a clay is measuring its *water of plasticity*. A clay's percentage of water of plasticity (%WP) equals the weight percentage of water required to develop optimum plasticity in a dry clay (Rice 1987: 62). Table 3.3 shows the water of plasticity of several clay types. Two tests were performed to measure the water of plasticity (Rice 1987: 61–63). During the first test, water was added to a standard amount of clay powder (50 g) until the resulting mass just started to become workable. The amount of added water was recorded. More water was added until the clay mass started to become sticky, and the additional amount was again recorded (Table 3.4). As 1 cc of volume equals 1 g of weight, the amount of water used can be directly converted into weight percentages (Table 3.4). The two quantities represent the range of workability from initial plasticity to stickiness; the higher the range of workability, the more versatile the clay (Rice 1987: 60–63). In general, fine clays require more water to develop plasticity than coarse clays, as they have more particles per unit volume and a more extensive pore or capillary system. However, the range of plasticity thus obtained is not an absolute measure, because the evaluation of initial workability and stickiness is highly subjective. This subjectivity is partially overcome when one person conducts all the tests.

Table 3.3. Water of Plasticity of Several Clay Types

Clay Type	%WP
Washed kaolin	44.48–47.50
White sedimentary kaolin	28.60–56.25
Ball clays	25.00–53.50
Plastic fire clays ·	12.90–37.40
Flint fire clays	8.89–19.04
Saggar clays	18.40–28.56
Stoneware clays	19.16–34.80
Brick clays	13.20–40.70

NOTE: After Nelson (1984: 322) and Rice (1987: 62).

Table 3.4. Plasticity of Tested Clays

Sample No.	%WP (Test 1)	Weight (g) wet	dry	%WP (Test 2)	Observations
Archaeological clays analyzed in 1989					
FN 621	35-38	44.34	33.64	31.81	Workable, very plastic
FN 802	25-28	43.05	34.79	23.75	Workable, good
FN 854 (temp.)	Used soaked	41.26	30.53	35.16	Workable, good
FN 907	29-32	44.19	34.07	29.70	Workable, good
FN 1223	30-32	40.25	31.19	36.89	Workable, good
Source clays analyzed in 1989					
89-1	31-34	44.91	34.35	30.74	Workable
89-2	32-39	43.12	31.85	35.38	Workable
89-3	27-30	44.82	35.92	24.77	Workable
89-4	26-30	46.18	37.35	23.64	Workable
89-5	24-26	47.47	39.37	20.57	Workable
89-6	36-42	45.88	5.34	29.82	Workable
89-7	33-37	44.89	33.38	34.45	Workable
89-8	26-40	43.26	34.35	25.93	Workable
89-9	36-41	42.52	34.61	22.85	Workable
Source clays analyzed in 1993					
1	24-27	42.50	33.10	27.19	Workable, sandy
2	23-27	41.10	32.50	26.46	Workable, sandy
3	25-28	42.40	32.50	30.46	Workable
4	24-29	46.80	36.00	30.00	Not very fat
5	35-41	39.60	26.20	51.15	Workable, good
6	37-40	41.60	28.60	45.45	Workable, good
7	33-39	38.00	26.60	34.76	Workable, good
8	38-42	39.50	26.30	50.19	Workable
9	24-28	42.20	32.80	28.66	Workable
10	34-38	40.40	28.50	41.75	Workable
11	28-34	40.30	30.00	34.30	Workable, good
12	28-34	42.30	31.20	35.58	Workable, good
13	24-27	44.30	35.90	23.40	Silty
14	20-22	43.20	35.80	20.67	Silty
15	25-27	45.50	35.60	27.81	Silty

A second method of establishing the water of plasticity is to determine the difference in weight between the wet clay specimen and the dried specimen. The weight loss caused by the evaporation of noncrystal water equals the amount of water originally needed to reach plasticity. This test does not give as exact a measure of workability as does the first test, because the amount of water added to develop plasticity is not controlled. To perform the second test and to measure the clays' drying shrinkage, the wet clay samples were formed into tiles of standardized form and size. The tiles were weighed, weighed again when completely dry, and the percentage of water of plasticity was calculated (Table 3.4). Most of the analyzed clays were fine grained and fat, and their plasticity was good to excellent (compare Tables 3.3 and 3.4).

Loss of noncrystal water during the drying process of a plastic clay causes shrinkage of the body, which can be measured as *linear drying shrinkage* (%LDS), also referred to as linear air shrinkage (Rice 1987: 71). Table 3.5 shows the linear drying shrinkage of several types of clay. To determine the linear drying shrinkage of the clays, the wet tiles were each marked with two parallel lines, 1 cm apart from each other. After the tiles were completely dry, the distance between the marks was measured and the difference converted into percentages (1 cm = 100%), which represent the linear drying shrinkage (Table 3.6). The shrinkage of all the clays tested was comparatively low, and only a few samples showed small drying cracks (compare Tables 3.5 and 3.6). These results indicate that the tested clays possess a high material flexibility, especially as the

Table 3.5. Linear Drying Shrinkage of Several Clay Types

Clay Type	%LDS
Crude kaolin	5.00–7.60
Ball clay	5.25–12.00
Refractory clay	4.25–11.00
Stoneware clay	4.80–9.30
Flint fire clay	0.78–6.59
White sedimentary kaolin	4.50–12.50
Saggar clays	2.80–10.80

NOTE: After Ries (1927: 227) and Rice (1987: 71).

Table 3.6. Linear Drying Shrinkage of Tested Clays
(Air Drying)

Sample No.	%LDS	Observations
Archaeological clays analyzed in 1989		
FN 621	5.0	
FN 802	5.0	
FN 854	10.0	
FN 907	7.5	
FN 1223	10.0	
Source clays analyzed in 1989		
89-1	6.0	
89-2	2.0	
89-3	2.0	
89-4	4.0	
89-5	6.0	
89-6	8.0	Drying cracks
89-7	10.0	Drying cracks
89-8	10.0	
89-9	6.0	
Source clays analyzed in 1993		
1	6.7	Small drying cracks
2	6.7	
3	10.0	
4	12.0	
5	13.3	Drying cracks, tile broke
6	13.3	Drying cracks, tile broke
7	10.0	Warped, drying cracks, tile broke
8	13.3	Drying cracks, spalling, tile broke
9	6.7	
10	13.3	Drying cracks, tile broke
11	12.0	
12	10.0	Tile broke
13	6.0	Powdery, silts?
14	6.7	Powdery, silts?
15	8.0	Powdery

clays tested were untempered and their linear drying shrinkage was not reduced by the addition of nonplastic materials.

Firing Performance of Clays

To observe possible property changes during firing, the previously formed tiles were cut into 11 pieces and all but one placed in an electric furnace. They were fired piece by piece at increments of 50°C (122°F) from 500°C to 950°C (932° to 1742°F) under an oxidizing atmosphere. Every piece of each sample was fired for 30 minutes at a specific temperature to ensure that all specimens were totally oxidized. This time period seemed to be sufficient, considering that under conditions of an open fire or a shallow pit the maximum temperature could probably only be maintained about 5 to 20 minutes (Shepard 1939: 264, 1985: 84). After the projected temperature was reached and held for that time, the pieces were left in the furnace until they had cooled down to about 300°C (572°F); they were then removed from the furnace to cool to room temperature. This cooling regimen approximates prehistoric firing conditions. Using the Munsell color charts, I recorded the changes in color to observe patterns of oxidation and to compare the color range of the analyzed clays with paste colors of ceramics found at Grasshopper Pueblo (Table 3.7). This color comparison provides a rough measure to evaluate whether sampled source clays could have been used for the production of ceramics in the Grasshopper assemblage. In general, the tested clays performed well within the firing range used by prehistoric potters. Only a few clays showed structural weakness such as cracks or bloating in the upper temperature ranges. The observed color range in the tested clays paralleled the paste colors of refired utilitarian and painted ceramics from Grasshopper except for ceramics with light-firing pastes (Triadan 1989: 64–66).

To summarize, the experiments on the workability and firing performance of the sampled source and archaeological clays demonstrated that all the tested clays could have been used to produce pottery.

MATERIAL ANALYSES

The entire collection of whole and reconstructed vessels from Grasshopper Pueblo was visually examined and 403 were identified as White Mountain Red Ware, Grasshopper Polychrome, or Kinishba Polychrome; a few of these vessels could not be assigned unambiguously to a specific ware or type. Form, ware and type, completeness of vessel, size (maximum diameter, rim diameter, height), core color, temper observations, preservation and color of slips and paints, classification of paint (mineral or carbon), observations regarding

Table 3.7. Color Changes in Fired Clays
(Munsell Color Charts 1975)

Sample No.	20°	500°	550°	600°	650°	700°	750°	800°	850°	900°	950°
Archaeological clays analyzed in 1989											
FN 621	10YR 6/6	2.5YR 5/6									
FN 802	7.5YR 5/2	5YR 6/4		5YR 6/6					2.5YR 5/8		
FN 854	7.5YR 5/4	7.5YR 5/6		5YR 5/6					5YR 5/8		2.5YR 5/8
FN 907	5YR 7/1	10YR 7/1		10YR 8/1							
FN 1223	5YR 5/2	7.5YR 6/4			7.5YR 6/6				5YR 6/8		
Source clays analyzed in 1989											
89-1	2.5YR 7/2	10YR 7/2			10YR 8/3			7.5YR 8/4		10YR 8/4	
89-2	7.5YR 3/4	2.5YR 4/6				2.5YR 4/8				2.5YR 5/8	
89-3	5YR 7/1	5YR 7/2	5YR 7/3					5YR 8/3			10YR 7/3
89-4	7.5YR 5/4	5YR 6/6						5YR 7/6			
89-5	5Y 6/1	5Y 7/2			2.5YR 8/2	10YR 8/3					10YR 8/4
89-6	5Y 7/1	10YR 7/2			10YR 7/3			7.5YR 6/6			5YR 6/6
89-7	5YR 5/2	5YR 6/2				5YR 6/3			2.5YR 5/4		
89-8	5Y 7/1	10YR 7/2	7.5YR 8/2		10YR 7/4			7.5YR 7/2			
89-9	5Y 4/1	2.5Y 7/4	10YR 7/3						7.5YR 5/6	7.5YR 6/6	7.5YR 8/4
Source clays analyzed in 1993											
1	7.5YR 5/4	7.5YR 6/4		5YR 6/4	5YR 6/6						
2	5YR 6/4	5YR 6/4		5YR 6/6							
3	5YR 5/4	2.5YR 5/6	2.5YR 4/6		2.5YR 4/8						2.5YR 5/8
4	10YR 5/2	7.5YR 6/4		5YR 6/4				5YR 7/6	5YR 6/6		
5	10YR 4/2	5YR 4/3	7.5YR 4/4		5YR 3/4			2.5YR 4/6	5YR 5/6		
6	10YR 3/2	10YR 4/3		7.5YR 4/4				5YR 4/6			
7	10YR 4/3	5YR 4/4	5YR 4/6		2.5YR 4/6			5YR 5/6	2.5YR 4/8	2.5YR 5/8	
8	10YR 5/4	7.5YR 5/4									2.5YR 5/8
9	7.5YR 4/2	7.5YR 5/4	5YR 5/4	5YR 6/6							
10	10YR 4/2	5YR 5/4	5YR 5/6		10YR 7/3			7.5YR 7/6	5YR 5/8		
11	2.5Y 7/2	10YR 7/4			10YR 7/3	7.5YR 8/4	7.5YR 7/4	7.5YR 7/6	5YR 6/6		2.5YR 3/8
12	2.5Y 5/2	7.5YR 6/4					5YR 6/6	5YR 5/6			
13	10YR 7/2	10YR 7/3						7.5YR 8/4			
14	7.5YR 6/4	5YR 5/4		5YR 6/6							
15	5YR 4/3	5YR 5/4	2.5YR 5/6								2.5YR 5/8

[25]

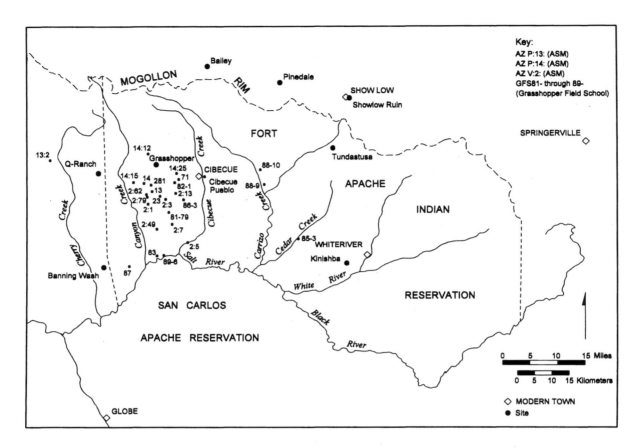

Figure 3.3. Locations of sampled sites.

black mineral paint (iron, copper carbonates), decoration, and archaeological context and provenience were recorded for these vessels. These data provided the base from which samples were chosen for neutron activation analysis and for some of the analyses outlined in Chapter 4. In addition to reconstructible vessels, sherds from controlled surface collections were chemically and petrographically analyzed.

Chemical Characterization

Neutron Activation Analysis (NAA)

Neutron activation analysis is based on the properties of the atomic nucleus. A substance is bombarded by neutrons during which a small fraction of the nuclei of certain constituent elements is transformed into unstable radioactive isotopes that decay with characteristic half-lives. During decay, each of these isotopes emits gamma rays with discrete energies that are uniquely characteristic for each respective isotope. The gamma-ray energy identifies the element present, and the actual

number of gamma rays detected is proportional to the amount of that specific element present in the substance. By measuring and counting the emitted gamma rays, the elemental composition of a substance can be determined both qualitatively and quantitatively. In principle, as many as 77 elements can be detected by neutron activation analysis, but the number of elements that can be determined simultaneously is fewer and depends on the composition of the analyzed material and the analytical procedures followed (Alfassi 1990; Ehmann and Vance 1991; Glascock 1992; Goles 1977; Kruger 1971; Parry 1991). In routine analyses of ceramic materials, usually 20 to 35 elements are determined quantitatively.

To assess the production and distribution of White Mountain Red Ware at Grasshopper Pueblo and the surrounding region, 331 samples were submitted to neutron activation analysis (Appendix B). The samples included 122 reconstructible vessels and sherds from Grasshopper Pueblo, 186 sherds from surface collections from 33 contemporaneous sites of the Grasshopper region and adjacent areas (Fig. 3.3, Table 3.8), 16 source clays from Grasshopper Pueblo and a surround-

Table 3.8. Samples from Sites in the Grasshopper Region and Adjacent Areas Analyzed by NAA

	Site	No. of Samples
GFS 82-1	Spring Creek Pueblo	7
AZ V:2:7	Ruin's Tank Pueblo	9
AZ P:14:25	Red Canyon Tank Pueblo	5
AZ V:2:62		6
AZ P:14:281		7
AZ V:2:13	Blue House Mtn. Pueblo	6
AZ V:2:79	Double Springs Cliff Dwelling	2
AZ P:14:15	Oak Creek Pueblo	4
AZ P:14:71		5
GFS 88-9	Carrizo Creek Pueblo	5
GFS 88-10	Blue Spring Pueblo	5
GFS 85-3	Cedar Creek Pueblo	5
	Cibecue Pueblo	5
TDT	Tundastusa	5
BW	Banning Wash Pueblo	3
PD	Pinedale Ruin	9
SL	Showlow Ruin	5
K	Kinishba	7
Q	Q-Ranch	6
AZ V:2:3	Spotted Mountain Pueblo	7
AZ P:14:13	Brush Mountain Pueblo	9
AZ V:2:1	Canyon Creek Cliff Dwelling	7
AZ P:14:12	Hilltop Pueblo	8
GFS 86-3	Black Mtn. Pueblo	8
AZ V:2:49	Canyon Butte Pueblo	6
AZ V:2:87		7
GFS 81-79		5
AZ V:2:23		4
AZ V:2:5	Hole Canyon Cliff Dwelling	3
AZ V:2:83		6
GFS 89-6		1
AZ P:13:2		3
AZ P:14:14	Red Rock House	6
Total		186

Table 3.9. Total Number of Samples Analyzed by NAA

		Number of samples				
Assemblage	No. of Sites	Whole Vessels	Sherds	Clays	Temper	Total
Grasshopper Pueblo	1	106	16	4	1	127
Grasshopper Region	26		148	10	6	164
Periphery	7		38	2		40
Total	34	106	202	16	7	331

NOTE: Sherds are from controlled surface collections.

ing catchment area of about 7 km (4.3 miles), and 5 samples of sands and 2 samples of weathered diabase that may have provided tempering materials (Table 3.9). For Grasshopper Pueblo, slightly over 20 percent (106) of the 403 vessels classified as White Mountain Red Ware, Grasshopper Polychrome, or Kinishba Polychrome were sampled, as well as 16 sherds from varying contexts. The 106 sampled vessels were all partial, because whole vessels could not be drilled to obtain powdered samples of the pastes. (Vessels less than 50% complete were classified as partial). Even though this restriction reduced the number of vessels from which to choose, I was able to sample about 20 percent of each of the different White Mountain Red Ware types present in the collection, as well as about 20 percent of the Grasshopper Polychrome vessels. White Mountain Red Ware vessels were also sampled to determine if any were produced locally. Of the 403 recorded vessels, 219 were identified as White Mountain Red Ware. Of these, 142 had a light paste and 77 had a dark paste; 33 (23.24%) of the light-paste White Mountain Red Ware and 23 (29.87%) of the possibly local dark-paste White Mountain Red Ware were sampled. Also, six of the Kinishba Polychrome vessels (50%) were sampled. All sherd samples (202) from Grasshopper Pueblo and the regional sites were also analyzed by weak-acid extraction ICP (Appendix B). The samples submitted for NAA were analyzed at the University of Missouri Research Reactor Center (MURR) in Columbia, Missouri.

Sample Preparation

Samples were assigned a six digit alphanumerical identification code, their analytical ID (ANID). Except for the sands and diabase, all samples were sherds or pieces from reconstructible vessels. (Clay samples had been fired into tiles.) A piece of about 2 square centimeters was broken off every sherd and if there was a portion remaining, it was retained for future reference.

Procedurally, all surfaces of the sherds are removed using a silicon-carbide drill burr. The scraping of the sherd surface is undertaken for two reasons: (1) the outer surface may be slipped and the slip may differ in composition from the clay body, and (2) contamination may have occurred during the vessel's use or while it was resting in the ground. The burred specimens are washed in deionized water and left to air dry for several hours. Each sample is then put into an agate mortar and ground to a fine powder to homogenize the sample, and finally the powder is transferred to a sterile glass vial. Researchers at MURR prefer this method to drilling directly into the sherd body, as drilling with a tungsten carbide drill can cause occasional contamination (Glascock 1992: 13) by Tungsten (W) and Cobalt (Co). Tungsten increases background counts, thus decreasing the measuring sensitivity, whereas cobalt is useful in discriminating clay sources and it is desirable to obtain accurate measurements of cobalt concentrations.

During all sample preparation, extreme caution is taken to avoid cross-contamination. Usually about 400 mg of the powdered sample are obtained, of which approximately 200 mg are used for short irradiations and 200 mg are used for long irradiations. The amount of about 200 mg of homogenized sample is considered to be sufficient to account for the possible heterogeneity occurring in relatively coarse ceramics and to represent a reliable chemical profile with low analytical errors (Glascock 1992: 13).

Irradiation

Two analytical procedures are used at MURR to measure various elements. The first procedure involves the determination and quantification of elements that form short-lived radioisotopes when exposed to neutrons. Approximately 200 mg of each powdered sample are weighed into a sterile 2/5-dram high-density polyethylene vial and sealed. By way of a pneumatic tube irradiation system, samples are irradiated sequentially for five seconds at a thermal neutron flux of $8 \times 10^{13} n/cm^2/s$. Generally, 12 primary (6 SRM–1633a [Flyash], 6 SRM–688 [Basalt]) and 2 quality control standards (Ohio Red Clay) are irradiated per about 64 unknown samples. The samples are allowed to decay for 25 minutes and are then placed in front of a high-resolution germanium detector to be counted for 12 minutes to collect a spectrum of emitted gamma rays. This short irradiation method allows the determination of aluminum (Al), barium (Ba), calcium (Ca), dysprosium (Dy), potassium (K), manganese (Mn), sodium (Na), titanium (Ti) and vanadium (V).

To identify elements with medium- and long-lived isotopes, a second set of samples is prepared. The analytical error between two distinct powdered samples of one specimen are smaller than the error rate that occurs when samples are transferred from polyethylene vials to quartz vials, because of possible contamination during this process. Moreover, as the whole sherd sample is powdered and homogenized and is treated as a representative sample of a whole ceramic vessel, it should be irrelevant which portion of the powdered sample is analyzed.

Approximately 200 mg of powdered sample are weighed into a high-purity quartz vial, which is then sealed under a slight vacuum using an oxygen torch. The samples are irradiated for 24 hours at a thermal neutron flux of $5 \times 10^{13} n/cm^2/s$. Samples are irradiated in groups of 50 to 60 with 4 primary (SRM–1633a [Flyash]) and 2 quality control standards (1 Ohio Red Clay and 1 SRM–278 [obsidian]) per batch. After seven days, the sample vials are cleaned in *aqua regia* to remove all possible surface contamination, placed in test tubes, and gamma ray emissions for each sample are counted for 1,800 seconds. The samples are counted by a germanium detector that is coupled to an automatic sample changer. Elements determined by this counting episode include arsenic (As), lanthanum (La), lutetium (Lu), neodymium (Nd), samarium (Sm), uranium (U), and ytterbium (Yb). Following an additional three-week to four-week decay period, the samples are recounted for 10,000 seconds each to measure the gamma ray emission spectrum for long-lived radioisotopes; elements determined are cerium (Ce), cobalt (Co), chromium (Cr), cesium (Cs), europium (Eu), iron (Fe), hafnium (Hf), nickel (Ni), rubidium (Rb), antimony (Sb), scandium (Sc), strontium (Sr), tantalum (Ta), terbium (Tb), thorium (Th), zinc (Zn), and zirconium (Zr). Thus, 33 elements are routinely quantified through these analytical procedures by MURR for the chemical characterization of pottery (Glascock 1992: 14).

A standard-comparator method is applied to quantify elemental concentrations. Unknown specimens, together with standards with known element concentrations, are irradiated and measured under identical conditions. The element concentrations in the unknown sample are then determined by means of ratios: the measured activities per unit weight of the unknown sample to the activities for a reference standard with known concentrations.

Standard reference material (SRM) 1633a Flyash and SRM–688 Basalt Rock from the National Institute of Standards and Technology (NIST) are used at MURR as primary reference standards for pottery. The SRM–1633a standard provides concentrations for 32 of the 33 elements mentioned above. For the reference concentration of calcium (Ca), SRM–688 is used. Furthermore, SRM–278 Obsidian Rock and Ohio Red Clay (a commercial clay) are analyzed with the unknown samples to control for possible systematic errors between batches of samples. Both of these standards provide a means to evaluate the precision of measurement for each element. The calculated analytical errors are generally small between batches of samples, ranging from one percent to two percent. (For more details on NAA techniques and procedures conducted at MURR, see Glascock 1992: 11–15).

Data Analysis

After counting was completed and the elemental concentrations of all samples were determined (Triadan 1994, Appendices C, D), bivariate plots of elemental concentrations and multivariate statistical methods were used to process the data. All concentrations were converted into base log 10 values. Using log values rather than absolute ppm concentrations tends to normalize the distribution for trace elements (Bishop and Neff 1989: 63; Harbottle 1976; Sayre 1975). Because ceramic material is compositionally very complex, to account for the diversity and high elemental correlation of pottery (Bishop and others 1982: 296) the data are interpreted by using multivariate statistical analyses. Multivariate statistical techniques encompass the variance within the data and define compositional groups on the basis of all elemental variables. Thus, compositional groups are defined on the basis of differences of the elemental composition as a whole and not on the basis of concentration differences between a few elements; group shape as well as group location is taken into consideration (Bishop and Neff 1989).

As a first step, cluster analysis involving average linkage was used to obtain preliminary information on compositional groupings based only on the absolute magnitude of elemental concentrations. Then principal components were calculated on the basis of 325 samples, 31 elements, and a variance-covariance matrix. Table 3.10 shows the eigenvalues for the principal components and the variance for the data set. It is necessary to note

here that although different compositional groups were apparent within the cluster dendrogram, no samples were preassigned to these tentative groups before they were submitted to principal component analysis. Four samples (DTR170, DTR197, DTR207, and DTS019) were not included in the principal component calculations, because they were obvious outliers that had few or no similarities with the rest of the sample group. Nickel (Ni) and strontium (Sr) were excluded as variables due to an unacceptable number of missing values (Triadan 1994, Appendix C). Missing values for a sample generally indicate that the gamma peak for certain elements was below the detection limit in that sample.

Compositional patterns in the sample set were thus established and compositional group membership probabilities were subsequently calculated through the determination of the Mahalanobis distance (Davis 1986: 485–487) for each sample to its group centroid. The Mahalanobis distance is defined as the measure of the squared Euclidian distance between a group centroid and a specimen, divided by the group variance in the direction of the specimen (Glascock 1992: 18, following Sayre 1975). In contrast to the simple Euclidian measure, the Mahalanobis distance calculation incorporates information about the correlations between pairs of elements derived by the off-diagonal terms of the variance-covariance matrix. Thus, the probability that a particular specimen belongs to a group can be calculated based not only on its proximity to the group centroid in Euclidian terms, but also on the rate at which the density of data points decreases from the group centroid toward that specimen. The significance of differences between groups of specimens can be tested by Hotteling's T^2 statistic (the multivariate equivalent of the Students t test; Davis 1986: 43–496). Because Hotteling's T^2 statistic is essentially equivalent to the Mahalanobis distance for individual data points, group membership probabilities can be calculated after transforming the T^2 statistic into the related F-value (Glascock 1992: 18-19).

Results

On the basis of principal component analysis, four major compositional groups were separated (Figs. 3.4, 3.5). These groups can also be clearly demonstrated through bivariate elemental plots (Figs. 3.6–3.8). Table 3.11 lists the mean elemental concentrations for each group. The compositional groups encompass samples with acceptable group membership probabilities (> 1%) for their own compositional group and lower probabilities or none of belonging to any of the three other

Table 3.10. Principal Eigenvalues and Associated Variance

Eigenvalue	Variance (%)	Cumulative Variance (%)
1.254	68.11	68.11
0.1541	8.365	76.48
0.09255	5.025	81.50
0.08571	4.654	86.16
0.04668	2.534	88.69
0.03616	1.963	90.65
0.03376	1.833	92.49
0.02259	1.227	93.71
0.02146	1.165	94.88
0.01691	0.9179	95.80

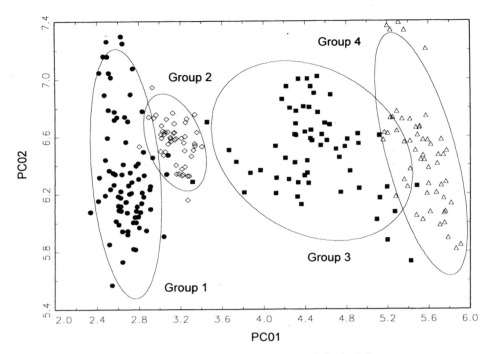

Figure 3.4. NAA compositional groups, Principal Components (PC) 1 and 2. Ellipse shows confidence interval of 90 percent.

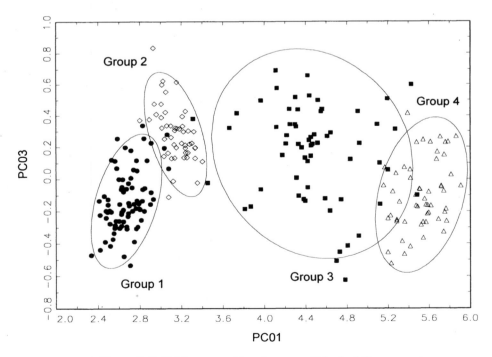

Figure 3.5. NAA compositional groups, Principal Components (PC) 1 and 3. Ellipse shows confidence interval of 90 percent.

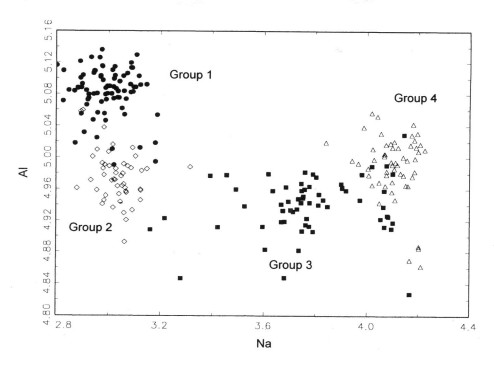

Figure 3.6. NAA compositional groups, Na and Al concentrations.
Element concentrations are plotted as base log 10 values.

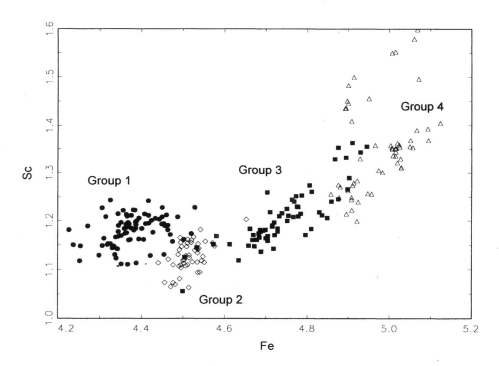

Figure 3.7. NAA compositional groups, Fe and Sc concentrations.
Element concentrations are plotted as base log 10 values.

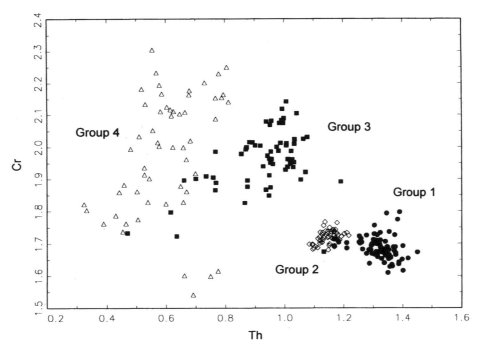

Figure 3.8. NAA compositional groups, Th and Cr concentrations.
Element concentrations are plotted as base log 10 values.

compositional groups (Appendix C). Samples that did not meet these criteria were excluded from the compositional groups. Thus, 248 samples (81.31% of the ceramics) were assigned to one of the four compositional groups; 57 samples (18.69%) remained unassigned. However, judgmentally almost all samples can be assigned to one of the four different groups (Appendix C). The chemical profiles of the analyzed source clays were projected against the four compositional groups, and group membership probabilities for each of the groups were calculated for each sample (Table 3.12).

Compositional Groups 1 and 2 consist of the White Mountain Red Ware that was imported into the Grasshopper region and Kinishba Polychrome. Most of these ceramics have a light paste or, as in the case of Group 2, the paste is sometimes light orange to orange. They were probably manufactured from kaolinitic clays that fire white to light orange under a predominantly oxidizing atmosphere. The nearest geological formations that bear kaolinitic clay deposits are cretaceous shales about 34 km (21 miles) northeast of Grasshopper Pueblo (Plate 2; Moore 1968: 72–73, Plate 1). Also, none of the source clays from the Grasshopper region or Kinishba showed any probability of belonging to either Group 1 or 2. A comparison of the iron contents of Compositional Groups 1 and 2 shows clearly that, on average,

the Group 2 ceramics are higher in iron concentrations (Fig. 3.9, Table 3.11), about two percent in Group 1 versus about three percent in Group 2, which accounts for the light orange to orange paste of some of the sherds assigned to Group 2. Ceramics that were originally classified visually as having a dark paste and as probably local, but that compositionally belonged to Group 1 or 2, were refired under oxidizing conditions at 900°C (1652°F) for 30 minutes to clarify the paste color (Table 3.13). It became apparent that all these ceramics had been incompletely oxidized, because they turned light orange-beige or orange during refiring.

Interestingly, all the analyzed Kinishba Polychrome vessels (n = 6) could be assigned to the imported ceramics, more specifically to Group 1. They were manufactured with the same raw materials as a large number of the imported White Mountain Red Ware and thus most certainly came from the same resource procurement zone as Group 1 ceramics. These findings stand in contrast to the assumption that Kinishba Polychrome was locally produced at Kinishba Ruin, about 50 km (31 miles) east of Grasshopper Pueblo (Baldwin 1938a; Cummings 1940: 87). The analyzed source clays from Kinishba (DTC001 and DTC002) do not match compositionally with either Compositional Group 1 or 2 (Table 3.12).

Table 3.11. Mean Elemental Concentrations (ppm) of Compositional Groups

Elements	Group 1, n = 81 Mean	SD	Group 2, n = 49 Mean	SD	Group 3, n = 63 Mean	SD	Group 4, n = 55 Mean	SD
As	7.20	3.15	15.35	9.46	*12.66	7.72	*4.96	3.16
La	41.40	15.1	41.6	3.7	30.0	6.5	21.1	5.1
Lu	0.529	0.093	0.481	0.039	0.425	0.065	0.383	0.112
Nd	31.0	13.5	37.8	5.2	28.8	7.0	24.8	9.8
Sm	6.56	2.49	7.34	0.82	6.30	1.37	6.03	1.87
U	7.31	1.65	4.15	0.60	3.00	1.40	*1.19	0.65
Yb	3.31	0.71	3.35	0.33	2.87	0.53	2.54	0.78
Ce	78.9	30.4	84.0	8.7	63.8	15.4	47.0	12.1
Co	4.60	1.64	9.81	2.13	24.60	9.00	50.40	7.64
Cr	48.7	4.1	52.4	2.5	93.1	18.9	104.5	40.9
Cs	31.24	7.68	15.84	2.18	9.38	5.60	3.11	0.90
Eu	1.161	0.447	1.485	0.174	1.483	0.294	1.893	0.498
Fe (%)	2.42	0.35	3.28	0.28	5.66	1.28	9.56	1.54
Hf	6.98	0.74	6.39	0.40	7.41	1.65	5.45	1.41
Ni	*2.1	9.0	*10.3	17.2	*59.0	33.3	*76.9	30.8
Rb	113.5	26.0	118.9	9.8	64.0	22.5	41.4	14.1
Sb	1.053	0.134	0.983	0.081	0.624	0.190	0.342	0.139
Sc	15.17	1.09	13.42	0.96	16.30	2.45	*23.12	5.48
Sr	*68.0	41.3	*50.6	29.7	214.9	112.1	*326.3	133.0
Ta	1.635	0.181	1.208	0.090	0.925	0.164	0.810	0.243
Tb	0.673	0.360	0.921	0.188	0.827	0.256	0.876	0.309
Th	21.12	2.58	14.13	1.17	8.87	2.27	4.16	1.12
Zn	63.2	16.4	74.6	10.1	80.6	16.8	98.4	18.3
Zr	194.8	32.2	170.8	22.1	188.0	42.2	140.3	33.3
Al (%)	12.12	0.82	9.46	0.71	8.73	0.70	9.79	0.86
Ba	445.2	222.6	465.5	71.2	460.6	162.3	351.1	95.7
Ca (%)	0.53	0.15	0.60	0.20	2.69	1.79	3.34	0.73
Dy	5.37	1.46	5.44	0.58	4.84	0.97	4.64	1.42
K (%)	1.86	0.32	1.97	0.10	1.25	0.33	1.00	0.37
Mn	113.5	46.1	198.9	62.6	668.5	267.2	1473.5	254.8
Na	1005.5	202.8	1100.2	206.8	6754.4	3265.7	12902.5	2201.9
Ti	4546.2	356.5	4221.3	247.9	7584.5	2305.5	14858.7	5811.1
V	94.9	10.1	92.5	7.9	143.5	31.6	227.8	60.9

* Missing values in data set. NOTE: Fe, Al, Ca, and K concentrations are recorded in percent.

Table 3.12. Group Membership Probabilities of Clays
(Probabilities are expressed in %)

Sample No.	Group 1	Group 2	Group 3	Group 4	Provenience	Color	Geologic Formation
DTC001	0	0	0.527	0	Kinishba Ruin	Light orange-beige	Recent Alluvium
DTC002	0		0.045	0	Kinishba Ruin	Light orange-beige	Recent Alluvium
DTC003	0.007	0	0.086	0	NW of 3 Way Tank, Road 011	Red	Martin
DTC004	0	0	0.281	0	3 Way Tank, Road 011	Dark gray-brown	Redwall Limestone
DTC005	0	0	0.047	0.060	South peak of Spotted Mountain	Dark brown	Mafic-Younger Gravel
DTC006	0	0	3.415	0.613	North peak of Spotted Mountain	Dark brown	Mafic-Younger Gravel
DTC007	0	0	0.022	0	North Spring Creek	Yellowish brown	Coconino-Upper Rim Gravel
DTC008	0	0	0.042	0	North Spring Creek	Yellowish brown	Coconino-Upper Rim Gravel
DTC009	0	0	45.936	0	Grasshopper Pueblo (P:14:1)	Brown	Supai (alluvial)
DTC010	0	0	11.388	0	Grasshopper Tank No. 2	Dark olive-brown	Naco (alluvial)
DTC011	0	0	0.847	0	South of Mud Tank	Gray	Naco (stream bed)
DTC012	0	0	0.102	0	1 Mile Tank	Dark olive-brown	Supai (alluvial)
DTC013	0	0	0	0	Rm 414, NEQ, Grasshopper Pueblo	Gray	
DTC014	0	0	0.050	0	Rm 420, SEQ, Grasshopper Pueblo	Brown	
DTC015	0	0	36.133	0	Rm 18, NEQ, Chodistaas (P:14:24)	Orange-brown	
DTC016	0.333	0	0	0	Rm 113, Grasshopper Pueblo	Yellow	Slip clay

NOTE: Mahalanobis distance calculations are based on the first six principal components (90.65% of variance).

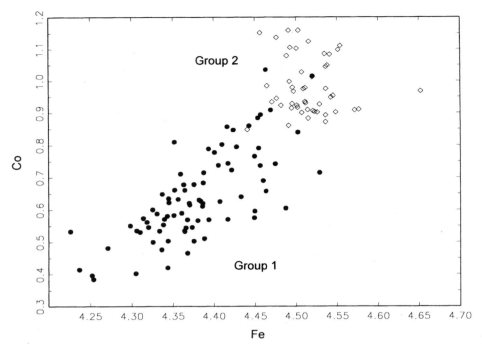

Figure 3.9. Difference in Fe concentrations in Compositional Groups
1 and 2. Element concentrations are plotted as base log 10 values.

Table 3.13. Core Color of Refired Sherds

Sample No. (ANID)	Original Core Color (Munsell Color Co. 1975)	Core Color after Refiring at 900°C for 30 Minutes
DTF023	7.5YR 6/ (light gray/gray)	5YR 6/8 (reddish yellow)
DTF038	7.5YR 6/ (light gray/gray)	2.5Y 8/2 (white)
DTB062	2.5Y 3/ (very dark gray)	10YR 8/3 (very pale brown)
DTB065	7.5YR 4/ (dark gray)	7.5YR 7/6 (reddish yellow)
DTB068	5YR 7/8 (reddish yellow)	7.5YR 8/6 (reddish yellow)
DTZ071	10YR 7/3 (very pale brown)	7.5YR 7/6 (reddish yellow)
DTW082	7.5YR 7/6 (reddish yellow)	7.5YR 7/6 (reddish yellow)
DTR162	7.5YR 4/ (dark gray)	7.5YR 8/6 (reddish yellow)
DTR194	7.5YR 4/ (dark gray)	10YR 8/2 (white)
DTR202	2.5Y 4/ (dark gray)	5YR 6/8 (reddish yellow)
DTR210	core: 7.5YR 5/ (gray)	5YR 6/8 (reddish yellow)
	edge: 7.5YR 6/ (light gray/gray)	
DTR211	7.5YR 7/ (light gray)	5YR 6/8 (reddish yellow)
DTR212	core: 7.5YR 6/ (light gray/gray)	5YR 5/8 (yellowish red)
	edge: 5YR 6/8 (reddish yellow)	
DTP216	2.5Y 4/ (dark gray)	5YR 6/8 (reddish yellow)
DTP217	7.5YR 3/ (very dark gray)	10YR 8/6 (yellow)
DTP223	7.5YR 3/ (very dark gray)	7.5YR 8/4 (pink)
DTR255	7.5YR 3/ (very dark gray)	7.5YR 8/6 (reddish yellow)
DTR276	7.5YR 4/ (dark gray)	5YR 6/8 (reddish yellow)
DTR279	10YR 6/3 (pale brown)	7.5YR 7/6 (reddish yellow)
DTR282	7.5YR 4/ (dark gray)	7.5YR 8/4 (reddish yellow)
DTR295	7.5YR 4/ (dark gray)	5YR 7/6 (reddish yellow)
DTP298	7.5YR 6/ (light gray/gray)	7.5YR 8/4 (pink)
DTR304	7.5YR 7/ (light gray)	5YR 6/8 (reddish yellow)
DTP313	5YR 6/6 (reddish yellow)	5YR 6/8 (reddish yellow)
DTP315	5YR 6/8 (reddish yellow)	5YR 7/8 (reddish yellow)
DTP317	7.5YR 4/ (dark gray)	7.5 YR 8/4 (pink)

Compositional Groups 3 and 4 consist of Grasshopper Polychrome and brown-core White Mountain Red Ware (Appendix B) and represent local production. Grasshopper Polychrome, which archaeologists assumed was produced at Grasshopper Pueblo (Whittlesey 1974: 105), does not form its own compositional group but crosscuts Groups 3 and 4. This distribution provides a strong argument for the local production of the brown-paste variety of White Mountain Red Ware. Moreover, clays from the area around Grasshopper have sufficiently high probabilities of belonging to Group 3 (Table 3.12), especially DTC009, a clay from a stratum directly underlying the site (Figs. 3.10, 3.11).

As all samples were assigned to their respective compositional groups with sufficiently high probabilities, a more refined analysis of the data set was necessary to assess whether subdivisions within the four compositional groups could be discerned. Principal components for Groups 1 and 2 (the imported ceramics) were therefore calculated on the basis of the concentrations of *only* the samples belonging to Groups 1 and 2, and principal components for Groups 3 and 4 (the locally produced ceramics) were calculated on the basis of the concentrations of *only* the samples belonging to Groups 3 and 4. Subgroups within the four compositional groups can be distinguished on Principal Components 1 and 2 (Figs. 3.12–3.14), which account for 76.48 percent of the variance within the whole data set (Table 3.10).

In addition to my own samples, I included in my analysis NAA data of ceramics and specifically clays from Room 113 at Grasshopper Pueblo that were generated by Zedeño at the Conservation Analytical Laboratory (CAL) of the Smithsonian Institution (Zedeño 1991, 1994a). Zedeño's data were calibrated on the basis of the standard Ohio Red Clay data to fit the MURR data. My data set had to be reduced by seven elements, dysprosium (Dy), aluminum (Al), nickel (Ni), strontium (Sr), manganese (Mn), titanium (Ti), and vanadium (V), because CAL routinely determines 26 of the 33 elements that are determined by MURR. Furthermore, calcium (Ca) was excluded because of too many missing values, and lutetium (Lu), neodymium (Nd), and uranium (U) were eliminated because they exhibited problematic values that may reflect possible analytical errors. Thus, a combined database with 22 elemental variables was used for comparative analyses.

Zedeño's study (1991, 1994a) was concerned with the production and circulation of Cibola White Ware. She concluded that almost all the white ware ceramics found at Chodistaas Pueblo (AZ P:14:24) were imported into the settlement. Besides Cibola White Ware whole ves-

sels, Zedeño also analyzed samples of utilitarian brown wares and several archaeological clays from Grasshopper Pueblo and Chodistaas Pueblo in addition to her source clays. These data provided a welcome opportunity to evaluate the two local compositional groups established for Grasshopper and to test whether clays from Room 113 could have provided the raw material for the local vessels. It should be noted that Compositional Groups 3 and 4 are comprised exclusively of decorated ceramics and therefore their pastes may be slightly different from the pastes of locally produced utilitarian brown ware vessels. Moreover, Chodistaas Pueblo predates Grasshopper Pueblo and is located about 1.6 km (1 mile) northeast of Grasshopper. The pastes of the brown ware vessels from Chodistaas may not closely resemble the pastes of the later brown ware vessels from Grasshopper and different source clays may have been used for their manufacture. Clay DTC015, which comes from Room 18 at Chodistaas Pueblo, shows a probability of 36.133 percent of belonging in Group 3, but its group membership probability is lower than that for the Grasshopper clay DTC009 (Table 3.12). Hence, any interpretations regarding the local ceramics should be drawn with these facts in mind.

Zedeño's compositional data for the late Pueblo III Cibola White Ware was used to test whether any of these ceramics were chemically similar to Compositional Group 1 or Group 2 White Mountain Red Ware ceramics, which would imply the same ceramic source or sources for both of these wares. Cibola White Ware is assumed to have come at least in part from the same area as White Mountain Red Ware, the southern Colorado Plateau. (For a detailed discussion of the origins of Cibola White Ware, see Zedeño 1994a: 72, 93.)

The results of the comparative analysis demonstrate that, in addition to clay DTC009 (from a stratum underlying Grasshopper Pueblo), two brown clays from Room 113 at Grasshopper Pueblo (PCC802 and PCC854) show a sufficiently high probability of belonging to Compositional Group 3 (Table 3.14). This attribution strongly supports the argument that Compositional Group 3 ceramics were manufactured at Grasshopper Pueblo. With the exception of three samples (PCN140, PCN031, and PCN264) that show a slight probability of belonging to Compositional Group 4, the chemical composition of utilitarian brown corrugated vessels from Chodistaas does not match that of the local decorated ceramics produced at Grasshopper (Table 3.15). However, when the archaeological clays from Grasshopper and Chodistaas and modern source clays from the vicin-

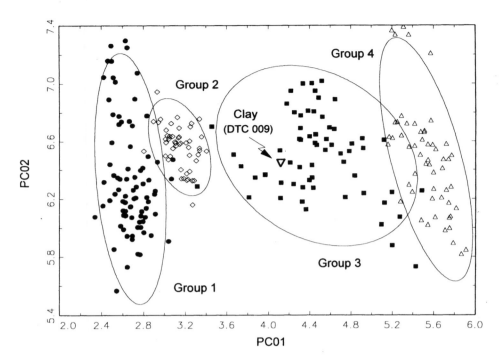

Figure 3.10. Source clay from Grasshopper Pueblo in relation to NAA compositional groups, Principal Components (PC) 1 and 2. Ellipse shows confidence interval of 90 percent.

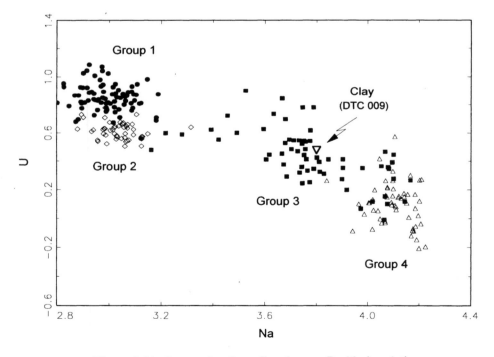

Figure 3.11. Source clay from Grasshopper Pueblo in relation to NAA compositional groups, Na and U concentrations. Element concentrations are plotted as base log 10 values.

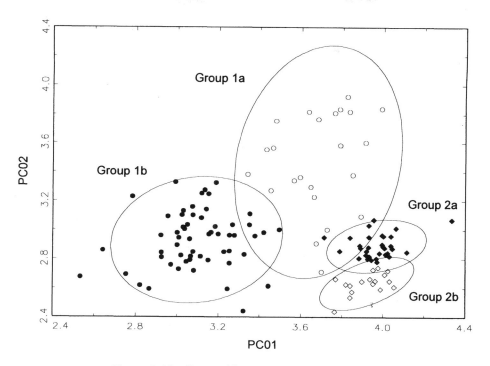

Figure 3.12. Compositional subgroups of NAA Groups 1 and 2, Principal Components (PC) 1 and 2. Ellipse shows confidence interval of 90 percent.

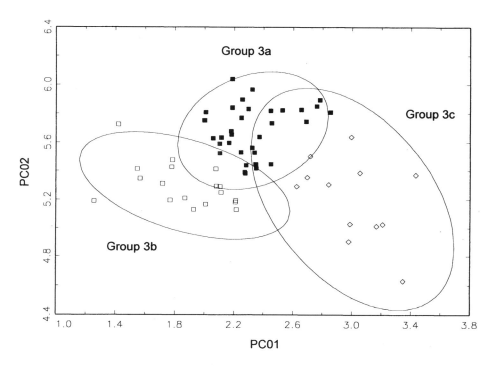

Figure 3.13. Compositional subgroups of NAA Group 3, Principal Components 1 and 2. Ellipse shows confidence interval of 90 percent.

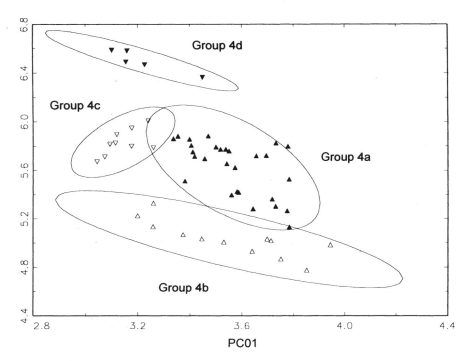

Figure 3.14. Compositional subgroups of NAA Group 4, Principal Components (PC) 1 and 2. Ellipse shows confidence interval of 90 percent.

**Table 3.14. Group Membership Probabilities: Local
Source Clays Compared to NAA Groups 3 and 4**
(Probabilities are expressed in %)

Sample No.	Group 3	Group 4	Provenience
DTC009	7.423	0	Grasshopper Pueblo (P:14:1)
DTC010	0	0	Grasshopper Tank No. 2
DTC015	0.097	0	Room 18, NEQ, Chodistaas Pueblo (P:14:24)
PCC802	6.592	0	Room 113, FN 802, Grasshopper Pueblo (P:14:1)
PCC854	2.156	0	Room 113, FN 854, Grasshopper Pueblo (P:14:1)
PCCTP5	5.519	0	Test pit 88–5, Chodistaas Pueblo (P:14:24)
PCC010	0	0	Room 10, Chodistaas Pueblo (P:14:24)
PC1223	0.002	0	Room 113, FN 1223, Grasshopper Pueblo (P:14:1)

NOTE: Mahalanobis distance calculations based on base log 10 concentrations of 22 elements. PC clays analyzed by Zedeño (1994a: 115–120).

ity of these two sites were compared with the brown corrugated pottery from Chodistaas, all the clays showed a high probability of belonging to the brown corrugated compositional group (Table 3.16). This broader, more regional match of clays with the brown corrugated ceramics, which stands in contrast to the local decorated ceramics from Grasshopper Pueblo (Compositional Group 3) that match very specific clays, can be explained by the small sample size (14 samples)

and the compositional heterogeneity of this group (Zedeño 1994a: 62–64). It is possible that if more samples were analyzed and added to the data set, the brown corrugated pots from Chodistaas could be divided into more than one compositional group, which may correspond to more specific source locations. In sum, brown corrugated ceramics from Chodistaas were definitely local to the area and were probably produced at least in the vicinity of Grasshopper and Chodistaas pueblos.

Table 3.15. Group Membership Probabilities: Brown Corrugated Pottery from Chodistaas Pueblo (AZ P:14:24) Compared to NAA Groups 3 and 4
(Probabilities are expressed in %)

Sample No.	Group 3	Group 4
PCN084	0	0
PCW137	0	0.002
PCN170	0	0
PCN258	0	0.036
PCN140	0	1.271
PCN216	0	0
PCN226	0	0
PCN031	0	1.102
PCN197	0	0
PCN267	0	0
PCN264	0	0.674
PCW267	0	0
PCW263	0	0
PCN307	0	0

NOTE: Mahalanobis distance calculations based on base log 10 concentrations of 22 elements.

Table 3.16. Group Membership Probabilities: Local Source Clays Compared to Brown Corrugated Pottery
(Probabilities are expressed in %)

Sample No.	Brown Corrugated	Provenience
DTC009	51.097	Grasshopper Pueblo (P:14:1)
DTC010	16.560	Grasshopper Tank No. 2
DTC015	25.235	Rm. 18, NEQ, Chodistaas Pueblo (P:14:24)
PCC802	42.698	Rm. 113, FN 802, Grasshopper Pueblo
PCC854	49.385	Rm. 113, FN 854, Grasshopper Pueblo
PCCTP5	76.539	Test pit 88–5, Chodistaas Pueblo
PCC010	43.810	Rm. 10, Chodistaas Pueblo
PC1223	40.275	Rm. 113, FN 1223, Grasshopper Pueblo

NOTE: Mahalanobis distance calculations based on Principal Components 1 through 13 (98.61% of variance). PC clays analyzed by Zedeño (1994a: 115–120).

Clay PCCTP5, from a test pit at the foot of the bluff on which Chodistaas is situated, was the best match (76.54% probability) with the brown corrugated ceramics. Because the brown corrugated ceramics do not match the chemical composition of the local decorated ceramics from Grasshopper, the utilitarian pottery at Chodistaas was probably manufactured with slightly different source clays, or the potters from Chodistaas used different paste recipes than those used by the potters from Grasshopper.

Except for two samples (PCN506 and PCN718; Table 3.17), the Cibola White Ware vessels form their

Table 3.17. Group Membership Probabilities: Cibola White Ware Compared to NAA Compositional Groups
(Probabilities are expressed in %)

Sam. No.	Group 1	Group 2	Group 3	Group 4	Site
PCN097	0	0	0	0	P:14:24
PCN101	0	0	0	0	P:14:24
PCN107	0	0	0	0	P:14:24
PCN134	0	0	0	0	P:14:24
PCN139	0	0	0	0	P:14:24
PCN157	0	0	0	0	P:14:24
PCN158	0	0	0	0	P:14:24
PCN172	0	0	0	0	P:14:24
PCN173	0	0	0	0	P:14:24
PCN175	0	0	0	0	P:14:24
PCN183	0	0	0	0	P:14:24
PCN236	0	0	0	0	P:14:24
PCN237	0	0	0	0	P:14:24
PCN265	0	0	0	0	P:14:24
PCN301	0	0	0	0	P:14:24
PCN346	0	0	0	0	P:14:24
PCN350	0	0	0	0	P:14:24
PCN390	0	0	0	0	P:14:24
PCN392	0	0	0	0	P:14:24
PCN393	0	0	0	0	P:14:24
PCN535	0	0	0	0	P:14:24
PCN595	0	0	0	0	P:14:24
PCN667	0	0	0	0	P:14:24
PCX310	0	0	0	0	P:14:24
PCX392	0	0	0	0	P:14:24
PCG206	0	0	0	0	P:14:8
PCN026	0	0	0	0	P:14:8
PCN131	0	0	0	0	P:14:24
PCN310	0	0	0	0	P:14:24
PCN313	0	0	0	0	P:14:24
PCN841	0	0	0	0	P:14:1
PCN891	0	0	0	0	P:14:1
PC2010	0	0	0	0	P:14:8
PCN006	0.002	0	0	0	P:14:197
PCN034	0	0	0	0	P:14:1
PCN063	0	0	0	0	P:14:24
PCN108	0	0	0	0	P:14:24
PCN135	0	0	0	0	P:14:24
PCN177	0	0	0	0	P:14:24
PCN253	0	0	0	0	P:14:24
PCN263	0	0	0	0	P:14:24
PCN304	0	0	0	0	P:14:24
PCN339	0	0	0	0	P:14:24
PCN425	0	0	0	0	P:14:24
PCN308	0	0	0	0	P:14:24
PCN338	0	0	0	0	P:14:24
PCN506	0	0	59.145	0	P:14:1
PCN718	0	0	58.437	0	P:14:1
PCN074	0.001	0	0	0	P:14:24
PCN256	0	0	0	0	P:14:24
PCN334	0.523	0	0	0	P:14:24

NOTE: Mahalanobis distance calculations based on base log 10 concentrations of 22 elements.

own distinct compositional groups (Zedeño 1994a: 73–77) that do not overlap with the two import White Mountain Red Ware groups (Compositional Groups 1 and 2). PCN506 and PCN718, two black-on-white jars from Grasshopper Pueblo, show almost a 60 percent probability of belonging to local Compositional Group 3 (Table 3.17). Zedeño (1994a: 74) had classified these two vessels together with two jars from Chodistaas (PCN338 and PCN308) as locally produced. Interestingly, the two local jars from Chodistaas show no probability of belonging to either of the two local polychrome groups (Compositional Groups 3 and 4). These results indicate that the two black-on-white jars from Grasshopper Pueblo were probably manufactured there with the same paste as the polychrome Group 3 vessels. The two earlier local jars from Chodistaas were produced elsewhere. The rest of the analyzed Cibola White Ware ceramics, including three more jars from Grasshopper, were imported into the Grasshopper region but from a different source or sources than the imported White Mountain Red Ware. The wider inferences that can be drawn from the compositional evidence for differential manufacturing loci of imported White Mountain Red Ware and Cibola White Ware and from the local production of some Cibola White Ware at Grasshopper are discussed below.

In conclusion, neutron activation analysis of a large sample of reconstructible vessels and sherds from Grasshopper Pueblo and sherds from surrounding sites resulted in the clear distinction of four compositional groups. Compositional Groups 1 and 2 comprise the imported White Mountain Red Ware. Compositional Group 3 and 4 ceramics were produced locally. A match of source clays from Grasshopper Pueblo with Group 3 and the occurrence of Grasshopper Polychrome in both Compositional Groups 3 and 4 provide a strong argument for the local production of White Mountain Red Ware. A more detailed discussion of the compositional groups, especially Group 4 that does not match any of the local source clays, is presented below in conjunction with the results of the petrographic analysis.

Inductively-coupled Plasma Emission Spectroscopy (ICP)

Dr. James H. Burton of the Laboratory for Archaeological Chemistry of the University of Wisconsin in Madison recently developed a weak-acid extraction technique for inductively-coupled Plasma Emission Spectroscopy (ICP) to be used for the chemical characterization of ceramics (Burton and Simon 1993). ICP elemental analysis normally involves the total digestion of the powdered ceramic or silicious sample material by a strong hydrofluoric acid solution and the consequent qualitative and quantitative elemental analysis of the resulting "liquid sample." It provides a true quantitative chemical bulk analysis (Jarvis and others 1992: 176; Thompson and Walsh 1989: 95–100, 232–237), similar to other instrumental techniques such as neutron activation, atomic absorption, and powdered X-ray fluorescence. In contrast, the weak-acid extraction method developed by Burton uses, as the name indicates, a weak hydrochloric acid solution. It should be emphasized that the samples are not dissolved by the hydrochloric acid, but that unknown portions of constituent elements are leached from each powdered sample and analyzed. Burton and Simon (1993: 45, 46) maintain that this method generates reproducible solutions that provide precise, quantitative results. They also postulate that "elemental abundances exhibited by the acid extracts are strongly related to the original geologic context in which they were formed. Firing influences on the chemical signature are minor" (Burton and Simon 1993: 52).

A total of 655 White Mountain Red Ware and Grasshopper Polychrome ceramics was submitted for weak-acid extraction ICP analysis at the Laboratory for Archaeological Chemistry of the University of Wisconsin in Madison (Triadan 1994, Appendix D). The samples included 33 ceramics from Grasshopper Pueblo and 622 specimens from 33 contemporary sites in the Grasshopper region and adjacent areas (Table 3.18). Of the ceramics submitted to weak-acid extraction ICP, 202 were also analyzed by NAA (Appendix B) of which 157 could be assigned to the four compositional NAA groups presented above. A comparison of the ICP and NAA data sets provided the opportunity to evaluate the weak-acid extraction technique for sourcing ceramics. It is fully acknowledged that weak-acid ICP and NAA are not directly comparable. Weak-acid ICP is not a "whole-sherd analysis," because only portions of the elemental constituents of the ceramics are leached and analyzed. Moreover, mainly major and minor elements were determined by ICP as opposed to a wide range of trace elements that were determined by NAA. Nevertheless, if weak-acid ICP provides reliable chemical characterization, major compositional trends in the data should parallel results from neutron activation analysis.

Sample Preparation

Procedurally, the surface and slip of portions of each sherd are removed with a drill burr and each sample is

Table 3.18. Total Number of Samples Analyzed by ICP

Site		No. of Samples
AZ P:14:1	Grasshopper Pueblo	33
GFS 82-1	Spring Creek Pueblo	30
AZ V:2:7	Ruin's Tank Pueblo	49
AZ P:14:25	Red Canyon Tank Pueblo	39
AZ V:2:62		43
AZ P:14:281		41
AZ V:2:13	Blue House Mtn. Pueblo	24
AZ V:2:79	Double Springs Cliff Dwelling	16
AZ P:14:15	Oak Creek Pueblo	10
AZ P:14:71		11
GFS 88-9	Carrizo Creek Pueblo	19
GFS 88-10	Blue Spring Pueblo	16
GFS 85-3	Cedar Creek Pueblo	12.
	Cibecue Pueblo	19
TDT	Tundastusa	11
BW	Banning Wash Pueblo	7
PD	Pinedale Ruin	19
SL	Showlow Ruin	5
K	Kinishba	19
Q	Q-Ranch	20
AZ V:2:3	Spotted Mountain Pueblo	20
AZ P:14:13	Brush Mountain Pueblo	41
AZ V:2:1	Canyon Creek Cliff Dwelling	18
AZ P:14:12	Hilltop Pueblo	26
GFS 86-3	Black Mtn. Pueblo	21
AZ V:2:49	Canyon Butte Pueblo	15
AZ V:2:87		12
GFS 81-79		12
AZ V:2:23		16
AZ V:2:5	Hole Canyon Cliff Dwelling	4
AZ V:2:83		9
GFS 89-6		1
AZ P:13:2		4
AZ P:14:14	Red Rock House	13
Total		655

ground in an agate mortar to a fine powder. One-hundred mg of each sample are then placed into a polyethylene vial, to which 20 ml of 1-molar hydrochloric acid are added. The vials are shaken and left at room temperature, under intermittent agitation, for two weeks, after which the solution is decanted and only the solution is analyzed by ICP. Based on the analysis of the extraction solutions of the ceramic samples, 12 elements (Al, Ba, Ca, Fe, K, Mg, Mn, Na, P, Sr, Ti, and Zn) are usually determined (Burton and Simon 1993: 47–48).

Results

Statistical analysis of the ICP data followed the procedures described for the NAA analysis. First, the general patterning of the ICP data was examined by calculating principal components on the basis of all 655 samples and all 12 elemental variables. Principal components plots indicate three potential compositional groups (Fig. 3.15).

To compare the ICP and NAA data sets, base log 10 values of element concentrations were bivariately plotted, and principal components were calculated for the ICP data of the 202 samples analyzed by both techniques on the basis of the 12 elemental variables.

A principal component plot of the ICP data of the 202 samples shows the same general structure as the whole data set (compare Figs. 3.15 and 3.16). When the samples are plotted with their NAA compositional group identification, it is clear that the general division of imported (NAA Groups 1 and 2) and local ceramics (NAA Groups 3 and 4) in the data set prevails (Fig. 3.17). Although this seems to indicate a general correspondence of the NAA and ICP data, there are curious differences between the relative elemental abundances in the two data sets. These differences can be demonstrated most graphically by the aluminum (Al) concentrations.

Ceramics assigned to NAA Groups 1 and 2 were manufactured from light-firing kaolinitic clays. Kaolinitic clays contain a higher alumina:silica ratio than orange-brown clays, which contain mainly smectites and illites (Rice 1987: 45–50; Shepard 1985: 374–377). The expected difference in aluminum content is present in the NAA data (Fig. 3.18). In contrast, the ICP data show almost an inversion of the Al concentrations (Fig. 3.19). Some aluminum values for samples classified as imports (belonging to either NAA Group 1 or Group 2) are as low as 724 ppm (0.07%, see Triadan 1994, Appendix D). Considering the fact that alumina (Al_2O_3) is a major constituent of clays and ranges from 28.3 percent to 39.4 percent (Rice 1987: 45–50), such low concentrations for aluminum are unrealistic.

Though the general division between local and imported ceramics is replicated by weak-acid ICP analysis, in light of the inverted aluminum concentrations it is likely that rather than actual compositional difference, the original firing temperature of the ceramics is a major factor in this distribution. Refiring experiments conducted on Grasshopper ceramics in 1989 demonstrated that both Grasshopper Polychrome and the brown-paste or locally produced White Mountain Red Ware vessels were considerably lower fired than the imported White Mountain Red Ware vessels (Triadan 1989: 66–67, Fig. 21). (The brown-paste variety vessels were probably fired at a slightly higher temperature than

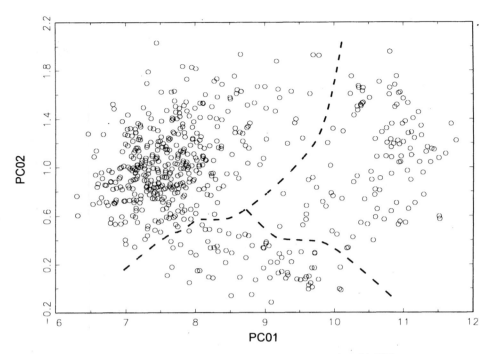

Figure 3.15. Samples analyzed by weak-acid ICP,
Principal Components (PC) 1 and 2; n = 655.

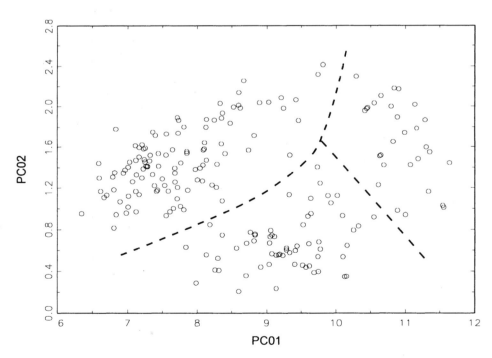

Figure 3.16. ICP data, samples also analyzed by
NAA, Principal Components (PC) 1 and 2; n = 202.

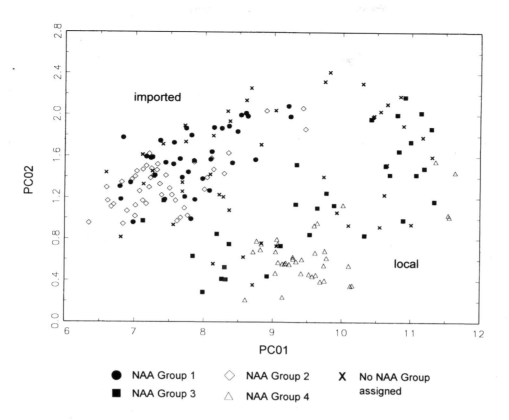

Figure 3.17. ICP data, samples also analyzed by NAA. Samples are identified by NAA group membership, Principal Components (PC) 1 and 2, n = 202.

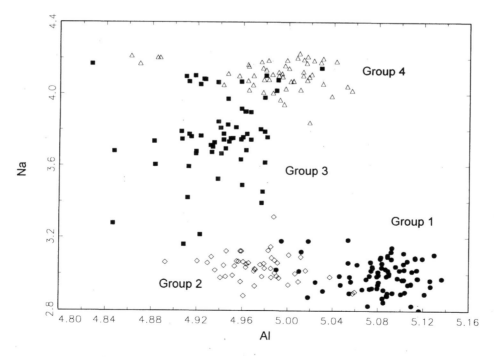

Figure 3.18. NAA compositional groups, Al and Na concentrations. Element concentrations are plotted as base log 10 values.

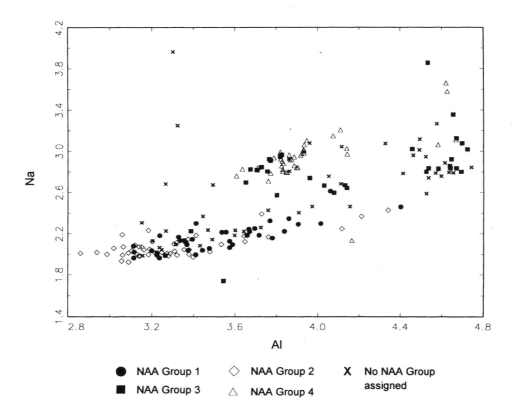

Figure 3.19. ICP data, samples also analyzed by NAA. Samples are identified by NAA group membership, Al and Na concentrations. Element concentrations are plotted as base log 10 values; n = 202.

the Grasshopper Polychrome vessels. In contrast to the local brown-paste White Mountain Red Ware, Grasshopper Polychrome is decorated with organic paint. It was most certainly fired below 750°C [1382°F], as otherwise the carbon would have burned off under predominantly oxidizing firing conditions [Rice 1987: 88]. Core color observations suggest an original firing temperature below 700°C [Triadan 1989: 69]. All ceramics were refired in an oxidizing atmosphere.) The ICP data seem to reflect this difference in firing temperature. It is probable that elements in the lower fired sherds (the local ceramics) are more easily leached and that these samples are therefore characterized by an overall higher extraction amount of elements. This is one logical explanation for the abnormally low aluminum concentrations determined by ICP in the imports (see also Neff and others 1996: 398).

A further review of the results of the weak-acid ICP analysis reveals additional problems. Though samples assigned to NAA Groups 1 and 2 are present in the import group, no compositional differentiation in the ICP data can be discerned. For instance, the clear dif-

ference in iron (Fe) content (Fig. 3.20) between these two groups (as determined by NAA) is not reflected in the ICP data (Fig. 3.21). (The mean difference in iron between NAA Groups 1 and 2 is about one percent; Table 3.11). Even though ICP seems to pick up the macro groupings (imported versus local) in ceramics, arguably for technological rather than compositional reasons, the clear compositional differentiation within the nonlocal subset is not detected.

The ICP data do seem to suggest some compositional differentiation within the local ceramics (Figs. 3.16, 3.17, 3.19), but the two local groups in the ICP data are not concordant with the two local NAA groups. Samples assigned to NAA Groups 3 and 4 occur in both of the local ICP groups (Figs. 3.17, 3.19). Also, most samples of Grasshopper Polychrome cluster in one of the two groups (the group farthest to the right in Figure 3.17), though the group is not made up exclusively of Grasshopper Polychrome. Samples in this group tend to be enriched in all measured elements. Because the Grasshopper Polychrome vessels were fired at lower temperatures than the local White Mountain Red Ware

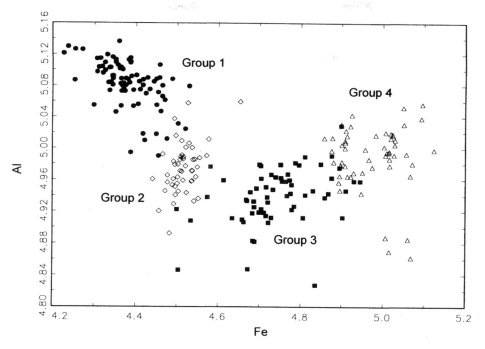

Figure 3.20. NAA compositional groups, Fe and Al concentrations. Element concentrations are plotted as base log 10 values.

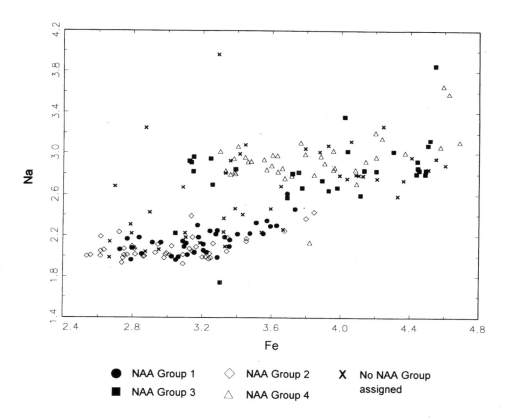

Figure 3.21. ICP data, samples also analyzed by NAA. Samples are identified by NAA group membership, Fe and Na concentrations. Element concentrations are plotted as base log 10 values; n = 202.

vessels, the differentiation between the two local ICP groups appears again to be essentially technological; the measured elements were more easily leached from the Grasshopper Polychrome and other specimens in the enriched group.

Relying solely on weak-acid ICP data, one could interpret the two local groups as representing two different production loci, one for Grasshopper Polychrome and the other for the brown-paste variety of White Mountain Red Ware. Based on a preliminary subset of the ICP data, Burton and Simon (1993: 57–58) indeed differentiated three compositional groups: imported or "true" White Mountain Red Ware, the brown-paste variety, and Grasshopper Polychrome. Clearly, this interpretation is quite different from the one based on the NAA data. As mentioned above, locally produced White Mountain Red Ware and Grasshopper Polychrome occur in both of the local compositional groups (NAA Groups 3 and 4).

To conclude, the comparative analysis demonstrated inherent problems with the weak-acid extraction method for sourcing ceramics and, as a result, for archaeological interpretations of the compositional data. (Neff and others 1996 present a methodological critique of the technique.) First, the elemental analysis of extraction solutions resulted in chemical profiles that do not accord with the geological materials used in the production of White Mountain Red Ware. Second, major compositional differences within the imported and locally produced White Mountain Red Ware are not reflected in the ICP data. Thus, the imported ceramics, for instance, could be interpreted as coming from a single resource procurement zone (Bishop and others 1982) rather than from at least two different sources. Third, groups that were formed in the ICP data set yielded erroneous information about the local production of White Mountain Red Ware.

Petrographic Analysis

Mineral classification of naturally occurring nonplastic inclusions and temper within ceramic pastes is a vital analytical tool in conjunction with chemical characterization. Ceramic sourcing studies often entail the comparison of raw materials with ceramic pastes. However, in most cases, ceramics are a complex composite of raw materials modified by human behavior. For instance, tempering agents may have been added by the potter. As elemental analysis usually is a bulk analysis of the ceramic materials, both clay and temper signatures are present in the resulting chemical profiles.

Petrographic analysis provides an invaluable means to evaluate compositional groups. (Bishop [1980] and Bishop and others [1982: 294–295, 299–300] present a more detailed discussion of the temper problem.)

In addition to the large number of samples submitted to chemical characterization, 80 polished thin sections were analyzed petrographically by Deborah Bergfeld at the Department of Geological Sciences, University of Missouri, Columbia. The samples consisted of 20 clays and 9 sand samples (Table 3.19) and 51 sherds (Table 3.20). Within the sherd samples, 29 came from Grasshopper Pueblo, the rest from 11 sites from areas adjacent to the Grasshopper region. All the sherds had been analyzed by ICP and a large portion of them by NAA (Table 3.20). The clay and sand samples included all those that had been analyzed by NAA. Eight of the clays came from archaeological contexts, predominantly Room 113 at Grasshopper Pueblo (Table 3.19).

The objectives of the petrographic analysis were to (1) identify the mineral components of nonplastic inclusions, and (2) determine if any mineralogical difference between ceramics local to Grasshopper and those coming from sites outside the Grasshopper region could be detected. Thin sections of fired source clays provided a means to determine the natural occurrence of nonplastic inclusions, against which thin sections of sherds could be contrasted. Sands were examined with respect to grain size and their principal mineral components. No detailed quantitative analysis, such as point counting, was carried out, but the petrographer provided quantitative estimates for the different mineral components and evaluated how much temper may have been added to the ceramic pastes.

Results

Petrographic analysis revealed three major temper groups. Temper Group 1 consists mainly of light sherd temper (grog) and quartz (Plates 3 and 4). Temper Group 2 consists of very fine-grained quartz (probably naturally present in the clay and derived from sandstone) and some diabase (Plate 5). Temper Group 3 consists predominantly of coarse diabase (Plates 6 and 7).

Table 3.20 demonstrates that the temper groups correspond well with the compositional groups. Imported White Mountain Red Ware (Compositional Groups 1 and 2) was sherd and quartz tempered. Local ceramics belonging to Compositional Group 3 were tempered with minor diabase (Temper Group 2). Local ceramics within Compositional Group 4 were tempered with high quantities of coarse diabase (Temper Group 3). Diabase

Table 3.19. Clays and Sands Analyzed by Petrography

Sample No.	NAA Sample No.	Provenience FN = Field No.	Observations (Percents are quantitative estimates by the petrographer; O.M. = Opaque minerals)
Clay			
1	DTC001	Kinishba Ruin	Very fine grained, quartz 10-15%, minor chert, carbonate 3-5%, plagioclase.
2	DTC002	Kinishba Ruin	Very fine grained, carbonate, plagioclase, muscovite, quartz. Nonplastics 15-20%.
3	DTC003	Martin Form., Road 011	Bimodal grain size, very fine-grained quartz and plagioclase, grains are subangular to subrounded, coarse grains of quartz that are subangular-rounded. Quartz 15-20%, plagioclase 2-3%. Large grains make up 5-10% of clay.
4	DTC004	3 Way Tank, Road 011	Fine grains are mostly quartz, 5-10%, larger clasts are carbonates, 10-15%, some are bioclasts. O.M. minor goethite.
5	DTC005	South peak, Spotted Mtn.	Too fine grained to see much, probably quartz and plagioclase, some goethite. Some volcanic inclusions and concentrated balls of plagioclase. Some **diabase.**
6	DTC006	North peak, Spotted Mtn.	Quartz 10-15%, chert 1%, plagioclase (mostly incorporated into very fine grained volcanic inclusions, but also some large mineral grains) 3-5%, minor clinopyroxene. Some **diabase.** Relatively coarse grain size.
7	DTC007	North Spring Creek	Large rounded quartz grains 20-25%, minor microcline, plagioclase, and chert. O.M. specular hematite 5% and minor goethite.
8	DTC008	North Spring Creek	Relatively coarse grained, much quartz, 20%, subrounded to rounded, chert 1-2%, and weathered plagioclase 10-15%, with minor clinopyroxene. O.M. goethite 3%, specular hematite 4-5%.
9	DTC009	Grasshopper Pueblo	Extremely fine grained, mostly quartz with some carbonate and muscovite but too fine grained to see much. Nonplastics 10-15%.
10	DTC010	Grasshopper Tank No. 2	Extremely fine grained, one large carbonate flake and an occasional large quartz grain, but overall the sample contains predominantly fine-grained subangular-subrounded quartz with a trace of muscovite. Nonplastics 10-15%.
11	DTC011	South of Mud Tank	Predominantly clay with some carbonate clasts 5-10%, many of the clasts are rounded; also some very fine-grained quartz mixed with carbonate (too fine grained to identify) 1-2%.
12	DTC012	1 Mile Tank	The majority of the slide is very fine grained, but large clasts of carbonate are present (2-3%), one is possibly a bioclast. The fine-grained material appears to be quartz, possibly mixed with carbonate 1-2%.
13	DTC013	P:14:1, Rm. 414, FN154	Very fine-grained matrix with some clasts of carbonate and quartz in roughly equal proportions and a trace of plagioclase. Nonplastics 10-12%.
14	DTC014	P:14:1, Rm. 420, FN206	Fine grain matrix with traces of muscovite and mixed carbonate and quartz. Occasional large clasts consisting of clay, carbonate, and quartz. Nonplastics 25-35%. **Good match with Temper Group 3.**
15	DTC015	P:14:24, Rm. 18	Predominantly quartz with a trace of muscovite. Very fine subangular grains with a few large quartz grains. Nonplastics 5-7%.
16	DTC016	P:14:1, Rm. 113, FN621	Extremely fine grains; quartz, plagioclase, and hematite 2-3%. Nonplastics 3-5%.
17		P:14:1, Rm. 113, FN802	Very fine grained quartz and carbonate, minor muscovite. Large carbonate clasts. Nonplastics 5-7%.
18		P:14:1, Rm. 113, FN854	Orthopyroxene and clinopyroxene 1-2%, plagioclase 1%, feldspar weathering to carbonate 3-5%, quartz 3-5%, and clay inclusions. Nonplastics 10-15%. **Diabase** but not in high concentrations. **Similar to Temper Groups 2 and 3.**
19		P:14:1, Rm. 113, FN907	Extremely fine grains; they appear to be quartz, some plagioclase, a piece of hornblende, and some goethite. Small black spots (possibly organic) throughout the clay, concentrated in some areas. Nonplastics 1%.
20		P:14:1, Rm. 113, FN1223	Very fine grains, appear for the most part to be quartz and carbonate, some carbonate clasts. Nonplastics 3-5%.
Sand			
21	DTS018	NW of 3 Way Tank	Chert, with hematite (lithic fragments), quartz, chert, minor carbonate.
22	DTS019	Oak Creek	Specular hematite, quartz, weathered plagioclase, pyroxene, hornblende, lithic fragments, goethite, and minor olivine.
23	DTS020	Oak Creek	**Diabase,** plagioclase, quartz, pyroxene, lithic fragments, hornblende, biotite, goethite, and minor carbonate.
24	DTS021	P:14:1, Rm. 107	Lithic fragments (clay and quartz), large quartz grains, minor muscovite, hornblende, and carbonate.
25		Q-Ranch, fine	**Diabase,** very large grains of plagioclase and clinopyroxene, smaller grains plagioclase, clinopyroxene, quartz, goethite, biotite, hornblende, olivine, specular hematite, siderite.
26		Q-Ranch, coarse	**Diabase,** very large grains of plagioclase and clinopyroxene, smaller grains plagioclase, clinopyroxene, quartz, goethite, biotite, hornblende, olivine, specular hematite, siderite.
27		Cibecue Creek	Quartz and carbonate.
28		Canyon Creek	**Diabase,** plagioclase, clinopyroxene, biotite, specular hematitie, siderite, goethite.
29		Forestdale Valley	Quartz and chert.

Table 3.20. Ceramics Analyzed by Petrography
(Description based on initial visual inspection of sherd cores)

Sample No.	NAA Sample No.	Description	Provenience	Temper Group*	NAA Group	Comments
30		Local Fourmile Polychrome	AZ P:14:1	3		
31	DTB128	Local Fourmile Polychrome	AZ P:14:1	1	3	White sherd temper, high probability for NAA Group 3 (21%)
32		Local Fourmile Polychrome	AZ P:14:1	3		
33		Local Fourmile Polychrome	AZ P:14:1	1		
34	DTB129	Local Fourmile Polychrome	AZ P:14:1	3	4	
35	DTB130	Local Fourmile Polychrome	AZ P:14:1	3	4	
36		Local White Mtn. Red Ware	AZ P:14:1	3		
37		Local Fourmile Polychrome	AZ P:14:1	3		
38	DTB131	Local Fourmile Polychrome	AZ P:14:1	3?		Sherd temper, low probability for NAA Groups 3 and 4
39	DTB132	Local Fourmile Polychrome	AZ P:14:1	3	4	
40	DTB133	Imported Fourmile Polychrome?	AZ P:14:1	2	3	
41		Imported Fourmile Polychrome	AZ P:14:1	1		
42	DTF134	Imported Fourmile Polychrome	AZ P:14:1	1	1	
43	DTF135	Imported Fourmile Polychrome	AZ P:14:1	1	1	
44	DTF136	Imported Fourmile Polychrome	AZ P:14:1	1	1	
45	DTF137	Imported Fourmile Polychrome	AZ P:14:1	1	1	
46		Imported Fourmile Polychrome	AZ P:14:1	1		
47		Imported Fourmile Polychrome	AZ P:14:1	1		
48		Imported Fourmile Polychrome	AZ P:14:1	1		
49	DTF138	Imported Fourmile Polychrome	AZ P:14:1	1		Low probability for NAA Group 1
50		Grasshopper Polychrome	AZ P:14:1	3		
51	DTG139	Grasshopper Polychrome	AZ P:14:1	3	4	
52		Grasshopper Polychrome	AZ P:14:1			
53		Grasshopper Polychrome	AZ P:14:1	3		
54	DTG140	Grasshopper Polychrome	AZ P:14:1	2		Low probability for NAA Group 3
55	DTG141	Grasshopper Polychrome	AZ P:14:1	2	3	
56	DTG142	Grasshopper Polychrome	AZ P:14:1	3		Low probability for NAA Group 3
57		Grasshopper Polychrome	AZ P:14:1	3		
58	DTG143	Grasshopper Polychrome	AZ P:14:1	2	3	
59	DTP216	Imported Fourmile Polychrome?	Tundastusa	1	1	
60	DTP217	Pinedale Polychrome or B/R	Tundastusa	1		Low probability for NAA Groups 1 and 2
61	DTP218	Grasshopper Polychrome?	Tundastusa	1		Low probability for NAA Group 2
62	DTP222	Local White Mtn. Red Ware	Banning Wash	1	2	
63	DTP223	Local? Pinedale Poly., B/R?	Banning Wash	1	1	
64	DTP229	Local White Mtn. Red Ware?	Pinedale	1		Low probability for NAA Group 2
65	DTP237	Local White Mtn. Red Ware?	Showlow	2	3	Some sherd temper?
66	DTP238	Local Fourmile Polychrome	Kinishba Ruin	1	2	
67	DTP239	Local Fourmile Polychrome?	Kinishba Ruin			Volcanic tuff
68	DTP245	Local Fourmile Polychrome?	Q-Ranch	2/3	3	
69	DTP249	Local Fourmile Polychrome?	Q-Ranch	3	4	
70	DTP250	Local Fourmile Polychrome?	Q-Ranch	3		Low probability for NAA Group 4
71		Local Pinedale Poly., B/R?	Q-Ranch	3		
72	DTP296	Local Fourmile Polychrome?	AZ V:2:87	3	4	
73	DTP297	Local White Mtn. Red Ware?	AZ V:2:87	1	2	
74	DTG300	Grasshopper Polychrome	AZ V:2:87	2	3	
75	DTP314	Imported Fourmile Polychrome	AZ V:2:5	1		Low probability for NAA Group 1
76	DTP316	Local White Mtn. Red Ware?	AZ V:2:83	1	2	
77	DTP317	Imported White Mtn. Red Ware?	AZ V:2:83	1		Low probability for NAA Group 2
78	DTG319	Grasshopper Polychrome	AZ V:2:83	1	3	Sherd temper
79	DTP321	Local White Mtn. Red Ware?	GFS 89-6	3	2	Should be NAA Group 4 but lots of quartz
80	DTP323	Imported Fourmile Polychrome	AZ P:13:2	1	1	

* Temper Group 1 = sherd and quartz
Temper Group 2 = fine-grained quartz and low quantities of weathered diabase
Temper Group 3 = high quantities of coarse diabase

outcrops occur about 5 km (3 miles) to the west of Grasshopper Pueblo along Oak Creek drainage (Plate 2 and discussion of regional geology herein; Moore 1968: 25, Plate 2). The contrast in the quantities of diabase temper in the two local groups is striking and easily detectable, even visually (Plates 5 and 6). However, the amount of temper does vary within both of these groups and there may be some overlap between the two groups. After petrographic analysis was completed and the correlation between Temper Groups 2 and 3 and Compositional Groups 3 and 4 became apparent, all samples analyzed by NAA were reexamined by binocular microscope. Consistently, samples assigned to Compositional Group 4 contained significantly higher amounts of temper than samples assigned to Group 3.

The imported ceramics, though probably produced from two different clay sources, show the same temper technology, predominantly crushed sherds. In contrast, the local ceramics contain crushed igneous rock as temper, but in differing quantities, which indicates two different paste recipes. The importance of temper for the chemical differentiation of Compositional Groups 3 and 4 is discussed below.

A few samples (Nos. 31, 38, 65, and 78) that were compositionally identified as being local (all but one belonging to NAA Group 3, see Table 3.20) had some sherd temper (Plates 8–11). Two of the samples (Nos. 31 and 38) actually showed light sherd temper in a local clay matrix. Sample 31 (DTB128) was securely grouped within NAA Group 3 (21% probability of group membership, Appendix C). This placement implies that within Compositional Group 3 the clay signature is very strong, because a considerable amount of foreign sherd temper did not pull this sample out of the local compositional group.

The analyzed source clays were generally very fine grained with few nonplastic inclusions. The clay from the stratum underlying Grasshopper Pueblo (No. 9, DTC009) contained predominantly very fine-grained quartz with some carbonates and muscovite (mica); nonplastics account for about 10 to 15 percent (Plate 12). One of the clays from Room 113 at Grasshopper Pueblo (No. 17, PCC802) is similar (Plate 13). A comparison of the quartz matrix of these two clays with that of the local ceramics shows that the clays could very well have provided the raw material for the local ceramics (compare Plates 5, 6, 12, and 13). A tempered clay from Room 113 (No. 18, PCC854) reveals some similarity with ceramics that belong to Temper Group 3 (compare Plates 14 and 6). However, this clay matches NAA Group 3 rather than NAA Group 4 (see

Table 3.14). The other two clays (No. 9, DTC009 and No. 17, PCC802) are a good chemical match with NAA Group 3 (Table 3.14).

DISCUSSION

Instrumental neutron activation analysis resulted in the identification of four distinct compositional groups for White Mountain Red Ware and Grasshopper Polychrome. Petrographic analysis distinguished three different temper groups, which supported the results of chemical characterization. A critical assessment of the weak-acid extraction ICP data revealed major problems with this extraction method. Chiefly, compositional groupings were formed in the data set that did not correspond with the NAA data. Because of these problems, I decided that the ICP data were unreliable and I did not use them for archaeological interpretations.

Compositional Groups 1 and 2 consist of light-paste White Mountain Red Ware imported into the Grasshopper region. Both groups reflect the same temper technology, sherd and quartz, although Group 2 ceramics may be somewhat more heavily tempered with sherds. These two import groups are compositionally well separated, which suggests that imported White Mountain Red Ware ceramics were produced with clays from at least two different sources. The exploitation of two different clay sources for the production of imported White Mountain Red Ware points to two different production zones and may indicate two different manufacturing loci, possibly two different villages. (The two different import production loci are further investigated by distributional analysis in Chapter 5.) Bivariate plots of certain elements (for example, Fig. 3.22) reveal that almost no overlap exists between the elemental concentrations pertaining to each respective group, which supports the claim that these two groups are compositionally distinct.

Compositional Group 3 and 4 ceramics are both tempered with crushed igneous rock (local diabase). However, the amount of temper differs significantly between the two groups. Group 3 corresponds with Temper Group 2 (mainly fine quartz and some weathered diabase) and Group 4 with Temper Group 3 (high quantities of coarse diabase).

The compositional data strongly indicate that the low-tempered Group 3 ceramics were produced at Grasshopper Pueblo. Clays from Grasshopper Pueblo match compositionally, whereas clays only about 1 km (0.6 mile) to the west and about 2 km (1.2 miles) to the north (DTC011 and DTC012) of the pueblo do not match

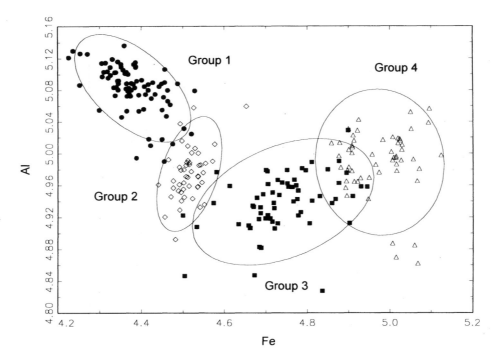

Figure 3.22. NAA compositional groups, Fe and Al concentrations. Element concentrations are plotted as base log 10 values. Ellipse shows confidence interval of 90 percent.

(Table 3.12). Clays from Chodistaas Pueblo show some probability of belonging to Group 3, but that probability is definitely lower than that of clays from Grasshopper Pueblo (Tables 3.12, 3.14). The argument for the production of Group 3 ceramics at Grasshopper becomes even stronger when additional, more circumstantial evidence is considered. The volume of fine-grained quartz in the source clay from Grasshopper Pueblo matches the quartz matrix observed in the ceramics. Moreover, refiring experiments on sherds and firing experiments on raw clays (Triadan 1989: 63–68) revealed that the color of clay sample 9 (NAA sample DTC009) matches the color of clay sample 802 from Room 113 at Grasshopper (Munsell color 5YR 6/; Table 3.7; and Triadan 1989: 64, Table 9), and it fits the color range of refired utilitarian brown wares, Grasshopper Polychrome, and local (brown-paste) White Mountain Red Ware (Munsell colors 5YR 5/6, 5YR 6/8, and 2.5YR 5/8 at 950°C [1742°F]; Triadan 1989: 66, Table 11). Physical properties tests also demonstrated that this source clay from Grasshopper was one of the best suited to produce pottery. It developed no drying cracks and fired well up to 950°C.

Although no source clay could be matched to the coarse-tempered Compositional Group 4 ceramics, I argue that these were also produced at Grasshopper Pueblo for the following reasons.

1. Grasshopper Polychrome as well as local White Mountain Red Ware are present in Compositional Group 4. Grasshopper Polychrome is a major constituent of the ceramic assemblage at Grasshopper Pueblo.

2. Petrographic analysis reveals some gradation in the amount of temper within the two local groups; some samples could be placed either on the high end for Temper Group 2 or on the low end for Temper Group 3. In other words, there seems to be some continuum between the two groups. Moreover, in contrast to the two import groups, bivariate elemental plots also show some overlap between individual elements (for example, Fig. 3.23).

3. Compositional Group 4 is probably only differentiated chemically because of its large quantities of diabase temper. The effects of massive temper addition on chemical profiles were tested with the following simulation. The specimens of Compositional Group 3 were "tempered" by mathematically adding the chemical profile of weathered diabase (DTP331) from Oak Creek drainage to the chemical profiles of the samples. Though no compositional match between the "tempered" Group 3 and Group 4 was obtained, Figure 3.24

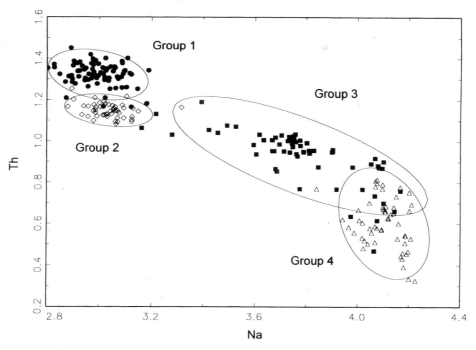

Figure 3.23. NAA compositional groups, Na and Th concentrations. Element concentrations are plotted as base log 10 values. Ellipse shows confidence interval of 90 percent.

shows a growing overlap of the two groups along Principal Components 1 and 2 (which account for 76.48% of the variance of the data), parallel to the amount of "temper" added. A shift can also be demonstrated on the basis of individual elements (Figs. 3.25, 3.26). Moreover, probability calculations based on the first six principal components (90.65% of the variance of the data) for Group 3 "tempered" with 40 percent diabase showed that most samples possess at least some probability of belonging to Compositional Group 4 (Table 3.21).

Table 3.21. Compositional Group Membership Probabilities: Group 3, with 40 Percent Diabase Temper, Compared to Group 4
(Probabilities are expressed in %)

Sample No.	Group 4	Sample No.	Group 4	Sample No.	Group 4	Sample No.	Group 4
DTB061	0.396	DTG099	5.459	DTB128	0.033	DTP247	0.084
DTB063	0.263	DTG100	0.054	DTB133	0.023	DTR251	0.364
DTB064	0.203	DTG101	7.953	DTG141	0.233	DTR252	3.200
DTZ071	0.003	DTG102	0.046	DTG143	2.988	DTR254	0.017
DTL075	0.122	DTG105	8.027	DTR145	9.799	DTR257	0.032
DTL077	0.007	DTG106	0.381	DTR147	3.648	DTR261	0.167
DTL079	0	DTG107	0.073	DTR148	0.015	DTR265	0.211
DTL081	7.974	DTG108	0.094	DTR149	1.168	DTR280	0.018
DTG085	9.567	DTG109	10.846	DTR161	0.005	DTG300	0.010
DTG088	3.156	DTG112	5.030	DTR163	43.193	DTG301	0.006
DTG089	6.190	DTG113	0.094	DTR167	0.045	DTG302	3.592
DTG090	20.188	DTG115	0.365	DTR183	5.567	DTG318	0.631
DTG092	0.461	DTG116	16.897	DTR186	1.093	DTG319	2.541
DTG095	2.540	DTG117	1.490	DTR193	0.021	DTP324	0.483
DTG096	3.135	DTG118	19.120	DTP237	0.004	DTR328	0.068
DTG098	8.960	DTG119	3.654	DTP245	0.331		

NOTE: Mahalanobis distance calculations are based on the first six principal components (90.65% of variance).

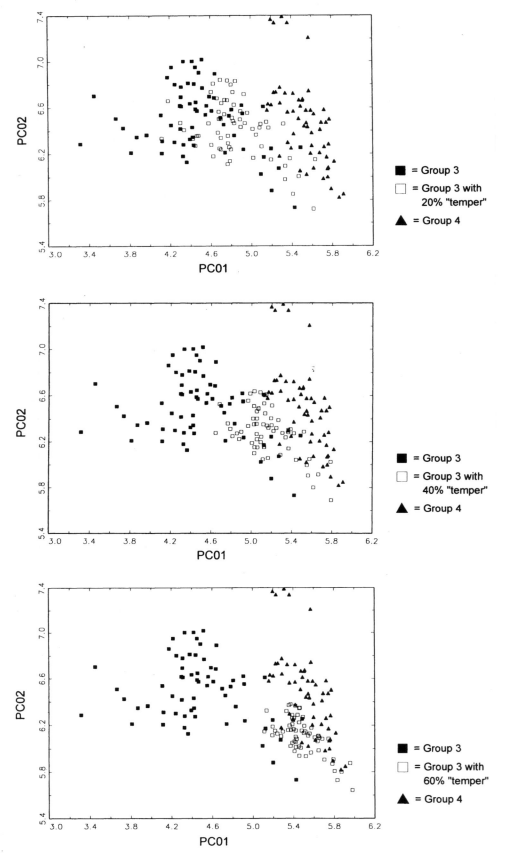

Figure 3.24. Influence of temper on the formation of compositional groups, Principal Components (PC) 1 and 2.

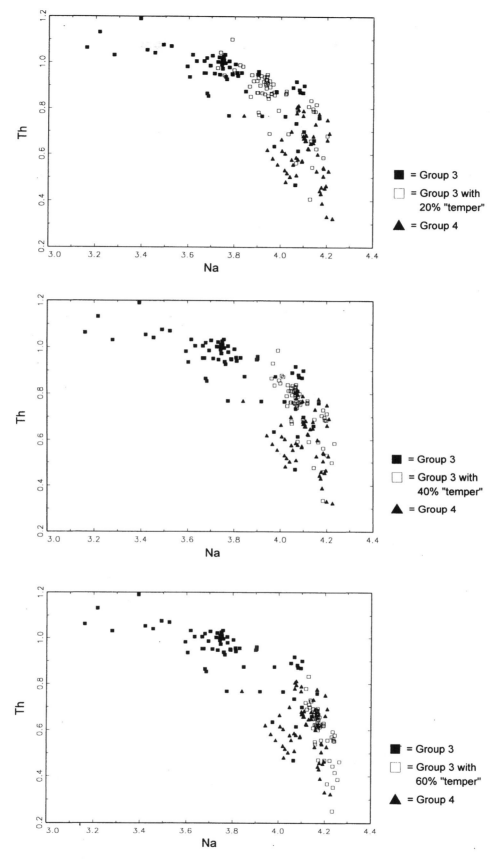

Figure 3.25. Influence of temper on the formation of compositional
groups, Na and Th concentrations (base log 10 values).

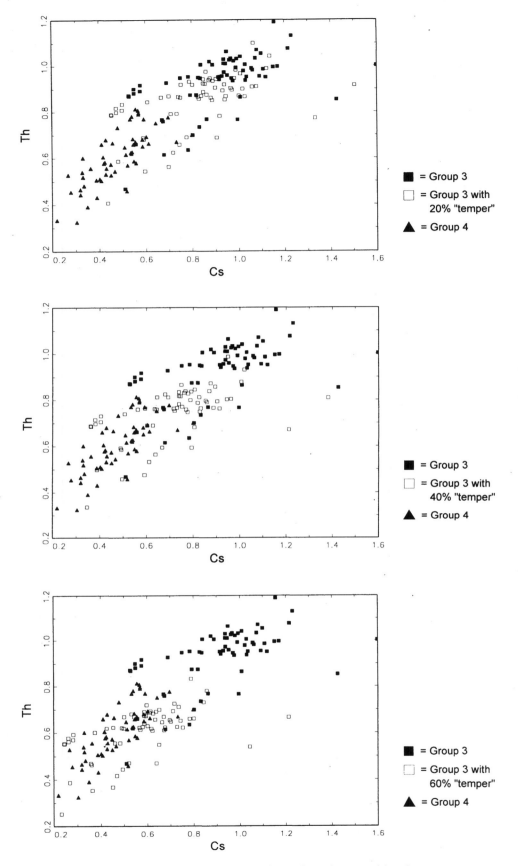

Figure 3.26. Influence of temper on the formation of compositional groups, Cs and Th concentrations (base log 10 values).

This simulation demonstrates that through the addition of a significant amount of temper, a new, totally different compositional group can be created. Obviously, to find the exact tempering material that was used prehistorically resembles the proverbial search for the needle in the haystack. (It is likely that a mixture of friable weathered diabase and other components, for example, quartz, was used as temper). However, this experiment provides some support for the claim that the same source of clay but two different paste recipes were used at Grasshopper Pueblo for the production of White Mountain Red Ware and Grasshopper Polychrome.

In conclusion, the material analyses demonstrate that both Grasshopper Polychrome and White Mountain Red Ware were produced at Grasshopper Pueblo. Contrary to traditional assumptions (Carlson 1970; Graves 1982), this implies at least two *regional* production zones for White Mountain Red Ware in the fourteenth century,

one in the mountains of east-central Arizona and one probably on the southern edge of the Colorado Plateau. Moreover, White Mountain Red Ware was produced at least at two different sources north of the Mogollon Rim during the A.D. 1300s. Cibola White Ware, which was imported earlier into the Grasshopper region, came from a third source. These results indicate a shift of the organization of production and circulation of decorated ceramics during the transition from Pueblo III to Pueblo IV times. Though significant amounts of imported White Mountain Red Ware are present in the Grasshopper ceramic assemblage, a change from import to local production of decorated ceramics seems to have occurred, a trend whose beginnings are observed at the earlier Chodistaas Pueblo (Zedeño 1991, 1994a). The wider behavioral implications of the local production of White Mountain Red Ware and Grasshopper Polychrome are explored in the following chapters.

CHAPTER FOUR

White Mountain Red Ware at Grasshopper Pueblo

The compositional and petrographic analyses of a large sample of polychrome ceramics from Grasshopper Pueblo and from contemporary sites in the Grasshopper and adjacent regions revealed that light-paste White Mountain Red Ware was imported into these areas. The results of the analyses also demonstrated convincingly that brown-paste White Mountain Red Ware and Grasshopper Polychrome were most likely manufactured at Grasshopper Pueblo. Large portions of the pueblo were excavated and controlled surface collections were made during 30 consecutive years of research at the site (Fig. 4.1). This research effort resulted in a wealth of archaeological material, including more than 1,000 reconstructible ceramic vessels, and probably provides the most complete information on large aggregated Pueblo IV period settlements in the east-central Arizona mountains to date. Because of this exceptional assemblage of well-documented ceramics, I was able to sample and analyze more than 100 provenienced White Mountain Red Ware and Grasshopper Polychrome vessels compositionally.

The available ceramic data from Grasshopper Pueblo provided an excellent basis to assess the broader implications of the import of White Mountain Red Ware and its local production at Grasshopper Pueblo between A.D. 1300 and 1400. For instance, what was the function of White Mountain Red Ware? Was it a readily available household item, or was it a status symbol and burial ware? What are the implications of the substantial local production of decorated ceramics at Grasshopper Pueblo? Are imported White Mountain Red Ware vessels and the local Grasshopper Polychrome copies contemporaneous? Do they differ in distribution and function? Could the presence of imported White Mountain Red Ware and local Grasshopper Polychrome indicate co-residence of different ethnic groups at Grasshopper Pueblo? More specifically, is it possible to identify ethnic residences within the site on the basis of the ceramic distribution?

In this chapter I use the results of the compositional analysis of the sampled ceramics and archaeological information on ceramics from room floors, room fill, controlled surface collections, and burials to: (1) establish the temporal relationship between imported White Mountain Red Ware and the locally produced copies, (2) assess the organization of production and distribution of White Mountain Red Ware and Grasshopper Polychrome, and (3) investigate the function of these ceramics within the prehistoric community.

INTRASITE CHRONOLOGY

To investigate the temporal relationship between imported White Mountain Red Ware and locally produced polychrome pottery, I analyzed decorated ceramics from different archaeological contexts at Grasshopper Pueblo and examined the distribution of the vessels belonging to the four compositional groups. As stated above, ceramics from Grasshopper Pueblo that were assigned to Compositional Groups 1 and 2 were imported into the settlement from at least two different sources. Ceramics assigned to Compositional Groups 3 and 4 were most likely produced at Grasshopper Pueblo, and the two compositional groups represent two distinct paste recipes. Compositional Group 3 and 4 ceramics represent a wide range of technological quality. Both groups contain ceramics that are indistinguishable from the imported White Mountain Red Ware except for their local brown pastes. Grasshopper Polychrome, on the other hand, represents the low end of the technological continuum in both compositional groups and often has heavily eroded surfaces (Plate 1). Some vessels in between these two extremes occur in both of the local compositional groups.

To reemphasize, the ceramics we classify as Grasshopper Polychrome were fired at fairly low temperatures because they were decorated with black carbon paint. The low firing temperature results in the poor preservation of Grasshopper Polychrome vessels as compared to the well-preserved, brown-paste copies that were decorated with mineral paint. Because Grasshopper Polychrome encompasses the lowest quality copies of Fourmile Polychrome and may represent the

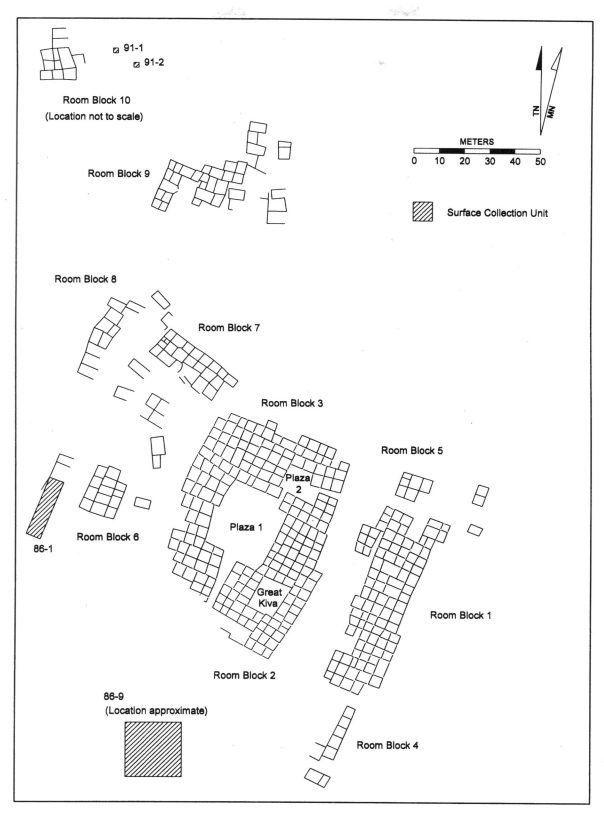

Figure 4.1. Location of systematic surface collection units
at Grasshopper Pueblo used as the basis for analysis.

last development in the manufacture of polychrome ceramics at Grasshopper Pueblo, I focused predominantly on imported White Mountain Red Ware and Grasshopper Polychrome for the temporal analyses.

Household Context

Discard and Refuse

Surface Refuse

Extramural areas of Grasshopper Pueblo are characterized by extensive trash middens and a high density of surface refuse scattered across the site. To establish discard patterns for the decorated ceramics, specifically White Mountain Red Ware and Grasshopper Polychrome, I examined four total collections of surface ceramics: two units collected in 1986 (one close to Room Block 6 and the other in a midden area south of Room Block 3) and two 2–m by 2–m units close to Room Block 10, collected under my supervision in 1991 (Fig. 4.1). I reclassified the ceramics from the two units collected in 1986 to eliminate possible bias that may have been caused by different people typing the ceramics. Brown-paste White Mountain Red Ware was recorded.

Light-paste White Mountain Red Ware constitutes between 7.10 and 28.43 percent of all ceramics found in the collected surface units, with an average of 24.53 percent. (These percentages are based on sherd weights; for a discussion of sherd quantification, see Rice 1987: 290–293). This ware constitutes 37.28 to 47.44 percent (with a mean of 44.31%) of the decorated ceramics. In stark contrast, the frequencies for Grasshopper Polychrome range from 0.14 to a maximum of 0.68 percent of the total ceramic assemblage, with an average occurrence of 0.36 percent. It represents between 0.60 and 2.70 percent of the decorated surface ceramics, averaging 1.45 percent. Slightly more than 6 percent of the decorated ceramics are brown-paste White Mountain Red Ware. Roosevelt Red Ware and black-on-white ceramics (mostly Pinedale Black-on-white jars) make up 19.02 and 26.78 percent of the decorated assemblage respectively. Figure 4.2 shows the mean percentages of decorated ceramics with regard to the total ceramic assemblage and the decorated ceramic assemblage from the surface.

The predominance of imported White Mountain Red Ware in the surface refuse strongly indicates that it was used and subsequently discarded earlier than Grasshop-

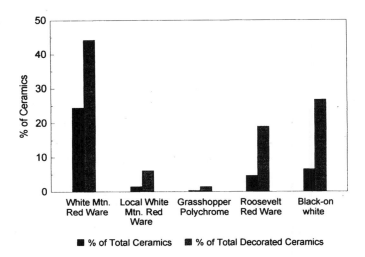

Figure 4.2. Mean percentages of decorated ceramics in surface refuse. Percentages are based on sherd weights.

per Polychrome (for a discussion of the temporal significance of surface ceramics, see Montgomery and Reid 1990). Also, among the local polychromes, brown-paste White Mountain Red Ware occurs in higher quantities (6.17% of the decorated ceramics) than Grasshopper Polychrome (1.45% of the decorated ceramics), which may imply that well-made local White Mountain Red Ware was produced slightly earlier than the low-fired Grasshopper Polychrome.

Room Fill

Reid (1973: 114–118) developed a relative room abandonment measurement for Grasshopper Pueblo. In principle, his model is based on the difference between the quantity of ceramics in floor assemblages and the number of sherds in room fill. Rooms with high frequencies of reconstructible and whole vessels on the latest occupational surface tend to have low sherd frequencies in the fill. They are interpreted as late abandoned, because floor assemblages were left in situ. Conversely, rooms with high sherd frequencies in the fill tend to have only a few floor vessels or none. They are interpreted as early abandoned. Most of the floor assemblage was removed and the rooms were subsequently used for trash deposition. In general, rooms at Grasshopper Pueblo seem to follow this pattern (Fig. 4.3; Montgomery 1993: 157–158, Fig. 12.2; Reid 1973: 115–116). Rooms in a third category have low sherd frequencies in the fill and few floor vessels and they are interpreted as having been functionally different

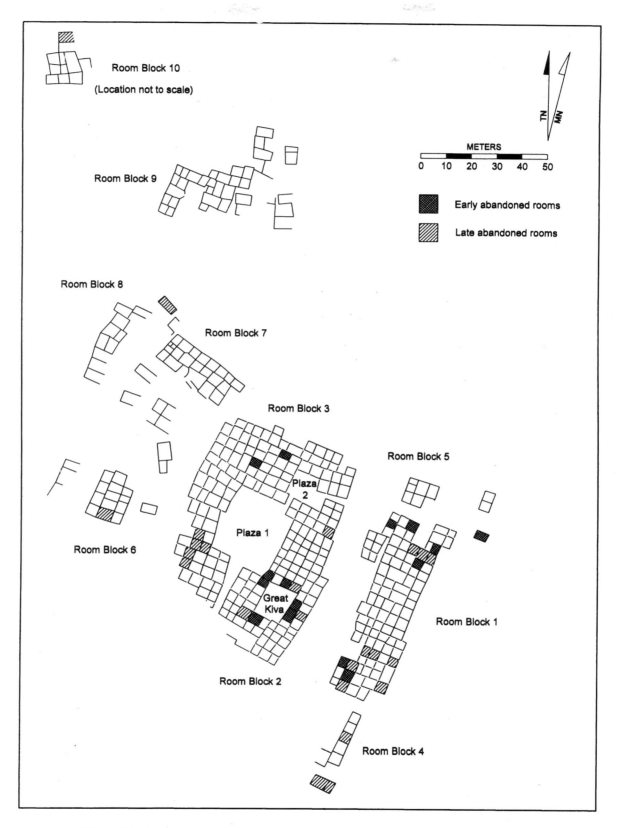

Figure 4.3. Early abandoned rooms and late abandoned rooms at Grasshopper Pueblo.

Table 4.1. Distribution of Decorated Ceramics in the Fill of Early Abandoned Rooms
Roosevelt Red Ware (Salado Polychrome) Excluded

Room	Total Sherds	Decorated Sherds	% of Total	White Mountain Red Ware	% of Decorated	Grasshopper Polychrome	% of Decorated	Black-on-white	% of Decorated
1	5313	1643	30.92	744	45.28	98	5.97	548	33.35
2	3019	721	23.88	232	32.18	217	17.24	117	16.23
10	5562	515	9.26	153	29.71	192	37.28	68	13.20
14	3863	952	24.64	236	24.79	298	31.30	195	20.48
16	2310	777	33.64	202	26.00	348	44.79	192	24.71
18 (kiva)	3547	1076	30.34	456	42.38	122	11.34	263	24.44
18, *trash only*	*2622*	*833*	*31.77*	*354*	*42.50*	*88*	*10.56*	*222*	*26.65*
20	6664	1370	20.56	227	16.57	765	55.84	197	14.38
23	12053	1786	14.82	425	23.80	730	40.87	186	10.41
28	8340	2223	26.66	454	20.42	1300	58.48	217	9.76
31	4567	943	20.65	227	24.07	614	65.11	145	15.38
41	3055	768	25.14	96	12.50	429	55.86	155	20.18
47	4351	668	15.35	134	20.06	233	34.88	140	20.96
146	6938	1230	17.73	409	33.25	483	39.27	128	10.41
270	4265	1136	26.66	319	28.18	133	11.71	313	27.55
274	2365	349	14.76	237	67.91	66	18.91	23	6.59
274, *trash only*	*1719*	*260*	*15.13*	*216*	*83.08*	*9*	*3.46*	*18*	*6.92*
Mean %			22.33		29.81		35.26		17.87

NOTE: Early Abandoned Rooms (Class 4), following Reid 1973: 116.

from domestic rooms; they were predominantly ceremonial rooms (Ciolek-Torrello 1985; Montgomery 1993: 159; Reid and Whittlesey 1982: 693).

I analyzed ceramics found in room fill to establish frequencies of White Mountain Red Ware and Grasshopper Polychrome in secondary household refuse and to test whether a temporal differentiation between these polychrome ceramics could be discerned in this context. Following Reid's relative room abandonment measure, I expected a higher frequency of White Mountain Red Ware in the fill of early abandoned rooms and a higher frequency of Grasshopper Polychrome in the fill of late abandoned rooms, if a temporal difference between White Mountain Red Ware and Grasshopper Polychrome existed and Grasshopper Polychrome was later, as indicated by the surface refuse.

Fill sherd frequencies of definitely early abandoned and definitely late abandoned rooms were analyzed by ware and type. Rooms that had been classified by Reid as probably early abandoned and probably late abandoned (Reid 1973: 116, Table 1) were not included in this analysis because their temporal position was ambiguous. Figure 4.3 shows rooms that were definitely early abandoned and late abandoned at Grasshopper Pueblo. I used sherd counts from past field seasons for this analysis and therefore cannot account for the possible mistyping of sherds. However, as a control I reclassified two collections of fill sherds from rooms that were excavated in the 1960s and did not encounter any mistyping of the decorated ceramics. Brown-paste

White Mountain Red Ware was not recorded separately from light-paste White Mountain Red Ware in these earlier counts.

Table 4.1 shows that the number of Grasshopper Polychrome sherds in the fill of early abandoned rooms is actually higher on average than the number of White Mountain Red Ware sherds. Some rooms have frequencies of more than 50 percent. These cases may include reconstructible Grasshopper Polychrome vessels from the roofs, which eventually collapsed into the rooms. A large number of Grasshopper Polychrome sherds may have come from later contexts (roofs still in use) than the discard in these rooms.

The late abandoned rooms show a slight increase in the occurrence of White Mountain Red Ware and a decrease in Grasshopper Polychrome (Table 4.2). Thus, based on a broad ware classification, the decorated ceramics are not distributed according to the temporal expectation formulated above. (Although Grasshopper Polychrome vessels are copies of Fourmile Polychrome, they are interpreted as a different ware because they are technologically different from White Mountain Red Ware. Vessels are rock-tempered and were painted with organic black paint that required firing at lower temperatures.) Black-on-white ceramics (mostly Pinedale Black-on-white), which are early, do show the anticipated decrease from early to late abandoned rooms. Figures 4.4 and 4.5 show the mean percentages and range of percentages of decorated wares and types in the fill of early and late abandoned rooms.

Table 4.2. Distribution of Decorated Ceramics in the Fill of Late Abandoned Rooms
Roosevelt Red Ware (Salado Polychrome) Excluded

Room	Total Sherds	Decorated Sherds	% of Total	White Mountain Red Ware	% of Decorated	Grasshopper Polychrome	% of Decorated	Black-on-white	% of Decorated
3	565	138	24.43	66	47.83	39	28.26	11	7.97
5	903	230	25.47	133	57.83	18	7.83	27	11.74
6	356	43	12.08	15	34.88	5	11.63	7	16.28
7	494	141	28.54	48	34.84	53	37.59	23	16.31
11	154	57	37.01	29	50.88	12	21.05	1	1.75
13	535	55	10.28	15	27.27	26	47.27	8	14.54
19	1751	755	43.12	84	11.13	306	40.53	82	10.86
21	772	255	33.03	25	9.80	38	14.90		
37	563	158	28.06	74	46.84	40	25.32	22	13.92
39	268	77	28.73	42	54.54	16	20.78	6	7.79
43	790	207	26.20	18	8.69	165	79.71	10	4.83
44	193	718	36.58	89	12.39	274	38.16	84	11.70
45	1039	286	27.53	29	10.14	198	69.23	5	1.75
97 (SWQ)	282	71	25.18	38	53.52	16	22.54	5	7.04
104 (NE/NW)	270	77	28.52	34	44.16	15	19.48	17	22.08
183	2496	348	13.94	104	29.89	105	30.17	42	12.07
198 (outl.)	632	100	15.82	33	33.00	47	47.00	10	10.00
205	543	159	29.28	50	31.45	26	16.35	54	33.96
210	1571	246	15.66	89	36.18	91	36.99	48	19.51
215	2802	485	17.31	82	16.91	189	38.97	88	18.14
216	234	76	32.48	21	27.63	10	13.16	10	13.16
218	499	250	50.10	62	24.80	68	27.20	34	13.60
319 (outl.)	483	78	16.15	11	14.10	13	16.60	48	61.54
359 (outl.)	1530	386	25.23	155	40.16	81	20.98	109	28.24
Mean %			26.28		31.62		30.49		14.95

NOTE: Late Abandoned Rooms (Class 1), following Reid 1973: 116.

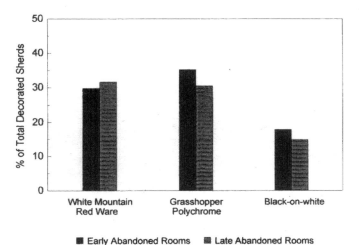

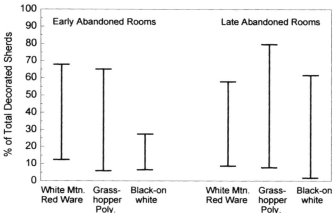

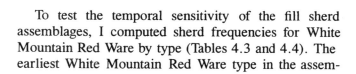

Figure 4.4. Mean percentages of White Mountain Red Ware, Grasshopper Polychrome, and black-on-white ceramics in room fill. Percentages are based on sherd counts.

Figure 4.5. Range of percentages of White Mountain Red Ware, Grasshopper Polychrome, and black-on-white ceramics in room fill.

To test the temporal sensitivity of the fill sherd assemblages, I computed sherd frequencies for White Mountain Red Ware by type (Tables 4.3 and 4.4). The earliest White Mountain Red Ware type in the assem-

blages, St. Johns Polychrome (Carlson 1970: 31–41), is rare (four sherds total) in the fill of early abandoned rooms and disappears completely in late abandoned rooms. Frequencies of Pinedale Black-on-red and Pine-

Table 4.3. Distribution of Selected Ceramic Types in the Fill of Early Abandoned Rooms
(Percentages are of Total Decorated Sherds)

Rm.	Total decor. sherds	White Mountain Red Ware													Indeter. White Mtn. Red Ware		Black-on-white		Cibicue Polychrome		Kinishba Polychrome	
		St. Johns Polychrome		Pinedale Black-on-red		Pinedale Polychrome		Cedar Creek Polychrome		Fourmile Polychrome		Showlow Polychrome										
		No.	%	No.	%	No.	%	No.	%	No.	%	No.	%	No.	%	No.	%	No.	%	No.	%
1	1643	1	0.06	36	2.19	6	0.37	6	0.37	463	28.18	37	2.25	195	11.87	548	33.35	84	5.11		
2	721			10	1.39			6	0.83	164	22.75	19	2.64	33	4.58	117	16.23	18	2.50	4	0.56
10	515			14	2.72	2	0.39	2	0.39	110	21.36	1	0.19	24	4.66	68	13.20	16	3.11	55	10.68
14	952			26	2.73	3	0.32	2	0.21	169	17.75	9	0.95	27	2.84	195	20.48	9	0.95	10	1.05
16	777			13	1.67	5	0.64	4	0.52	144	18.53	11	1.42	25	3.22	192	24.71	8	1.03	4	0.52
18	1076			57	5.30	4	0.37	?	?	321	29.83	11	1.02	63	5.86	263	24.44	58	5.39	2	0.19
trash	833			43	5.16			8	0.96	253	30.37	10	1.20	40	4.80	222	16.65	49	5.88		
20	1370			15	1.10			9	0.66	171	12.48	1	0.07	31	2.26	197	14.38	21	1.53	9	0.66
23	1786	2	0.11	14	0.78	2	0.11	4	0.22	61	3.42	103	5.77	239	13.38	186	10.41	13	0.73		
28	2223			39	1.75	1	0.05	6	0.27	274	12.33	19	0.86	115	5.17	217	9.76	19	0.86	1	0.05
31	943			24	2.55	8	0.85	25	2.65	106	11.24	11	1.17	53	5.62	145	15.38	16	1.70		
41	768			3	0.39	1	0.13	2	0.26	60	7.81	2	0.26	28	2.65	155	20.18			1	0.13
47	668	1	0.15	7	1.05			3	0.45	88	13.17	4	0.60	31	4.64	140	20.96	20	2.99	4	0.60
146	1230			41	3.33	2	0.16			289	23.50	10	0.81	67	5.45	128	10.41	21	1.71		
270	1136			15	1.32	22	1.94	2	0.18	211	18.57	2	0.18	67	5.90	313	27.55	39	3.43		
274	349			12	3.44	19	5.44	20	5.73	143	40.97	37	10.60	6	1.72	23	6.59				
trash	260			10	3.85	14	5.39	24?	9.23	126	48.46	37	10.60	5	1.92	18	6.92				
Mean			0.11		2.11		0.9		0.98		18.79		1.92		5.32		17.87		2.39		1.6

NOTE: Early Abandoned Rooms (Class 4), following Reid 1973: 116.

Table 4.4. Distribution of Selected Ceramic Types in the Fill of Late Abandoned Rooms
(Percentages are of Total Decorated Sherds)

| Rm. | Total decor. sherds | White Mountain Red Ware | | | | | | | | | | | | Indeter. White Mtn. Red Ware | | Black-on-white | | Cibicue Polychrome | | Kinishba Polychrome | |
| | | St. Johns Polychrome | | Pinedale Black-on-red | | Pinedale Polychrome | | Cedar Creek Polychrome | | Fourmile Polychrome | | Showlow Polychrome | | | | | | | | | |
		No.	%	No.	%	No.	%	No.	%	No.	%	No.	%	No.	%	No.	%	No.	%	No.	%
3	138			18	13.04	1	0.73	22	15.94	4	2.90	2	1.45	19	13.77	11	7.97	3	2.17		
5	230			30	13.04			3	1.30	69	30.00	11	4.78	20	8.70	27	11.74	3	1.30	2	0.87
6	43			1	2.33	4	9.30			9	20.93	1	2.33			7	16.28	2	4.65		
7	141			6	4.25	2	1.42			35	24.82			5	3.55	23	16.31	5	3.55		
11	57			5	8.77	1	1.75	1	1.75	20	35.09	1	1.75	1	1.75	1	1.75				
13	55			6	10.91					9	16.36					8	14.54				
19	755			10	1.33			1	0.13	44	5.83	3	0.40	26	3.44	82	10.86	46	6.09	49	6.49
21	255			8	3.14			1	0.39	6	2.35			10	3.92	?					
37	158			19	12.03			3	1.90	27	17.09	2	1.27	23	14.56	22	13.92	6	3.80		
39	77			5	6.49	1	1.30	1	1.30	15	19.48			20	25.97	6	7.79	3	3.90		
43	207			1	0.48					11	5.31			6	2.90	10	4.83				
44	718			10	1.39			1	0.14	41	5.71			37	5.15	84	11.70	18	2.51		
45	286							1	0.35	19	6.64			9	3.15	5	1.75	1	0.35		
97	71							3	4.23	20	28.17	4	5.64	11	15.49	5	7.04				
104	77							2	2.60	9	11.69	2	2.60	21	17.17	17	22.08				
183	348			5	1.44					89	25.58	2	0.58	8	2.30	42	12.07	2	0.58	12	3.45
198	100			4	4.00					19	19.00	1	1.00	9	9.00	10	10.00	1	1.00		
205	159			22	13.84			1	0.63	15	9.43	4	2.52	8	5.03	54	33.96	1	0.63	3	1.89
210	246			26	10.57	11	4.47	5	2.03	29	11.79			18	7.32	48	19.51	1	0.41		
215	485			10	2.06			1	0.21	29	5.98			42	8.66	88	18.14	16	3.30	15	3.09
216	76			3	3.95			1	1.32	7	9.21			10	13.16	10	13.16	13	17.11	4	0.53
218	250			8	3.20	3	1.20	1	0.40	20	8.00	18	7.20	12	4.80	34	13.60	3	1.20	4	1.60
319	78									2	2.56			9	11.54	48	61.54	1	1.28		
359	386			24	6.22	2	0.52	1	0.26	93	24.09	14	3.63	21	5.44	109	28.24				
Mean					8.50		2.59		2.05		14.50		2.70		8.49		15.60		3.17		2.56

NOTE: Late Abandoned Rooms (Class 1), following Reid 1973: 116.

[63]

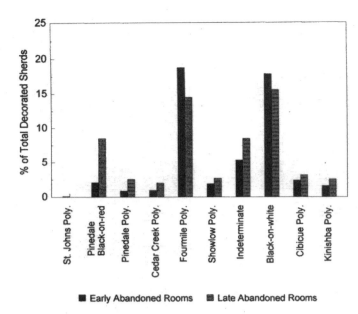

Figure 4.6. Mean percentages of ceramic types in room fill. Percentages are based on sherd counts.

dale Polychrome (dating generally from about A.D. 1275 to 1320, Appendix A; Carlson 1970: 47–57) increase slightly from early to late. Cedar Creek Polychrome, a temporally intermediate type between Pinedale Black-on-red or Pinedale Polychrome and Fourmile Polychrome, also increases slightly. However, Fourmile Polychrome, the most abundant White Mountain Red Ware type, decreases in frequency. Showlow Polychrome, contemporaneous with Fourmile, shows a slight increase through time. Interestingly, Cibicue Polychrome, a Pueblo IV period Mogollon type, occurs in higher frequencies in the fill of late abandoned rooms. Kinishba Polychrome also occurs in slightly higher numbers in the fill of late abandoned rooms than in the fill of early abandoned rooms. Figure 4.6 demonstrates these trends.

The analysis of frequencies of decorated ceramics from fill contexts of early and late abandoned rooms provided inconclusive results with regard to the temporal position of Grasshopper Polychrome. Though the average percentages of White Mountain Red Ware and Grasshopper Polychrome seem to be reversed with regard to the initial expectation, Fourmile Polychrome, the predominant White Mountain Red Ware type, does decrease in frequency in the late abandoned room fill assemblages. However, this trend may be partially modified by higher percentages of indeterminate White Mountain Red Ware in the late fill assemblages (compare Tables 4.3 and 4.4, Fig. 4.6).

Considering that the peak occupation of Grasshopper Pueblo lasted only about 30 to 50 years, the relative chronology provided by the room abandonment measure is not refined enough to pinpoint the transition from predominantly imported White Mountain Red Ware to locally produced Grasshopper Polychrome ceramics. Moreover, early abandoned rooms may have been used as trash dumps for a considerable amount of time and thus may represent assemblages that do not date exclusively to the early phases of pueblo occupation. On the other hand, Grasshopper Polychrome was discarded in the fill of early abandoned rooms in significant numbers, which may imply a production of these ceramics during the main occupation of the pueblo.

Room Floors

To further examine the temporal relationship between Grasshopper Polychrome and White Mountain Red Ware, more specifically Fourmile Polychrome, I analyzed the floor assemblages of 61 rooms that contained reconstructible vessels. These rooms are classified as late abandoned or probably late abandoned following Reid's (1973: 114–118) definition. Figure 4.7 shows that Grasshopper Polychrome was by far the most abundant decorated type on late room floors. Fourmile Polychrome and Showlow Polychrome occur only in small numbers. This distribution of decorated vessels on late room floors demonstrates that Grasshopper Polychrome was in use during the late occupation of the pueblo (Montgomery and Reid 1990), whereas use of Fourmile Polychrome declined.

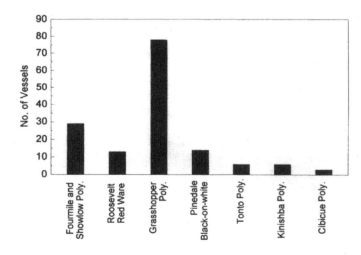

Roosevelt Red Ware includes Gila Polychrome and indeterminate Roosevelt Red Ware.

Figure 4.7. Number of decorated vessels on room floors.

Reviewing the results of the compositional analysis, most of the local ceramics from room contexts (assigned to Compositional Groups 3 and 4) are associated with late or possibly late abandoned rooms. With regard to the imported ceramics (assigned to Compositional Groups 1 and 2), the situation is not as clear. Six nonlocal Fourmile and three Kinishba Polychrome pots occur in definitely late abandoned rooms. The rest of the analyzed import vessels from rooms are either associated with unclear or problematic contexts within the rooms, or come from rooms that cannot be readily classified as early or late abandoned. Nonlocal Fourmile vessels on late room floors could have been heirlooms and not recent imports and thus would not contradict a hypothesis that imports were predominantly early and declined or even ceased to reach the community during the later parts of its occupation. Conversely, a few vessels of nonlocal White Mountain Red Ware could have been brought into the settlement up to its final abandonment while local polychrome ceramics were produced in considerable numbers.

Mortuary Context

I undertook a spatial analysis of decorated ceramics associated with burials to examine whether chronologically significant patterns could be identified. The analysis included 172 burials that contained White Mountain Red Ware, Grasshopper Polychrome, Pinedale Black-on-white, or Kinishba Polychrome pottery (Fig. 4.8). Figure 4.9 shows areas of the site excavated before 1979 in order to relate the burial locations in Figure 4.8 to these areas. After the 1978 season, no burials were excavated by the University of Arizona Archaeological Field School as part of an agreement with the White Mountain Apache tribe. Two burials (91 and 393) were not mapped because no provenience data were available.

The burial records from 1963 through 1978 provided the basis for this analysis. Although in most cases the types of decorated vessels associated with the burials were recorded, brown-paste White Mountain Red Ware vessels were not distinguished from light-paste vessels. Thus, White Mountain Red Ware in this analysis refers predominantly to imported vessels, but may include some locally produced brown-paste pots. It was hoped that the ceramics from burials, representing a tightly controlled archaeological context, would allow some temporal differentiation between early and late types and perhaps between Grasshopper Polychrome and Fourmile Polychrome.

Burial vessels were mapped by type according to their provenience (Figs. 4.10–4.16). A comparison of temporally sensitive ceramic types did not reveal a spatial differentiation within the analyzed burial population. Early types, such as black-on-white bowls and Pinedale Black-on-red occur in the same areas of the site as Fourmile Polychrome and Grasshopper Polychrome (Figs. 4.10, 4.11, 4.14, and 4.15).

To further test the potential of decorated ceramics for determining a temporal differentiation of the burials, the burials containing more than one, three, and five decorated vessels (n = 129, n = 52, and n = 16, respectively) were seriated and subjected to multidimensional scaling (Kendall 1971; Kruskal 1971; Kruskal and Wish 1978). Roosevelt Red Ware types were included in this analysis. Both Brainerd–Robinson and Jaccard coefficient matrices were used. Moreover, burials that contained vessels analyzed by neutron activation were studied to determine whether locally produced vessels could be temporally distinguished from nonlocal ones. Because the number of chemically characterized vessels from burials with multiple decorated vessels was small (n = 10), this attempt to temporally distinguish locally from nonlocally produced vessels was tenuous.

The results of the multidimensional scaling revealed that the ceramic types within the burials seriate temporally (Figs. 4.17a, b), with the exception of black-on-white bowls (very early) and Tonto Polychrome (thought to be very late). This discordance is probably caused by the small quantities of both of these types of vessels in the burial assemblage and their co-occurrence in some interments. Black-on-white bowls were probably heirlooms and therefore appear in burials together with late ceramics. Both Fourmile Polychrome and Grasshopper Polychrome are relatively late, Grasshopper Polychrome possibly a little later (Fig. 4.17b). The burials, on the other hand, do not seriate on the basis of ceramic types (Figs. 4.18a, b). Likewise, burials that contained vessels that were analyzed by neutron activation could not be differentiated temporally. Again, the quantity of compositionally analyzed vessels was probably too small to yield meaningful results.

The seriation of the decorated mortuary ceramics demonstrates that no horizontal stratigraphy can be discerned within the Grasshopper burials. Vessels of specific ceramic types are undoubtedly the most time-sensitive artifacts present in the assemblage. However, the total occupation of Grasshopper Pueblo may not have exceeded 75 years, from about A.D. 1300 to 1375. The vessels associated with burials represent ceramic

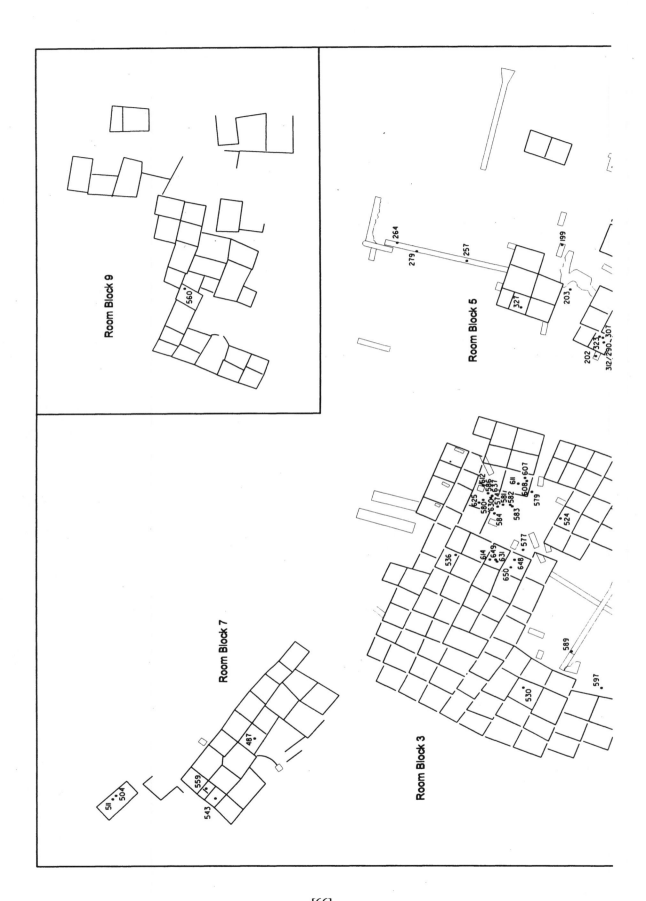

Room Block 9

Room Block 7

Room Block 5

Room Block 3

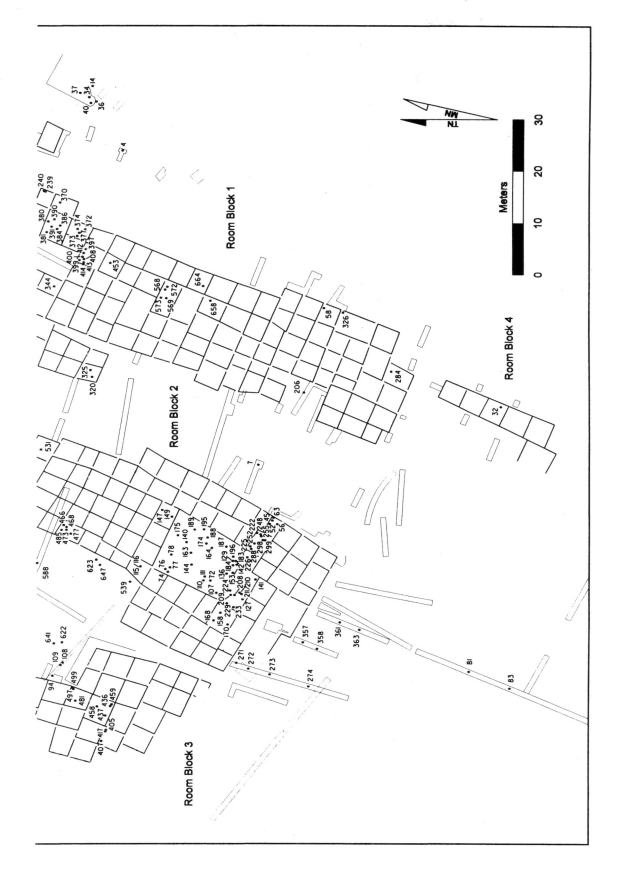

Figure 4.8. Locations of burials containing White Mountain Red Ware, Grasshopper Polychrome, Pinedale Black-on-white, and Kinishba Polychrome vessels.

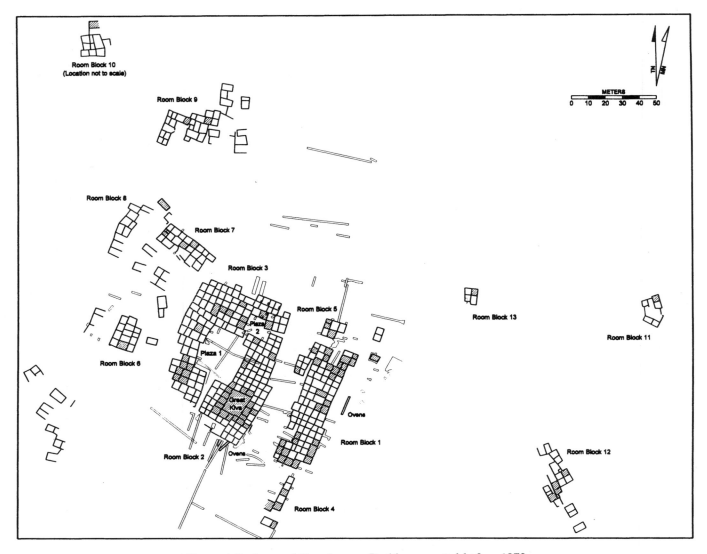

Figure 4.9. Areas of Grasshopper Pueblo excavated before 1979.

types that date to this time period and overlap considerably (Appendix A; Carlson 1970). It is thus not surprising that vessels of relatively early types should occur together with vessels of relatively late types in burials in an occupational context that spans little more than three generations. In the case of Grasshopper Pueblo, we are confronted with the complex situation of a large aggregated pueblo occupied for a short period of time (Reid and Whittlesey 1990), an occupation too short to allow a finer chronological division on the basis of ceramic types.

To summarize, the analysis of frequencies of decorated ceramics from room fill contexts of early and late abandoned rooms provided inconclusive results with regard to the temporal positions of Grasshopper Poly-

chrome and White Mountain Red Ware. Considering the short occupation of Grasshopper Pueblo and the fact that early abandoned rooms may have been used as trash dumps until the last stages of abandonment of the settlement, fill from early abandoned rooms may well represent a mixed assemblage and thus is not sensitive enough to trace the transition from imported, light-paste Fourmile Polychrome to Grasshopper Polychrome, a transition that may have occurred during the course of a few years.

Similarly, the analysis of pottery from burials did not result in a refined intrasite chronology on the basis of ceramic types. No horizontal stratigraphy could be discerned. The seriation of decorated ceramics from burials placed both Fourmile Polychrome and Grasshopper

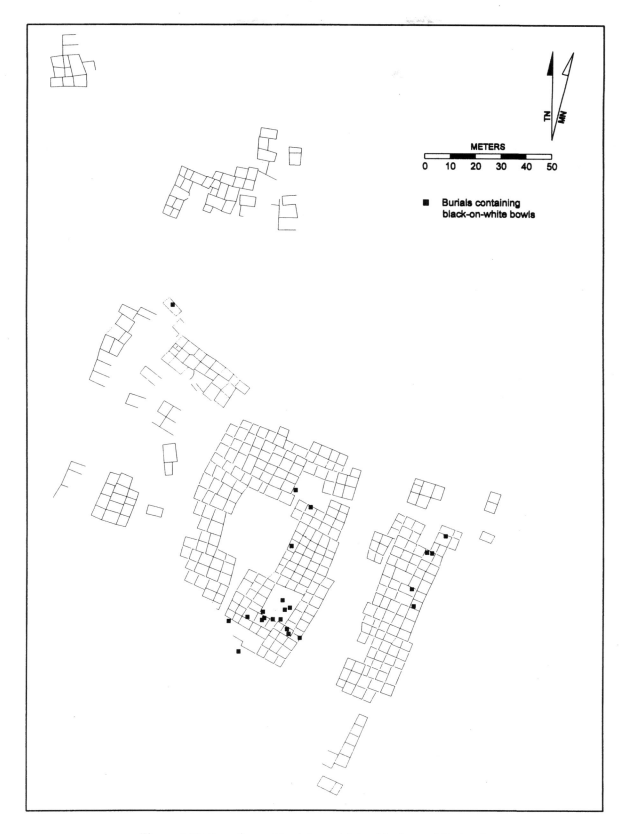

Figure 4.10. Locations of burials containing black-on-white bowls.

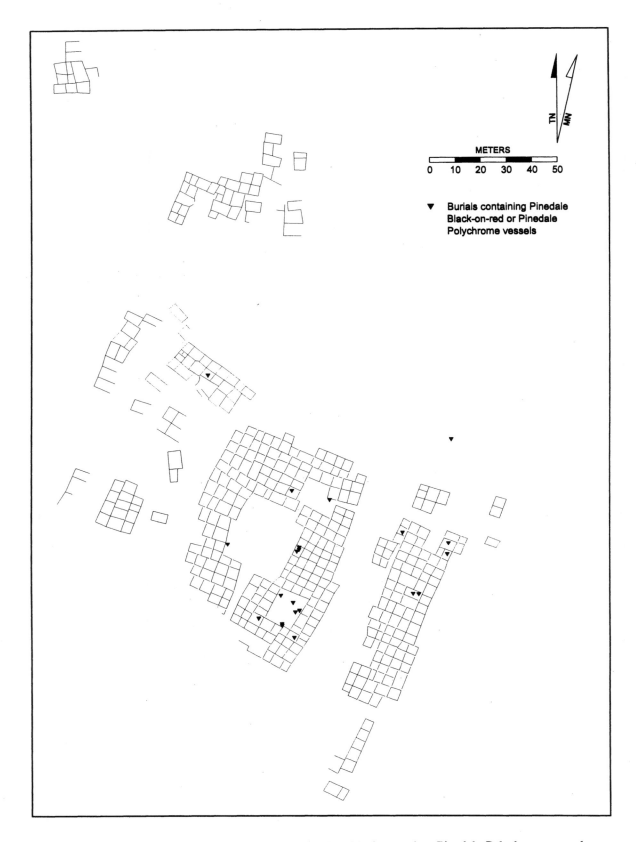

Figure 4.11. Locations of burials containing Pinedale Black-on-red or Pinedale Polychrome vessels.

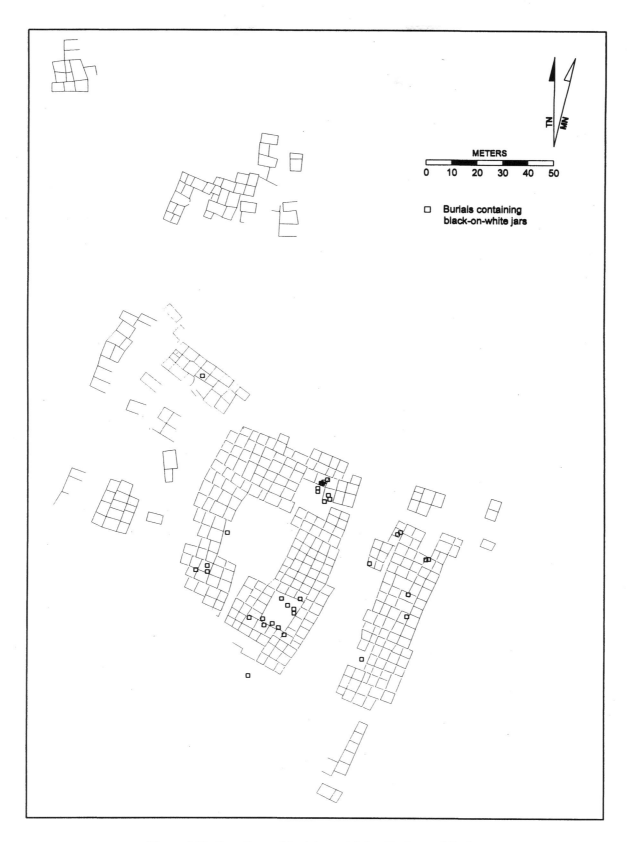

Figure 4.12. Locations of burials containing black-on-white jars.

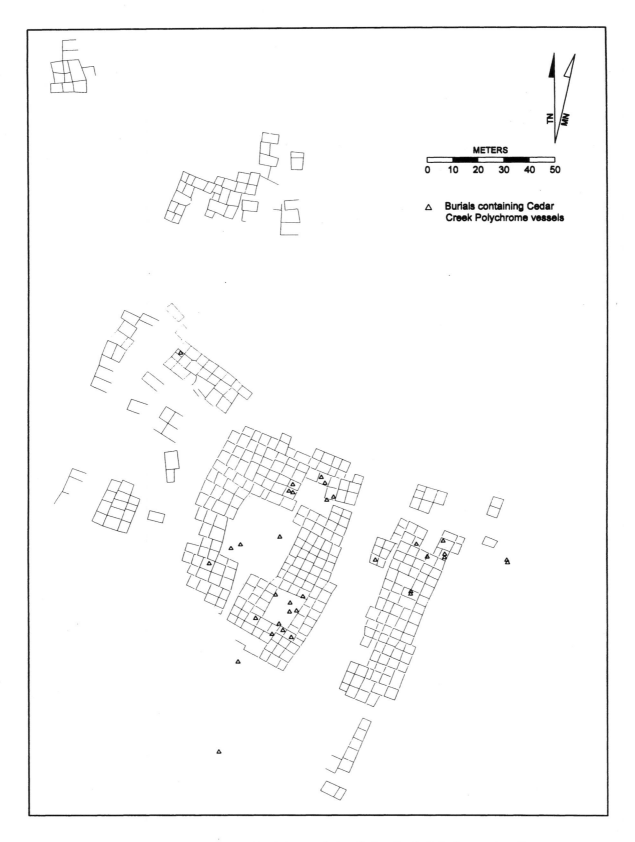

Figure 4.13. Locations of burials containing Cedar Creek Polychrome vessels.

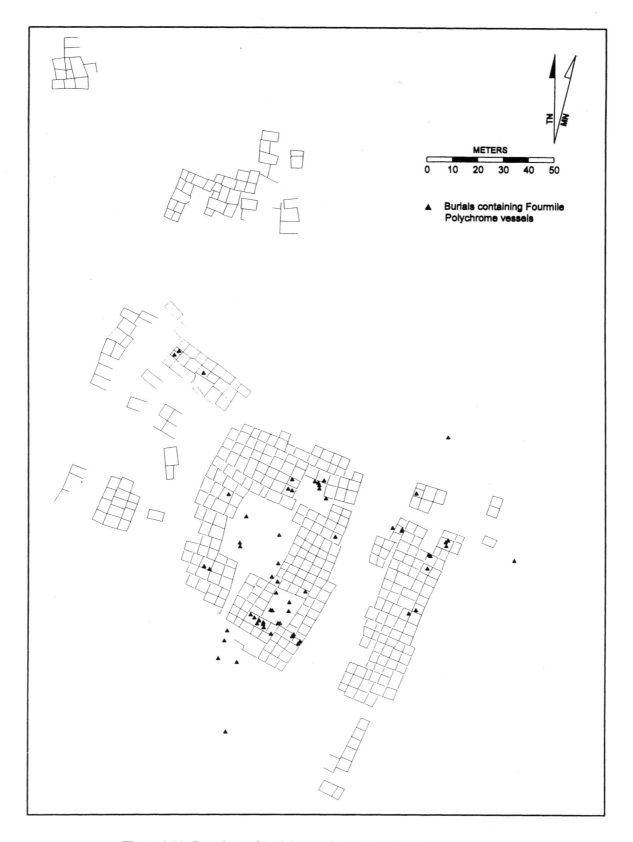

Figure 4.14. Locations of burials containing Fourmile Polychrome vessels.

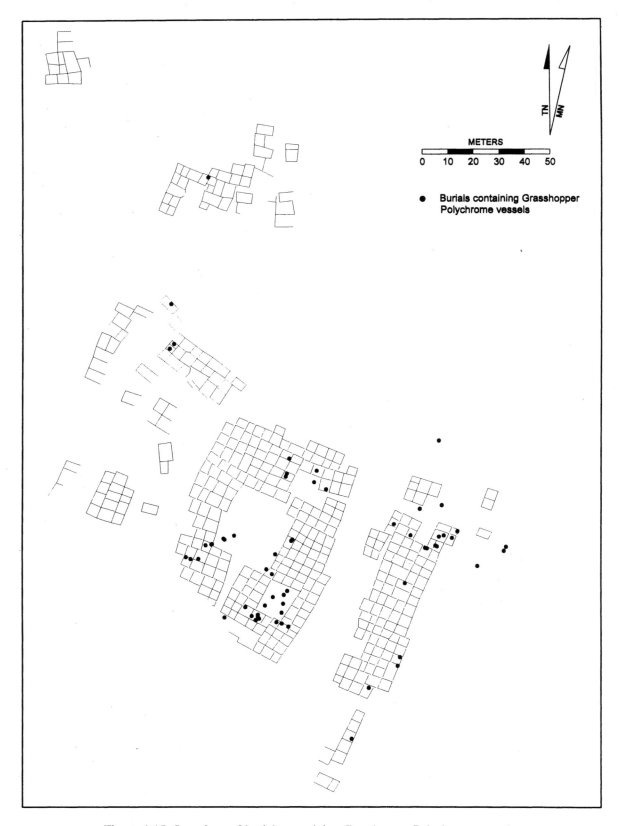

Figure 4.15. Locations of burials containing Grasshopper Polychrome vessels.

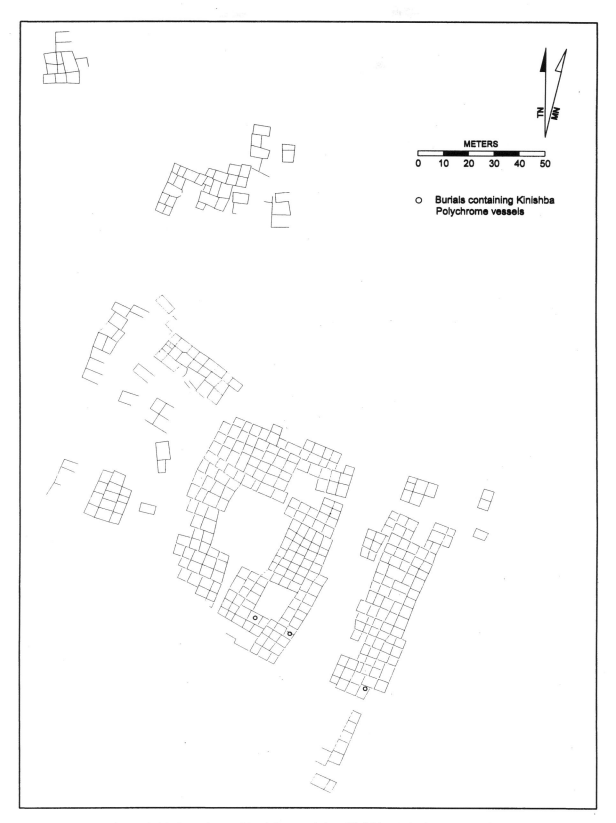

Figure 4.16. Locations of burials containing Kinishba Polychrome vessels.

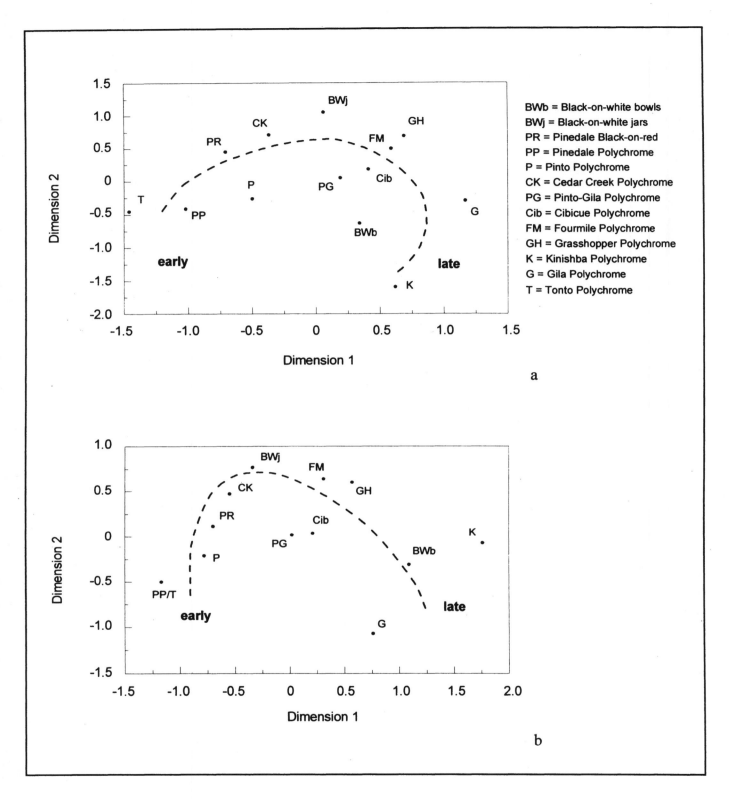

Figure 4.17. Multidimensional scaling of decorated ceramics within burials: *a*, Jaccard coefficient matrix, burials with more than one decorated vessel (n = 129); *b*, Brainerd-Robinson matrix, burials with more than five decorated vessels (n = 16).

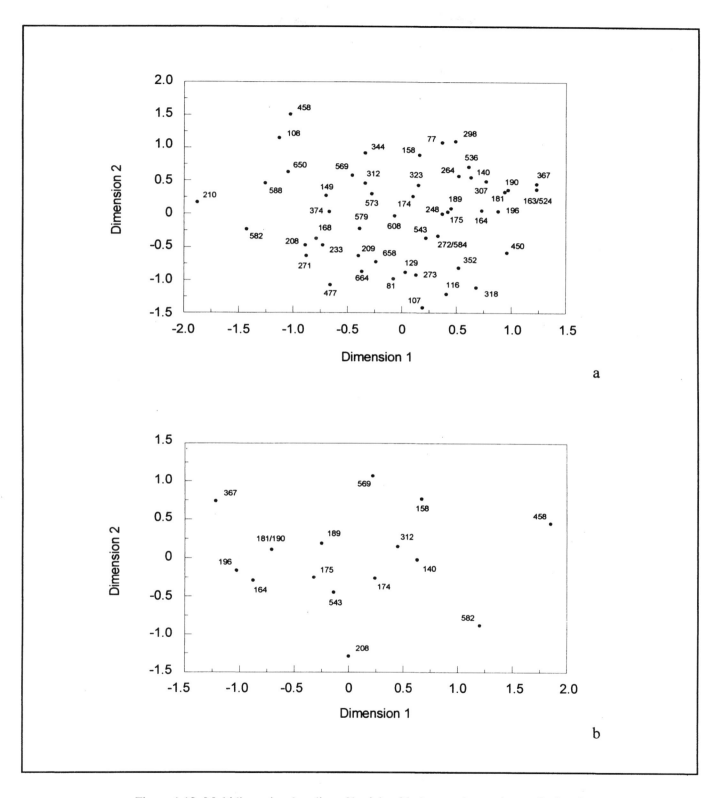

Figure 4.18. Multidimensional scaling of burials with decorated ceramics: *a*, Brainerd-Robinson matrix, burials with more than three decorated vessels (n = 52); *b*, Jaccard coefficient matrix, burials with more than five decorated vessels (n = 16).

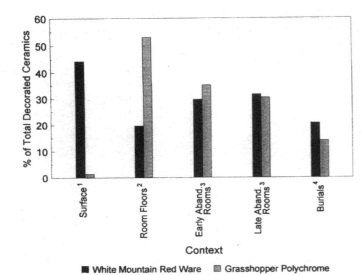

¹Sherds, percentages based on sherd weights
²Reconstructible vessels (total decorated vessels = 147)
³Sherds, percentages based on sherd counts
⁴Reconstructible vessels (total decorated vessels = 526)

Figure 4.19. Occurrence of White Mountain Red Ware and Grasshopper Polychrome at Grasshopper Pueblo.

Polychrome relatively late, but they could not be temporally distinguished from each other (although Figure 4.17*b* shows Grasshopper Polychrome as a little later). However, as Grasshopper Polychrome occurs in significant numbers in the fill of early abandoned rooms, and as it is present in burials (Fig. 4.19), production of this type may have started during the main occupation of the pueblo, possibly between A.D. 1320 and 1340.

A comparison of ceramics from late room floor assemblages and surface refuse does show a basic temporal distinction between White Mountain Red Ware and Grasshopper Polychrome. Grasshopper Polychrome was the most abundant decorated type on room floors, which implies that it was in use late during the occupation of the pueblo. The predominance of mostly imported White Mountain Red Ware in the surface refuse, on the other hand, indicates that White Mountain Red Ware was used and discarded earlier than the local Grasshopper Polychrome. In essence, White Mountain Red Ware occurs in high numbers in the surface refuse context, but in limited quantity on late room floors (Fig. 4.19). Conversely, Grasshopper Polychrome occurs sparsely in the surface assemblage but represents the majority of decorated vessels on room floors. On the basis of the room floor and surface assemblages, Grasshopper Polychrome was definitely

later than imported White Mountain Red Ware. (Montgomery and Reid [1990] demonstrate a case of rapid ceramic replacement at Chodistaas Pueblo on the basis of room floor and surface assemblages.)

PRODUCTION

White Mountain Red Ware, and particularly the chronologically latest type in the series, Fourmile Polychrome, became the predominant decorated pottery in settlements south of the Mogollon Rim during Pueblo IV times (Chapter 5). During the late A.D. 1200s, a rapid replacement of mostly black-on-white ceramics with black-on-red and polychrome ceramics occurred in the Grasshopper region (Montgomery and Reid 1990). At this time the black-on-red and polychrome ceramics were almost all Pinto Black-on-red or Pinto Polychrome, both Roosevelt Red Ware types. Cibola White Ware was the predominant black-on-white pottery before this transition (Zedeño 1994a: 29–32, Table 4.2). Zedeño demonstrated that Cibola White Ware vessels were almost exclusively imported into settlements that were located in the vicinity of Grasshopper Pueblo. She analyzed 47 of 51 Cibola White Ware vessels from Chodistaas Pueblo and found that 43 of them were nonlocal and may have come from three different sources, probably north of the Mogollon Rim (Zedeño 1994a: 73–77). Some of the Pinto Black-on-red and Pinto Polychrome vessels associated with deposits dating late in the occupation of Chodistaas Pueblo were probably locally produced.

The compositional and petrographic analyses on White Mountain Red Ware and Grasshopper Polychrome not only confirmed that the distribution of White Mountain Red Ware expanded southward during early Pueblo IV times (as reflected by the imported ceramics grouped in Compositional Groups 1 and 2), but demonstrated that, contrary to traditional assumptions, some White Mountain Red Ware and Grasshopper Polychrome (the low-fired copy of Fourmile Polychrome) were manufactured south of the Mogollon Rim at Grasshopper Pueblo. With regard to the late Pueblo III period patterns, these results raise questions about the organization and scope of local ceramic production at Grasshopper Pueblo.

The quantities of analyzed ceramics from Grasshopper Pueblo identified as either Compositional Group 3 or Group 4 provide a means to assess the volume of local ceramic production. Of 122 analyzed samples, 106 were assigned to one of the four compositional groups (Table 4.5). The rest were unassigned because of their

Table 4.5. Total Samples from Grasshopper Pueblo Analyzed by NAA

Source	Compositional Group	No. of Samples	Total	% of Assigned Ceramics	% of All Ceramics
Imports	Group 1	47			
	Group 2	3	50	47.17	40.98
Local	Group 3	36			
	Group 4	20	56	52.83	45.90
Total Assigned Ceramics			106	100	86.88
Unknown	Unassigned	16	16		13.12
Total		122	122		100

low or ambiguous group membership probabilities. Fifty (47.17%) of the compositionally assigned ceramics were imported (Groups 1 and 2) and 56 (52.83%) were locally produced. Only 3 of the 50 imported White Mountain Red Ware ceramics belong to Compositional Group 2. Thirty-six (64.29%) of the locally produced ceramics belong to Group 3 and 20 (35.71%) to Group 4 (Table 4.5). Clearly, slightly more than 50 percent of the analyzed ceramics were produced locally.

The total ceramic sample from Grasshopper Pueblo (n = 122) included 16 sherds from various contexts and 106 reconstructible vessels, of which 94 were assigned to compositional groups (Table 4.6). Information on archaeological context was available for 87 of these vessels. Nineteen (57.58%) of the vessels from mortuary contexts were imported and 14 (42.42%) were locally manufactured. In contrast, 25 (46.3%) vessels from room contexts were imported and 29 (53.7%) were local (Table 4.6). The slightly inverted relation-

ship between the sampled burial and room vessels again suggests that imported ceramics are somewhat earlier than the locally produced ceramics.

The fact that only 3 of the 50 imported ceramics were assigned to Compositional Group 2 implies that Grasshopper Pueblo was probably not part of a distribution network that moved vessels into the pueblo from the source of Group 2 ceramics. With regard to the locally manufactured pots, consistently higher quantities of Group 3 vessels in all contexts may indicate a preference for pastes with less temper for the manufacture of local decorated ceramics.

The most striking point is, however, that slightly more than half of the analyzed ceramics were locally produced. This observation is supported by the whole vessel assemblage from Grasshopper Pueblo. As mentioned previously, 403 of the reconstructed vessels were recorded and used as the basis for this study. Locally manufactured Grasshopper Polychrome represented 40.7

Table 4.6. Reconstructible Vessels from Grasshopper Pueblo Analyzed by NAA

Source	Compositional Group	Burials No.	Burials Total	Burials % of Assigned Vessels	Rooms No.	Rooms Total	Rooms % of Assigned Vessels	Unknown Context No.	Total
Imports	Group 1	17			24			2	43
	Group 2	2	19	57.58	1	25	46.30	0	3
Local	Group 3	9			20			3	32
	Group 4	5	14	42.42	9	29	53.70	2	16
Total Assigned Vessels		33		100	54		100	7	94
Unknown	Unassigned	8			3			1	12
Total		41			57			8	106

percent (n = 164) of the vessels. Light-paste and dark-paste White Mountain Red Ware constituted 35.2 percent (n = 142) and 19.1 percent (n = 77) respectively and Kinishba Polychrome accounted for 3.0 percent (n = 12) of the assemblage; the remaining 8 vessels (2%) could not be unambiguously typed. To compare these data with the compositional data, all of the samples analyzed by NAA (n = 331) were cross-checked to determine how consistently the ceramics that had initially been labeled as local or possibly local (based on the visual identification of dark pastes) were assigned to local production by elemental analysis. The percentage of misclassified samples provided a factor with which to adjust the number of dark-paste vessels in the whole vessel assemblage, leading to a more accurate measurement for local White Mountain Red Ware pots at Grasshopper Pueblo. About 36 percent of the NAA samples originally thought to be local were identified as nonlocal. Refiring revealed that the majority of these ceramics had been insufficiently oxidized (Chapter 3, Table 3.13), which caused the dark cores. Applied to the whole vessel assemblage from Grasshopper Pueblo, the adjusted number of local White Mountain Red Ware is 49, or 12.1 percent of the recorded reconstructible vessels. Local White Mountain Red Ware and Grasshopper Polychrome combined represent 52.8 percent of the vessels. The whole and reconstructible vessels as well as the compositionally analyzed samples (as they are a fraction of the whole vessel assemblage) came predominantly from mortuary and room contexts and thus date after the establishment of Grasshopper Pueblo.

To summarize, not only were White Mountain Red Ware and Grasshopper Polychrome manufactured at Grasshopper Pueblo, but, in comparison to late Pueblo III times, an enormous increase in the local production of decorated ceramics can be demonstrated (Zedeño 1994a). Slightly more than 50 percent of the vessels decorated in the White Mountain Red Ware stylistic tradition, more specifically that of Fourmile Polychrome, were produced at the pueblo, which underscores the importance of this tradition and may indicate the loss of access to such vessels from the original source or sources.

DISTRIBUTION

In general, the distribution of ceramics within a site, especially whole vessels found in situ, may provide information about where and how they were used. In turn, the distribution of *locally* produced ceramics may shed light on the organization of ceramic production at the settlement. The ceramic assemblage from Grasshopper Pueblo is characterized by a high variability of decorated vessels. Besides large quantities of imported White Mountain Red Ware and local Grasshopper Polychrome, the third most abundant decorated ceramics are Roosevelt Red Ware types; other types such as Cibicue Polychrome occur in smaller quantities (Chapter 2). This diversity in decorated ceramics reflects a marked increase in variability from that of ceramic assemblages of late Pueblo III period sites in the vicinity of Grasshopper Pueblo (Zedeño and Triadan, in press). At Chodistaas Pueblo, for instance, the decorated ceramics consisted predominantly of Cibola White Ware and some Roosevelt Red Ware that dated to the end of that pueblo's occupation (Zedeño 1994a: 29–31).

Reid and Whittlesey (Reid 1989: 87; Reid and Whittlesey 1982: 699) suggested that White Mountain Red Ware, Roosevelt Red Ware, and Grasshopper Polychrome were each associated with one of the three major room blocks and that they might represent different ethnic groups residing at the pueblo. To assess these ideas, I analyzed the distribution of decorated whole or reconstructible vessels from archaeological contexts to determine if White Mountain Red Ware and Grasshopper Polychrome were indeed associated with residential units or burial groups and if they could be considered ethnic markers. I also examined the distribution of compositionally analyzed decorated ceramics. A spatial difference in the distribution of import Groups 1 and 2 at the site, for instance, might imply that people associated with the two different nonlocal production areas lived in separate "quarters" or "*barrios*" of the settlement.

The volume of locally produced White Mountain Red Ware and Grasshopper Polychrome raised questions about the organization of production and consumption of these ceramics at Grasshopper Pueblo. For example, vessels assigned to the two local compositional groups or their respective subgroups (Chapter 3, Figs. 3.12–3.14) might be associated with different residential units, and, if so, could reflect groups of potters living in different parts of the pueblo using different paste recipes or exploiting different sections of the clay deposits to produce local polychrome pots. It should be kept in mind, however, that the sampled vessels (found predominantly on room floors and in burials), although they certainly represent consumption and discard, may not represent the actual place of manufacture. Perhaps not every household produced its own polychrome ceramics, and vessels may have circulated within the settlement.

Household Context

I examined the spatial distribution of decorated vessels from room floors throughout Grasshopper Pueblo to test whether I could discern significant patterns that could be linked to discrete residential units, for example the three major room blocks. I mapped the presence of Fourmile Polychrome and Showlow Polychrome (the latest types of White Mountain Red Ware), Grasshopper Polychrome, Gila Polychrome and Tonto Polychrome (the latest types of Roosevelt Red Ware), Cibicue Polychrome, Kinishba Polychrome, and black-on-white jars on room floors.

Figures 4.20 through 4.25 show that within the floor vessel assemblages no distinct patterns of distribution can be observed. Vessels of all wares and types occur in all parts of the site. Clusters of rooms with floor pots (Figs. 4.20 and 4.21) probably indicate general areas of late abandonment within the settlement.

Next, I explored the distribution of chemically analyzed vessels from room contexts. Figures 4.26 through 4.29 show that neither local nor imported ceramics pattern spatially within the site; they occur in all three major room blocks. The same is true for vessels of the two local groups and the compositional subgroups; they, also, cannot be associated with discrete sections of the site. It is interesting, however, that in three cases where two or more analyzed vessels came from the same room (Rooms 8, 21, and 23), Grasshopper Polychrome vessels and local brown-paste Fourmile Polychrome vessels both belonged to Compositional Group 3 and were manufactured using the same paste recipe.

Mortuary Context

If ethnically different groups with distinct material possessions resided at Grasshopper Pueblo, one would assume that those differences would be reflected in burial customs and consequently in the burial inventories. To assess whether decorated vessels functioned as "ethnic markers" and if individuals belonging to different groups were buried with their respective "emblematic" ceramics, I analyzed the combination of decorated vessels within the burials.

The Grasshopper burial population contained at least 16 individuals with lambdoidal head deformation (Birkby 1973: 12–14; Ezzo 1991: 220, 1993). Head deformations are caused by keeping infants in cradle boards. Lambdoidal head deformation is ascribed to the Anasazi. Reid (1989: 87) uses the occurrence of lambdoidal head deformation on human remains at Grasshopper

Pueblo to argue for the presence of Anasazi at the settlement. (Using head deformation to determine ethnic differentiation remains problematic, however, because osteological data in the Southwest, on which these assumptions are based, are scant and not representative.) Since these individuals possessed a physiological trait that might have characterized them as nonlocal to Grasshopper Pueblo, I examined their associated burial assemblages first to see if there were any significant patterns within the decorated ceramics. The funeral assemblages associated with the "Anasazi" contained White Mountain Red Ware, Roosevelt Red Ware, and Grasshopper Polychrome, often mixed within a single burial. Furthermore, after looking at the whole Grasshopper burial population, it became clear that the majority (n = 77) of the 129 burials with more than one decorated vessel contained pots belonging to at least two of the major decorated wares or types (Table 4.7). This even distribution and the co-occurrence of decorated ceramics within the burials support Whittlesey's (1978: 184–225, 1984: 282) conclusion that the burial population at Grasshopper is overall remarkably homogeneous.

To identify patterns that might be linked to residential groups or units, I undertook a spatial analysis of decorated ceramics associated with burials (Figs. 4.10–4.16). Figures 4.13 through 4.15 demonstrate that White Mountain Red Ware ceramics and Grasshopper Polychrome do not cluster within specific room blocks or subunits of major room blocks.

The distributional analyses revealed that decorated ceramic vessels from room floors do not pattern according to the three major residential units of the main pueblo. Likewise, the ceramics assigned to the four compositional groups did not pattern significantly. Both imported White Mountain Red Ware and locally produced polychrome vessels occurred in all areas of the site. Although two paste recipes were used at Grasshopper Pueblo to produce polychrome ceramics, and compositional subgroups within the two groups of local manufacture indicate variations in source exploitation or paste preparation, the identification of distinct production loci (for example, potters' workshops) within the site was not possible. The results of the mortuary analysis showed no correlation of ceramic wares with residential units or possible ethnic groups.

In sum, White Mountain Red Ware (local and imported) and Grasshopper Polychrome are fairly evenly distributed throughout the site. Their even distribution and co-occurrence suggest that all households had access to these ceramics and may indicate that the same people who used the imported ceramics made and used

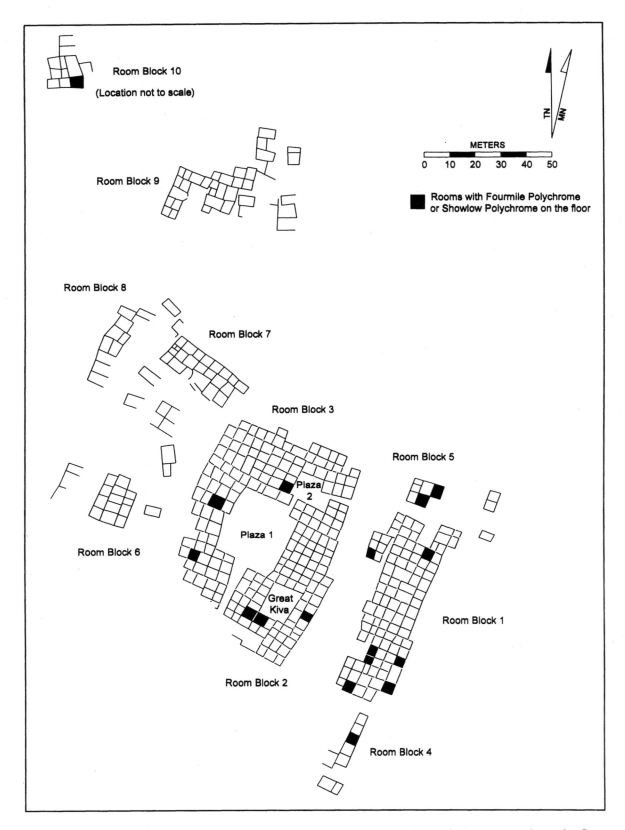

Figure 4.20. Distribution of rooms with Fourmile Polychrome or Showlow Polychrome vessels on the floor.

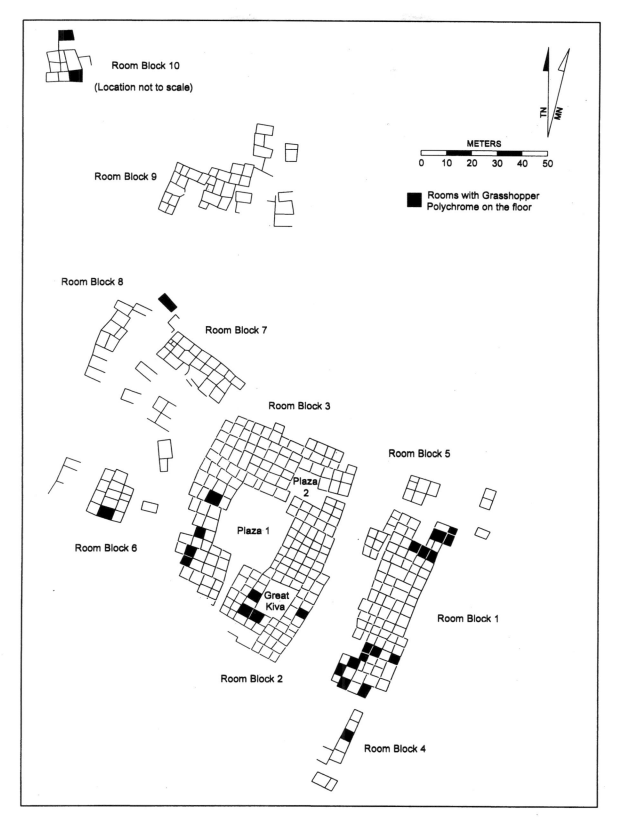

Figure 4.21. Distribution of rooms with Grasshopper Polychrome vessels on the floor.

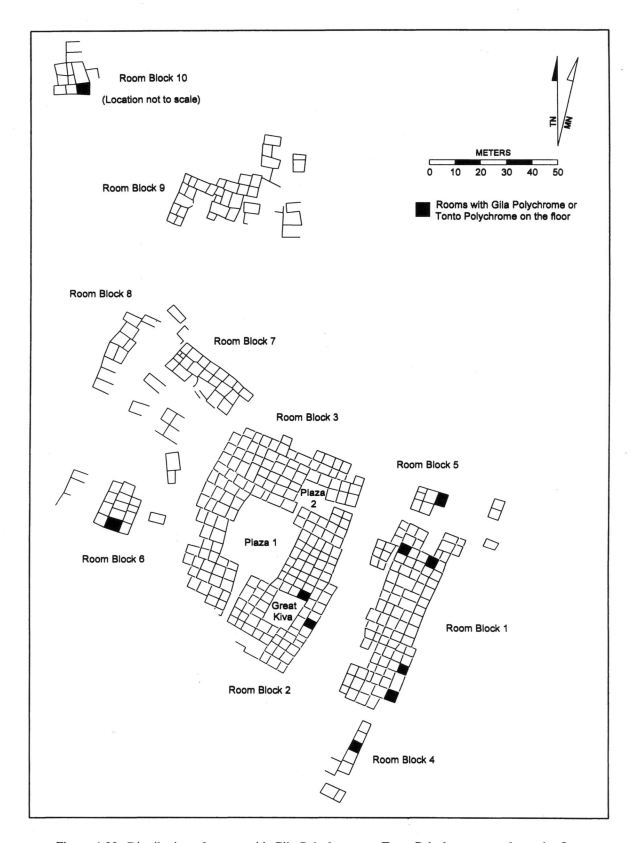

Figure 4.22. Distribution of rooms with Gila Polychrome or Tonto Polychrome vessels on the floor.

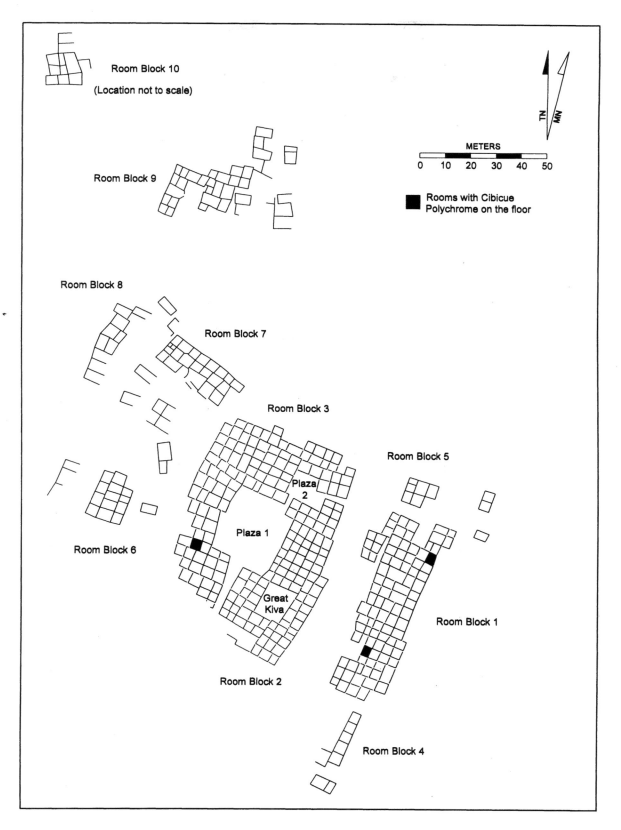

Figure 4.23. Distribution of rooms with Cibicue Polychrome vessels on the floor.

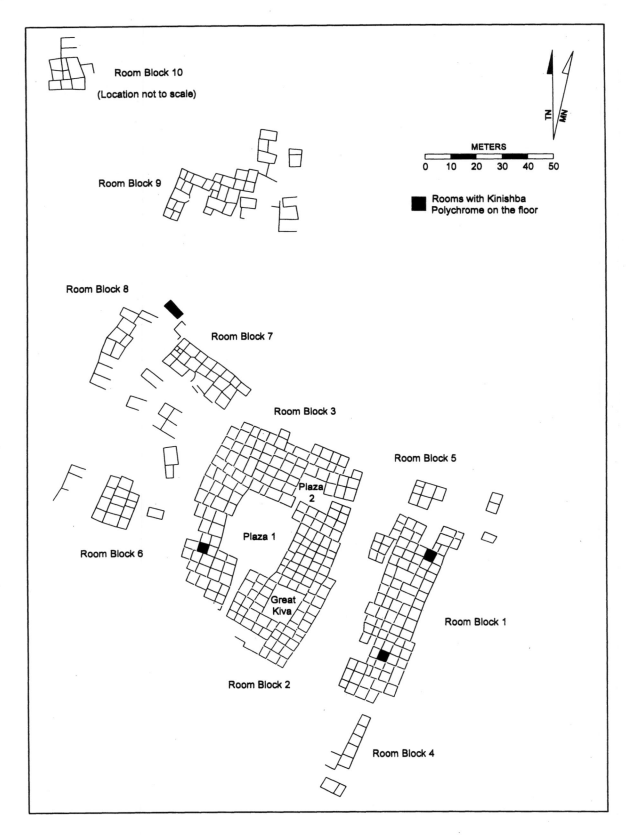

Figure 4.24. Distribution of rooms with Kinishba Polychrome vessels on the floor.

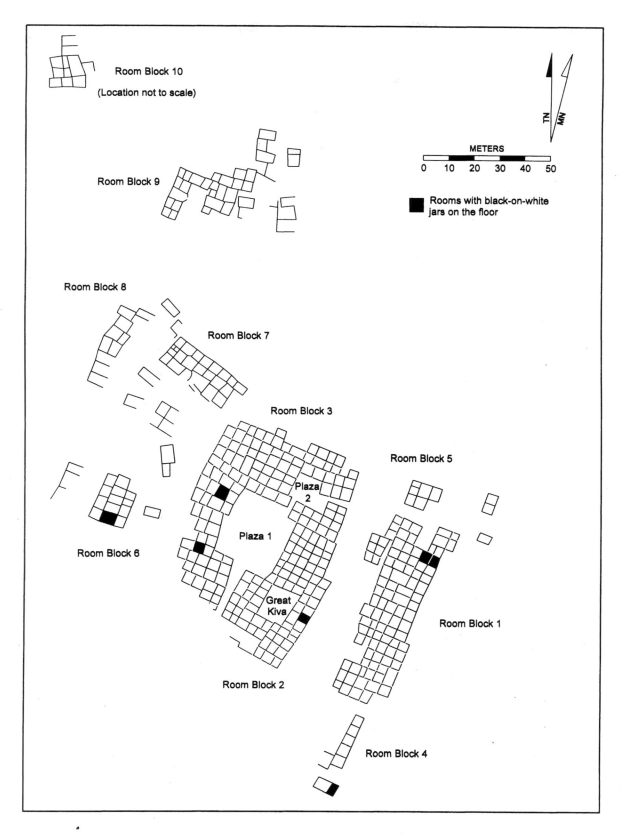

Figure 4.25. Distribution of rooms with black-on-white jars on the floor.

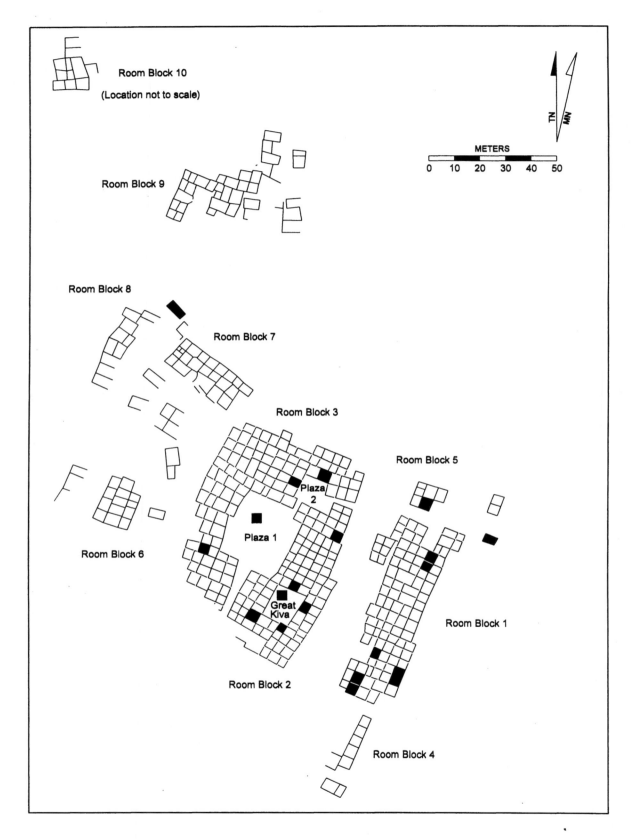

Figure 4.26. Provenience of vessels belonging to NAA Compositional Group 1.

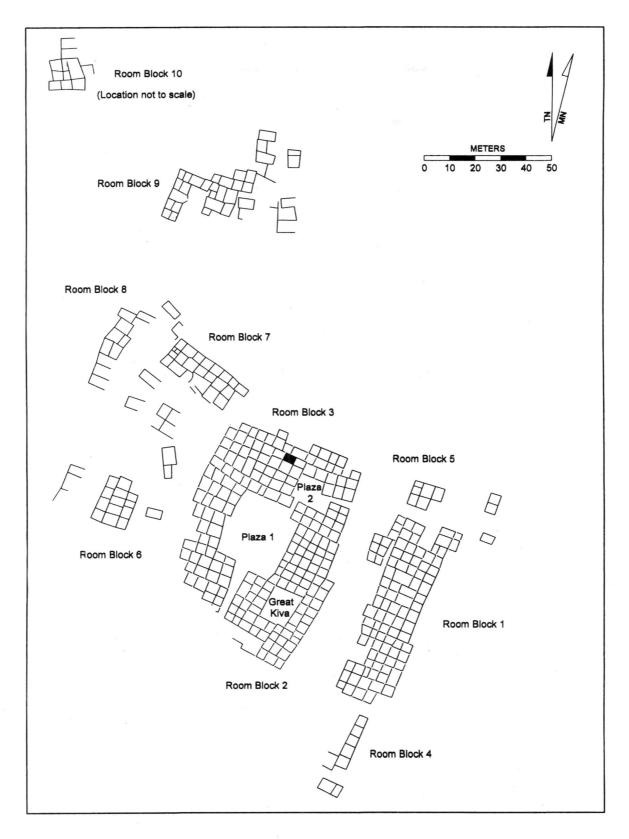

Figure 4.27. Provenience of vessels belonging to NAA Compositional Group 2.

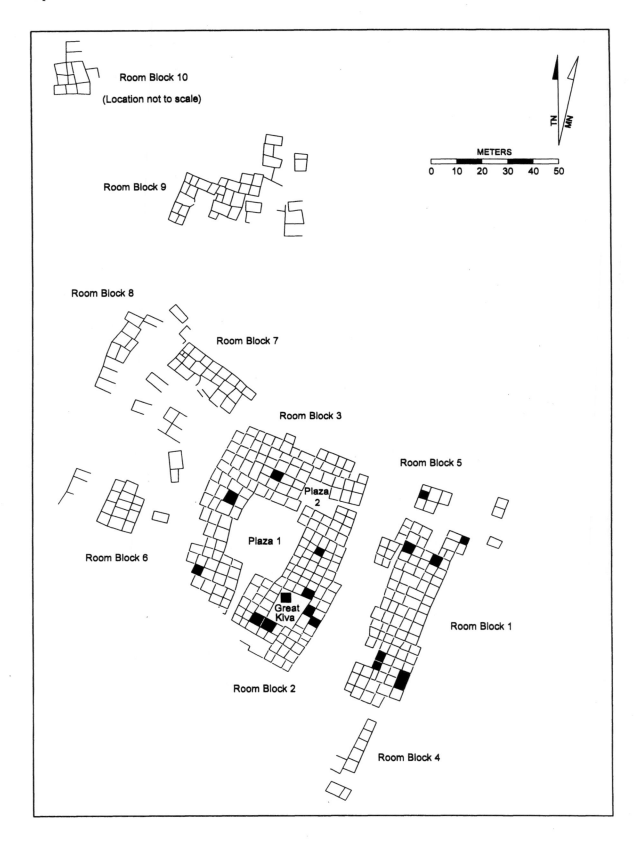

Figure 4.28. Provenience of vessels belonging to NAA Compositional Group 3.

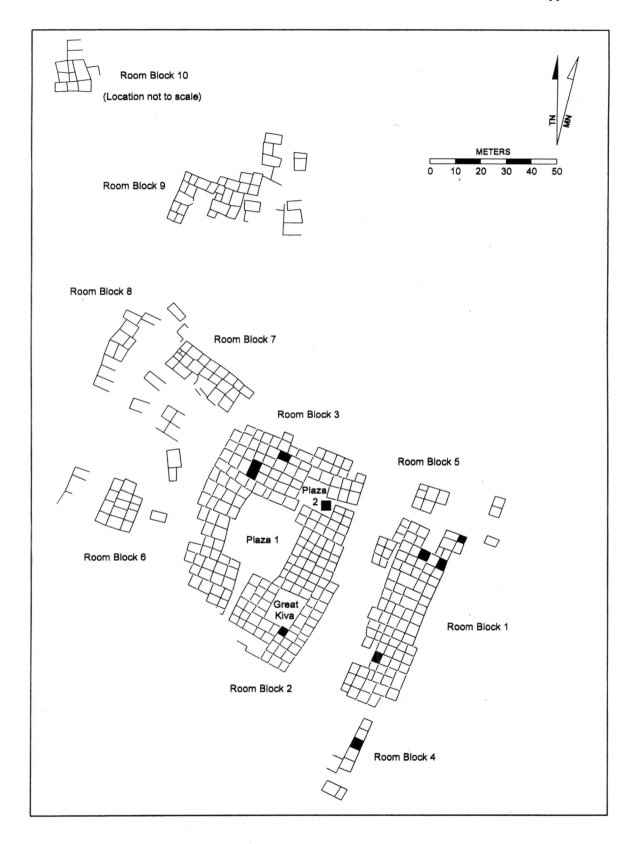

Figure 4.29. Provenience of vessels belonging to NAA Compositional Group 4.

Table 4.7. Association of Decorated Ceramic Wares and Types in Burials

Combination of Decorated Wares and Types	No. of Burials
White Mountain Red Ware, Roosevelt Red Ware	13
White Mountain Red Ware, Grasshopper Polychrome	8
White Mountain Red Ware, Cibicue Polychrome	12
Roosevelt Red Ware, Grasshopper Polychrome	3
Roosevelt Red Ware, Cibicue Polychrome	19
Grasshopper Polychrome, Cibicue Polychrome	1
White Mountain Red Ware, Roosevelt Red Ware, Grasshopper Polychrome	3
White Mountain Red Ware, Roosevelt Red Ware, Cibicue Polychrome	8
White Mountain Red Ware, Grasshopper Polychrome, Cibicue Polychrome	4
Roosevelt Red Ware, Grasshopper Polychrome, Cibicue Polychrome	2
White Mountain Red Ware, Roosevelt Red Ware, Grasshopper Polychrome, Cibicue Polychrome	4
Total	77

the later local copies. If different ethnic groups resided at Grasshopper Pueblo, the different decorated ceramics were not restricted to any discrete group.

FUNCTION

White Mountain Red Ware (imported as well as some local) and Grasshopper Polychrome occur in significant proportions in mortuary contexts (Fig. 4.19), and they constitute a high percentage of the decorated ceramics in the discard. This distribution indicates that these ceramics were readily accessible to everyone. Moreover, Grasshopper Polychrome and Fourmile Polychrome (both predominantly bowls) were definitely part of the household assemblage, because they were found in situ on the floors of late abandoned rooms (Fig. 4.19). However, because Grasshopper Polychrome was manufactured later than Fourmile Polychrome, it occurred in much higher numbers on the room floors. As both were present in the same contexts, no functional difference can be demonstrated between them. Decorated bowls were probably used as serving vessels for food consumption, as they have been by historic puebloan groups (Clemmer 1979: 545, Fig. 13; Cushing 1979: 239, Figs. 51, 241, 245, 248), and were eventually buried with their owners or given as part of the mortuary furniture by members of the mourning group of the deceased (Whittlesey 1978: 145, 231). Grasshopper Polychrome probably served as a late local substitute for Fourmile Polychrome.

A difference in vessel sizes between White Mountain Red Ware and Grasshopper Polychrome, however, indicates that they may have been manufactured to meet different transportation requirements. Whittlesey (1974: 108–110) reported that White Mountain Red Ware bowls from burials tended to nest within each other, and she interpreted this characteristic as a sign that the ceramics were produced for export. Large numbers of vessels could be easily transported if they fit into each other. A comparison of bowl sizes between imported White Mountain Red Ware and locally produced Grasshopper Polychrome clearly supports Whittlesey's observation. As I had recorded the sizes for all reconstructed White Mountain Red Ware and Grasshopper Polychrome vessels, I was able to analyze a sample somewhat larger than Whittlesey's for standardization within the imported ceramics.

The distribution of maximum vessel diameters was plotted for imported Fourmile Polychrome bowls and Grasshopper Polychrome bowls. Grasshopper Polychrome bowls show a more or less normal distribution in their sizes, with a majority of vessel diameters ranging from 20 cm to 30 cm (Fig. 4.30a). The distribution is unimodal and no different *size classes*, such as small, medium, or large, can be observed. The majority of imported Fourmile Polychrome bowls are in the same size range as the Grasshopper Polychrome bowls and also do not form standardized size classes. However, in contrast to the local vessels, distinct divisions about every 3 cm can be observed in the distribution plot of the maximum diameters of the bowls (Fig. 4.30b). Plots of rim diameters (which equal vessel apertures) of both types show a similar distribution (Fig. 4.31). The imported Fourmile Polychrome bowls fit into each other (Fig. 4.31b) and were manufactured for easy transport. The late local imitations duplicated the general size of Fourmile Polychrome bowls but did not emphasize nestability, which may indicate that they were not produced to be transported in large numbers over long distances.

Imported White Mountain Red Ware and Grasshopper Polychrome vessels were part of the everyday household assemblage of people living at Grasshopper Pueblo. The homogeneous spatial distribution of imported and locally manufactured ceramics within Grasshopper Pueblo indicates that households had equal and continuous access to White Mountain Red Ware or its substitutes throughout its occupation. The scale of local production of these polychrome ceramics suggests that they were important and popular items. A decrease in nestability occurred hand-in-hand with the shift of the production of Fourmile style ceramics from nonlocal to

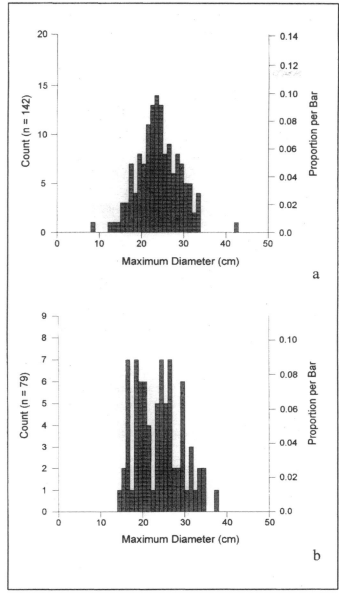

Figure 4.30. Distribution of bowl sizes: *a*, Grasshopper Polychrome; *b*, imported Fourmile Polychrome.

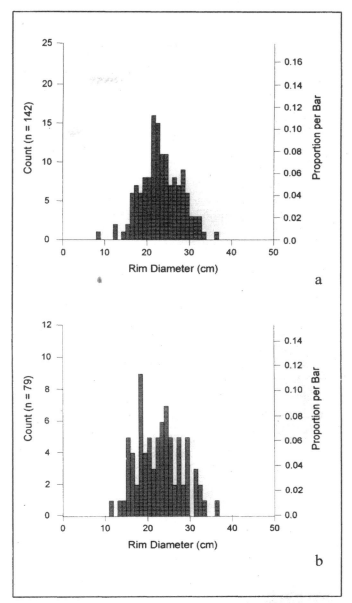

Figure 4.31. Distribution of bowl apertures: *a* Grasshopper Polychrome; *b*, imported Fourmile Polychrome.

local, which indicates a change toward production for local consumption rather than for long-distance transport.

DISCUSSION

The analysis of decorated ceramics in their archaeological context, in conjunction with results derived from material analyses (Chapter 3), contributed to interpretations of the function of White Mountain Red Ware and its local copies and of the behavioral mechanisms involved in its production and distribution. White Mountain Red Ware appears to have been imported into

Grasshopper Pueblo predominantly during the early stages of occupation, as indicated by its high frequencies in surface refuse. These light-paste ceramics probably came from areas along the Mogollon Rim, where light-firing kaolinitic clay deposits occur (Plate 2; Moore 1968: 72–73, Plate 1). The local production of brown-paste White Mountain Red Ware and Grasshopper Polychrome started later, possibly during the peak of occupation around A.D. 1320 to 1340. The presence of a few, well-made local copies of Cedar Creek Polychrome supports this hypothesis. Similarly, Point of Pines Polychrome seems to be a late local copy of imported Fourmile Polychrome in the Point of Pines area (Wendorf 1950: 49; Carlson 1970: 77–82). The volume of locally produced decorated ceramics following the White Mountain Red Ware stylistic tradition was substantial. Slightly more than 50 percent of the ceramics that were found in contexts dating after the establishment of the settlement and that were decorated predominantly in Fourmile style were produced at Grasshopper Pueblo.

The distributional analyses did not show any association of decorated ceramics with residential units or groups of burials; both White Mountain Red Ware and Grasshopper Polychrome were evenly distributed throughout the site in rooms and burials. Households had continuous and equal access to these ceramics; they were an integral part of the household assemblage and ended up as funerary goods. Imported White Mountain Red Ware vessels may have been manufactured to facilitate long-distance transport. Bowls fit into each other and large numbers of them could have been transported relatively easily. Grasshopper Polychrome bowls, on the other hand, were made in the same range of vessel sizes but did not emphasize nestability, which indicates that they were produced predominantly for local consumption and distribution.

Archaeologists usually use two basic frameworks to explain the circulation of ceramics: they moved either through some form of exchange (including trade) or they were distributed with moving people, in other words through migration. In reality, of course, there may have been a combination of both. During the late A.D. 1300s, Grasshopper Pueblo and other settlements south of the Mogollon Rim were established and became highly aggregated in a short period of time. The settlement aggregation coincides with high quantities of imported White Mountain Red Ware, predominantly Fourmile Polychrome, in these southern settlements. Because imported White Mountain Red Ware at Grasshopper Pueblo occurs predominantly in contexts associated with the early phases of occupation, it is probable that high quantities of these polychrome ceramics were brought in by people who moved into Grasshopper Pueblo from the southern areas of the Colorado Plateau rather than through trade or exchange. Incidentally, the nestability of these imported pots would have allowed the transport of a large number of vessels into the settlement. This interpretation is supported by the abandonment of a series of sites north of the Mogollon Rim during the early A.D. 1400s (Haury and Hargrave 1931; Martin and others 1961, 1964, 1967; Mills, in press). Also, artifact assemblages from the northern settlements still occupied during this time lack evidence of goods that

might have been exchanged for large quantities of White Mountain Red Ware vessels (Haury and Hargrave 1931).

Migration is a complex *process*, and often people may not have left their home communities all at once (see, for example, Anthony 1990; Cameron 1995; Duff, in press). It is conceivable that the communities north of the Mogollon Rim were abandoned gradually and that people moved into Grasshopper Pueblo over a period of several years, bringing White Mountain Red Ware vessels with them until the height of the occupation of the pueblo. People may also have maintained ties with the village or villages where the imported vessels were made, and some vessels may have come into Grasshopper as a result of exchange.

Eventually the immigrants started to make White Mountain Red Ware at Grasshopper Pueblo, using local clays but their own slip clays and mineral paints, which resulted in the well-fired, local brown-paste copies. During the later phases of occupation at Grasshopper Pueblo, people started to use all local materials, producing the pottery we classify as Grasshopper Polychrome. The poor preservation and inferior appearance of these ceramics today are caused by the low-firing temperature that was required to keep the organic paint, used for decoration, intact. In prehistoric times, when these pots were "new," they probably looked quite similar to the imported Fourmile Polychrome vessels. Perhaps potters decided that vessels decorated with carbon paint and local hematite (for the slips) did not look noticeably different from the earlier imported pots and that it was not worthwhile to go back north for minerals.

In general, locally produced vessels were tempered with igneous rock and diabase, whereas the imported vessels contained sherd and quartz temper. However, a few ceramics that belong to the low-tempered local Compositional Group 3 contained both sherd and diabase temper; one sample (DTB128) actually had white sherd temper in a local clay matrix. All these samples are well-fired brown-paste White Mountain Red Ware painted with mineral paint, and I argue that these ceramics signify the transition from imported light-paste White Mountain Red Ware to locally made Grasshopper Polychrome. They are evidence for an adaptation by potters to locally available materials and techniques. Moreover, two-thirds of the reconstructible vessels from Grasshopper Pueblo are decorated in Fourmile style (combining imported White Mountain Red Ware vessels and local copies), indicating that this stylistic tradition was important (see, for example, Adams 1991a: 96–101) and that immigrants from the north had a considerable impact on the community.

Production and Distribution of White Mountain Red Ware in the Grasshopper Region

The compositional and petrographic data discussed in Chapter 3 demonstrate that White Mountain Red Ware was imported into the Grasshopper region from at least two different production zones that were probably located along the Mogollon Rim and that some White Mountain Red Ware as well as Grasshopper Polychrome vessels were produced at Grasshopper Pueblo. In fact, the local production of polychrome ceramics was substantial, and it appears that more than half of the whole and reconstructible vessels decorated in Fourmile style found at Grasshopper Pueblo were produced locally. These vessels came predominantly from burials and from floors of late abandoned rooms, which indicates that they were discarded some time after the pueblo was established until its abandonment. In contrast, the highest frequencies of imported White Mountain Red Ware ceramics, mostly Fourmile Polychrome, were found in surface refuse, which means that the vessels were used and discarded in substantial quantities during the earliest times of occupation at Grasshopper Pueblo. These results demonstrate a shift from mainly imported decorated ceramics to local production and an increase in the variability of ceramics in the Grasshopper region during the transition between the late Pueblo III and Pueblo IV periods. Local production of decorated ceramics in the region started around A.D. 1280 (Zedeño 1991, 1994a) and coincided with a replacement of black-on-white ceramics with polychrome ceramics throughout the area (Montgomery and Reid 1990). As mentioned above, parallel to an increased local production of decorated ceramics, major aggregation occurred in the region, caused primarily by the immigration of people into the area. I consider next the regional dimensions of these processes.

The results of the ceramic analyses raised specific questions with regard to the regional production and distribution of imported White Mountain Red Ware and its locally produced variants. For instance, were the ceramics attributed to the two different sources of imported, light-paste White Mountain Red Ware distributed evenly throughout the Grasshopper region? If not, it may be possible to reconstruct patterns of circulation within the mountains of east-central Arizona, which in turn may point to the areas of production and the northern homelands of the immigrating groups.

What was the impact of the substantial local production of polychrome ceramics at Grasshopper Pueblo on the surrounding region? Did locally produced polychrome ceramics circulate from Grasshopper Pueblo and, if so, how far? Did settlements within the Grasshopper region produce their own local White Mountain Red Ware or were they part of a distribution network with Grasshopper Pueblo as its primary production center? Some of the contemporary settlements were very large and were probably established through the same demographic processes involved in the founding of Grasshopper. It is likely that their inhabitants produced their own utilitarian brown wares, although this idea remains to be tested. One may assume that they also produced decorated ceramics. Another question of interest is whether there were other communities south of the Mogollon Rim in areas adjacent to the Grasshopper region that produced White Mountain Red Ware.

To assess the regional aspects of the processes observed at Grasshopper Pueblo and their behavioral implications, I conducted instrumental neutron activation analysis on 186 samples from 33 contemporary sites within the Grasshopper region and from adjacent areas in the east-central Arizona mountains (Chapter 3, Fig. 3.3, Table 3.8, Appendix B), and I included 22 samples from sites outside the Grasshopper region in the petrographic analysis (Chapter 3, Table 3.20). These material analyses were undertaken to (1) examine the regional distribution of imported White Mountain Red Ware with regard to its different production sources, (2) determine if individual production loci apart from Grasshopper Pueblo existed within the Grasshopper region, and (3) assess if a boundary or boundaries of the circulation of local ceramics could be established.

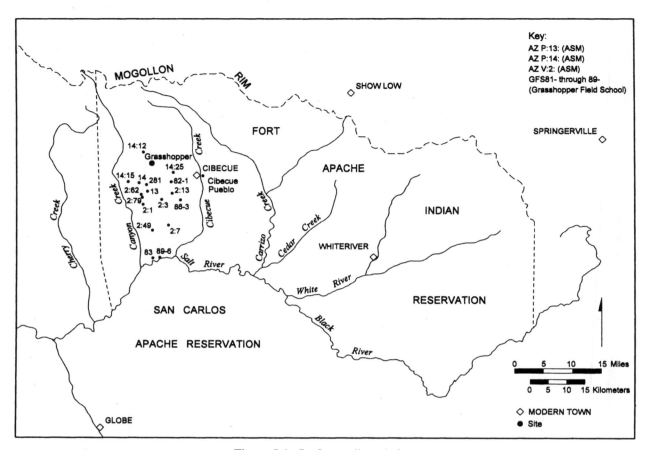

Figure 5.1. Surface collected sites.

Table 5.1. Systematic Surface Collections

Site	Collector	Year
AZ P:14:1, Grasshopper Pueblo	Triadan	1991
	Tuggle	1986
AZ P:14:15, Oak Creek Pueblo	Triadan	1991
AZ P:14:25, Red Canyon Tank Pueblo	Triadan	1991
AZ P:14:281	Triadan	1991
AZ V:2:7, Ruin's Tank Pueblo	Triadan	1991
AZ V:2:13, Blue House Mtn. Pueblo	Triadan	1991
AZ V:2:62	Triadan	1991
AZ V:2:79, Double Springs Cliff Dwelling	Triadan	1991
GFS 82-1, Spring Creek Pueblo	Triadan	1991
Cibecue Pueblo	Triadan	1991
AZ V:2:1, Canyon Creek Cliff Dwelling	Tuggle	1985
AZ V:2:3, Spotted Mtn. Pueblo	Tuggle	1968
GFS 86-3, Black Mtn. Pueblo	Welch	1986
AZ V:2:83	Welch	1989
GFS 89-6, Sanrace Cliff Dwelling	Welch	1989
AZ P:14:12, Hilltop Pueblo	Tuggle	1969
AZ P:14:13, Brush Mtn. Pueblo	Tuggle	1969
AZ V:2:49, Canyon Butte Pueblo	Tuggle	1979
AZ P:14:14, Red Rock House	Tuggle	1969

NOTE: AZ is Arizona State Museum Site Survey number; GFS is Grasshopper Field School number.

In addition to the ceramics that were characterized compositionally and petrographically, I analyzed ceramics from systematic surface collections from contemporary sites within the Grasshopper region to obtain data on the occurrence and frequencies of White Mountain Red Ware, the local brown-paste variety, and Grasshopper Polychrome. During the 1991 field season, I carried out controlled surface collections at nine contemporary sites in the Grasshopper region (Fig. 5.1., Table 5.1) and within two collection units at Grasshopper Pueblo (Fig. 4.1). In areas with the highest sherd densities, 2–m by 2–m grid units were set up and all ceramics within the units were collected. Sherds were typed, counted, and weighed. Nine additional sites and two other units at Grasshopper Pueblo are represented by systematic surface collections undertaken by David Tuggle in 1968, 1969, 1979, 1985, and 1986, and by John Welch in 1986 and 1989 (Table 5.1, Fig. 5.1); these collections were retyped, recounted, and weighed.

IMPORTED WHITE MOUNTAIN RED WARE IN THE GRASSHOPPER REGION

As a first step in evaluating the distribution and circulation of imported White Mountain Red Ware within the Grasshopper region, I analyzed the distribution of decorated ceramics and White Mountain Red Ware in contemporary sites of the area. Figure 5.2 shows percentages of decorated ceramics found on the surface, based on sherd weights. Decorated ceramics range from 1.08 percent at AZ V:2:83 to 63.09 percent at AZ P:14:13, with an average for all sites of about 17 percent. The high percentage of decorated ceramics in AZ P:14:13 may be caused by severe pothunting that introduced large quantities of sherds from burial vessels into the surface debris. Another possibility is that the collection unit analyzed for this site (collected by Tuggle in 1969) does not represent a total collection but one biased toward decorated ceramics.

In most of the sites, White Mountain Red Ware constitutes more than 50 percent of the decorated ceramics and in two sites, AZ V:2:49 and AZ V:2:79, more than 90 percent (Fig. 5.3). Although these sites, in general, reflect the trend seen at Grasshopper Pueblo (AZ P:14:1), most of them have significantly higher quantities of White Mountain Red Ware on the surface than does Grasshopper Pueblo. This predominance of White Mountain Red Ware may indicate that the decorated ceramic assemblages from these sites differed from the assemblage at Grasshopper Pueblo. Roosevelt Red Ware (or Salado Polychrome) is practically absent in the sur-

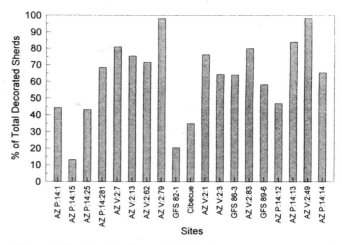

Figure 5.3. Distribution of White Mountain Red Ware in sampled sites in the Grasshopper region. Percentages are based on sherd weights. AZ is Arizona State Museum Site Survey number; GFS is Grasshopper Field School number.

face debris of some of the sites with high White Mountain Red Ware frequencies (Fig. 5.4), and perhaps only a few Roosevelt Red Ware vessels contributed to their decorated assemblage. In contrast, at Grasshopper Pueblo Roosevelt Red Ware constitutes 29.28 percent of the decorated burial vessels (Whittlesey 1978: 174–175, Table 7) and averages 19 percent on the surface (Fig. 5.4). In general, sites with high frequencies of White

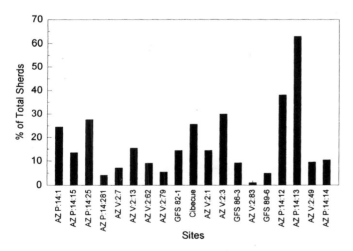

Figure 5.2. Distribution of decorated ceramics in sampled sites in the Grasshopper region. Percentages are based on sherd weights. AZ is Arizona State Museum Site Survey number; GFS is Grasshopper Field School number.

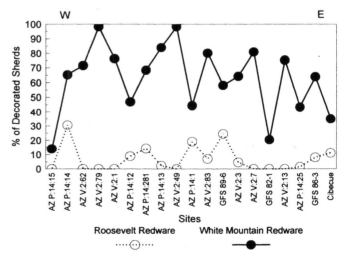

A few Roosevelt Red Ware sherds (9 and 1) were picked up in unsystematic grab collections from AZ V:2:7 and AZ V:2:13 respectively.

Figure 5.4. Distribution of Roosevelt Red Ware and White Mountain Red Ware in sampled sites in the Grasshopper region. Percentages are based on sherd weights. AZ is Arizona State Museum Site Survey number; GFS is Grasshopper Field School number.

Table 5.2. Compositional Group Membership (NAA) of Sampled Ceramics
from Sites in the Grasshopper Region and Adjacent Areas

Site	Compositional Group 1	Group 2	Group 3	Group 4	Unassigned	Total no. of samples
GFS 82-1, Spring Creek Pueblo			4	2	1	7
AZ V:2:7, Ruin's Tank Pueblo		6			3	9
AZ P:14:25, Red Canyon Tank Pueblo	3		2			5
AZ V:2:62	1		1	3	1	6
AZ P:14:281		2		5		7
AZ V:2:13, Blue House Mtn. Pueblo	1	2	1	2		6
AZ V:2:79, Double Springs Cliff Dwelling				1	1	2
AZ P:14:15, Oak Creek Pueblo	2		1		1	4
AZ P:14:71	3		1		1	5
GFS 88-9, Carrizo Creek Pueblo	1	1			3	5
GFS 88-10, Blue Spring Pueblo	2	1			2	5
GFS 85-3, Cedar Creek Pueblo		1			4	5
Cibecue Pueblo	1	3			1	5
TDT, Tundastusa	1	1			3	5
BW, Banning Wash Pueblo	1	2				3
PD, Pinedale Ruin	3				6	9
SL, Showlow Ruin	3		1		1	5
K, Kinishba		5			2	7
Q, Q-Ranch Pueblo			2	3	1	6
AZ V:2:3, Spotted Mtn. Pueblo	1	4		1	1	7
AZ P:14:13, Brush Mtn. Pueblo	2	3	2	1	1	9
AZ V:2:1, Canyon Creek Cliff Dwelling	1	1		4	1	7
AZ P:14:12, Hilltop Pueblo	1		1	5	1	8
GFS 86-3, Black Mtn. Pueblo	1	6			1	8
AZ V:2:49, Canyon Butte Pueblo	1	5				6
AZ V:2:87	1	1	3	1	1	7
GFS 81-79	1	1		2	1	5
AZ V:2:23		2			2	4
AZ V:2:5, Hole Canyon Cliff Dwelling	2				1	3
AZ V:2:83		2	2		2	6
GFS 89-6, Sanrace Cliff Dwelling		1				1
AZ P:13:2	1		1		1	3
AZ P:14:14, Red Rock House			1	5		6
Total	34	46	27	35	44	186

NOTE: GFS is Grasshopper Field School number; AZ is Arizona State Museum Site Survey number.

Mountain Red Ware in the surface debris seem to have low quantities of Roosevelt Red Ware or none (Fig. 5.4).

White Mountain Red Ware constitutes around 20 percent or less of the surface sherds on two of the collected sites. At Oak Creek Pueblo (AZ P:14:15) the low frequency for White Mountain Red Ware is probably caused by the small overall sample size. I recovered only 10 decorated sherds from the collection unit, 4 of which were White Mountain Red Ware. Sherd weight in this case skews the proportion considerably. (By sherd count, 40% of the collected surface sherds are White Mountain Red Ware). Spring Creek Pueblo (GFS 82–1), on the other hand, may be slightly earlier than the other sites, based on its considerable proportion (56.59%) of black-on-white ceramics in the surface assemblage. In sum, the analysis of surface collections

from fourteenth-century sites within the Grasshopper region demonstrates that White Mountain Red Ware is well represented in the surface refuse of all of them.

White Mountain Red Ware was imported into the Grasshopper region from two distinct sources. One is associated with ceramics that were assigned to Compositional Group 1 and the other source is associated with ceramics assigned to Compositional Group 2 (Chapter 3). An analysis of the distribution of the ceramics from the sampled sites within the Grasshopper region and adjacent areas that were assigned to these two compositional groups reveals an interesting pattern. Of the 50 imported vessels from Grasshopper Pueblo, only 3 belonged to Compositional Group 2 (Table 4.5). Analyzed imported ceramics from sites in close proximity to Grasshopper Pueblo (Table 5.2) were assigned predom-

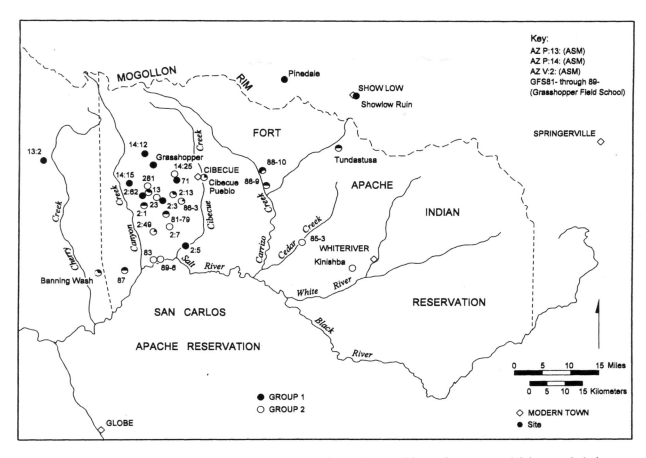

Figure 5.5. Quantities (in percent) of ceramics belonging to Compositional Groups 1 and 2 in sampled sites.

inantly to Compositional Group 1 (Fig. 5.5) and reflect the pattern seen at Grasshopper Pueblo. Site AZ P:14:281 is an exception; samples of imported White Mountain Red Ware from this site belong exclusively to Compositional Group 2 (Fig. 5.5, Table 5.2). Both Compositional Group 1 and Group 2 White Mountain Red Ware occur in sites farther to the south and east of Grasshopper Pueblo, with an increasing proportion of Compositional Group 2 ceramics (for example, AZ P:14:13, AZ V:2:49, and GFS 86–3; see Fig. 5.5). Imported ceramics from sites farthest to the east and along the Salt River belonged exclusively to Compositional Group 2. Noteworthy among these sites is Kinishba, a large pueblo of about 800 rooms, with a spatial arrangement similar to Grasshopper Pueblo (Baldwin 1938b, 1939; Cummings 1940). Kinishba was the largest fourteenth-century settlement in the eastern part of the Fort Apache Indian Reservation and imported White Mountain Red Ware seems to have come predominantly from the source of Compositional Group 2 ceramics. The sample size was small and this inter-

pretation has to be taken cautiously. However, the samples were taken randomly from a large collection, and the fact that all sherds belonged to Compositional Group 2 indicates that Group 2 ceramics were present at Kinishba in considerable quantities.

This geographical pattern of imported White Mountain Red Ware suggests two different distributional systems within the east-central Arizona mountains. Imported White Mountain Red Ware ceramics found at Grasshopper Pueblo and the surrounding sites, as well as at sites in the northern part of the Canyon Creek drainage and AZ P:13:2 west of Q-Ranch, may have come predominantly from a source directly to the north or northeast (Fig. 5.6). Interestingly, analyzed ceramics from both Pinedale Ruin and Showlow Ruin were assigned only to Compositional Group 1 (Table 5.2, Fig. 5.5). In contrast, imported White Mountain Red Ware found at the eastern sites may have come from a source farther east of Showlow Ruin, perhaps the Springerville area. Pots may have been moved along the north fork of the White River and then farther west along the

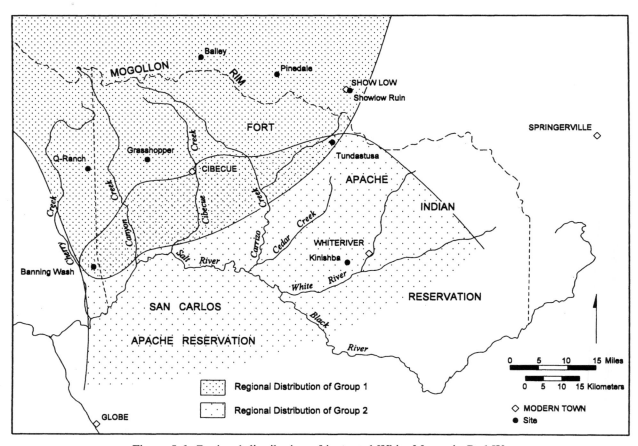

Figure 5.6. Regional distribution of imported White Mountain Red Ware.

Salt River (Fig. 5.6). Imported ceramics at sites in the intermediate area probably came from both sources.

Though this picture is at best preliminary and further analysis of larger samples is certainly required, including systematic sourcing of ceramics from sites north of the Mogollon Rim, it is intriguing and hints at complex distribution and interaction mechanisms among different mountain and plateau communities during the fourteenth century.

LOCALLY PRODUCED WHITE MOUNTAIN RED WARE AND GRASSHOPPER POLYCHROME IN THE GRASSHOPPER REGION

To evaluate whether contemporary sites in the Grasshopper region contained locally produced decorated ceramics and, if so, in what quantities, I tabulated the frequencies of brown-paste White Mountain Red Ware and Grasshopper Polychrome from the surface collections. The term "local" is used here to mean local to the Grasshopper region, not specifically to Grasshopper

Pueblo. Figure 5.7 shows that all sampled sites contained local ceramics in their assemblages. Both brown-paste White Mountain Red Ware and Grasshopper Polychrome were classified as local. Percentages for the brown-paste White Mountain Red Ware are adjusted (Chapter 4) and should reflect local production fairly accurately.

Compared to Grasshopper Pueblo (AZ P:14:1), the quantities of Grasshopper Polychrome and of brown-paste White Mountain Red Ware vary considerably in these sites. The quantities of local sherds in the surface debris of sites AZ V:2:62 and GFS 86-3, for instance, are similar to those at Grasshopper Pueblo, around 5 percent. In contrast, at Red Canyon Tank Pueblo (AZ P:14:25) and Hilltop Pueblo (AZ P:14:12), local ceramics constitute more than 17 percent of the decorated ceramics found on the surface. A possible explanation for the high numbers of locally produced decorated ceramics at some of the sites could be, again, that heavy pothunting introduced sherds from burial vessels into the surface assemblage. At Grasshopper Pueblo, where

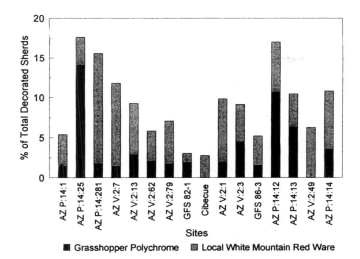

Figure 5.7. Local decorated ceramics in sampled sites in the Grasshopper region. Percentages are based on sherd weights. AZ P:14:15, AZ V:2:83, and GFS 89–6 are not plotted because of small samples.

slightly more than 50 percent of the reconstructed vessels of the Fourmile stylistic tradition from mortuary and domestic contexts were produced locally, the surface discard patterns do not reflect these numbers. (Only 5.4% of the decorated surface ceramics at Grasshopper were locally manufactured, Fig. 5.7). However, this divergence in quantities between the contexts reflects a temporal difference. Most of the local ceramics were probably produced after large quantities of imported White Mountain Red Ware had been introduced into the settlement and the local ceramics were in use until the final occupation of the settlement, which accounts for their small numbers in the surface refuse.

It is difficult to assess the scope of local production within the regional settlements based on surface material. As demonstrated by the analysis of different archaeological contexts at Grasshopper Pueblo, surface material does not necessarily reflect the scale of production and consumption of locally manufactured vessels. It may represent predominantly ceramics that were discarded early in the occupational history of a site. However, considering the frequencies of brown-paste White Mountain Red Ware and Grasshopper Polychrome at the contemporary surface-collected sites, one could speculate that at least the same proportion, if not in some cases a higher proportion, of local ceramics was present in the assemblages of these sites as was present at Grasshopper Pueblo. At any rate, the analysis of surface ceramics from the sampled sites demonstrated that a component of locally produced decorated ceramics was present at all of them.

Compositional analysis differentiated two groups of locally produced ceramics (Compositional Groups 3 and 4) that reflect two different paste recipes rather than two different raw material sources. Analyzed ceramics from 19 of the sampled sites within the Grasshopper region were assigned to Compositional Groups 3 or 4 (Table. 5.2, Fig. 5.8). Unlike Compositional Groups 1 and 2, no regional pattern of distribution could be discerned for these two groups. Sites located closer to the Oak Creek-Canyon Creek drainage tend to have slightly higher numbers of the heavy diabase-tempered Group 4 ceramics (Fig. 5.8). Extensive diabase outcroppings occur in this drainage (Plate 2). In general, ceramics assigned to both of the local compositional groups are present in these sites, with a minor preference for light-tempered paste, Compositional Group 3 ceramics.

GRASSHOPPER PUEBLO: CERAMIC PRODUCTION AND DISTRIBUTION CENTER?

Compositional Group 3 and Group 4 ceramics occur in sites within the Grasshopper region (Fig. 5.8). Vessels assigned to both of these groups were produced at Grasshopper Pueblo, probably from a secondary source clay from a stratum that underlies the site. The presence of Group 3 and Group 4 ceramics in sites within the Grasshopper region argues strongly for production at Grasshopper Pueblo and a subsequent distribution from there throughout the region. As discussed in Chapter 3, some source clays collected not far away from Grasshopper Pueblo, but close to some of the other sampled sites, do not match either of the two local compositional groups.

I could find no indication for a highly localized production of vessels in the Fourmile stylistic tradition within the Grasshopper region. Although sample size for each site was small, I would expect that if each settlement predominantly produced its own decorated ceramics, then production would have been reflected in the compositional data. It should have resulted in a much higher variability within the two local compositional groups than was present, and the respective data sets should have showed subdivisions that coincided with sample proveniences.

If on-site production of polychrome ceramics occurred in these settlements, it must have been on a relatively small scale. After large-scale local production of White Mountain Red Ware and Grasshopper Polychrome started at Grasshopper Pueblo, the community appears to have become a regional supplier of these vessels.

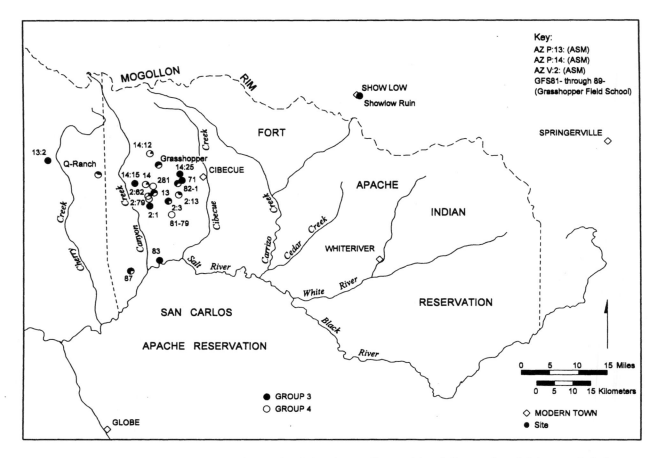

Figure 5.8. Quantities (in percent) of ceramics belonging to Compositional Groups 3 and 4 in sampled sites.

CIRCULATION OF LOCALLY PRODUCED WHITE MOUNTAIN RED WARE AND GRASSHOPPER POLYCHROME

No clear boundary of the circulation of the locally produced White Mountain Red Ware and Grasshopper Polychrome ceramics could be established, but some interesting trends were observed. Grasshopper-produced ceramics did not occur in sampled sites outside the Grasshopper region except in the western sites of Q-Ranch and AZ P:13:2, and one sherd found at Show-low Ruin (Table 5.2, Fig. 5.8). (All samples from Q-Ranch belonged to either Compositional Groups 3 or 4, except one that was unassigned). In fact, none of the analyzed ceramics from sampled sites east of Cibecue Creek, including Cibecue Pueblo, could be assigned to Compositional Groups 3 or 4.

Petrographic analysis supported these findings. Except for five samples, all analyzed sherds could be classified into three temper groups (Table 3.20). Temper Group 1 represents the imported White Mountain Red

Ware and consists of sherd and quartz. Temper Groups 2 and 3 are characterized by diabase, which occurs about 5 km (3 miles) west of Grasshopper Pueblo in the Oak Creek-Canyon Creek drainage (Plate 2). Except for two samples, all the local ceramics were classified either as Temper Group 2 or 3, and all the imported ceramics were classified as Temper Group 1. No other temper group was identified. None of the analyzed ceramics from sites outside the Grasshopper region except Q-Ranch belonged to Temper Groups 2 or 3 (Table 3.20).

Though conclusions should be drawn with caution, Grasshopper Pueblo seems to have been a center of production and distribution of White Mountain Red Ware and Grasshopper Polychrome ceramics. The circulation of these vessels encompassed mainly the Grasshopper region (Fig. 5.9). Cibecue Valley and the Mogollon Rim were probably the eastern and northern boundaries, whereas Q-Ranch and AZ P:13:2 apparently participated in a Grasshopper distribution sphere. The southern, and southwestern boundaries are not clear,

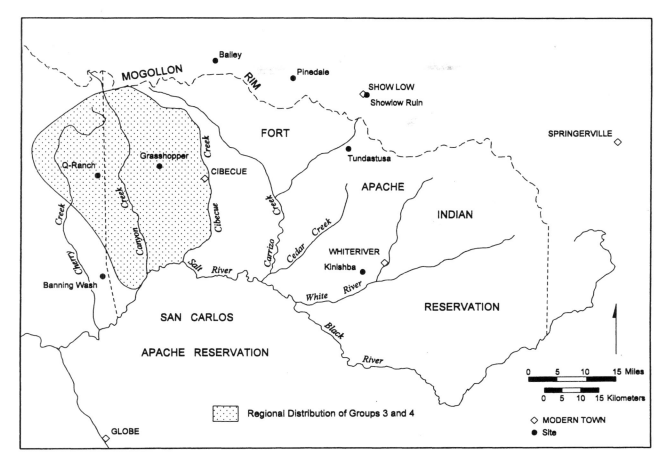

Figure 5.9. Regional distribution of locally produced White Mountain Red Ware and Grasshopper Polychrome.

although it is interesting to note that some analyzed ceramics from site AZ V:2:87 were assigned to Compositional Groups 3 and 4, whereas ceramics from Banning Wash about 8 km (5 miles) to the west (Fig. 5.9) could not be assigned to either of the local compositional groups. Salt River Canyon may have been a natural southern boundary of the Grasshopper region, but no sites south of the Salt River were sampled. The one local sherd found at Showlow Ruin may indicate that even during the later phase of occupation at Grasshopper Pueblo, contacts with communities north of the Mogollon Rim existed.

These observations are tentative and larger samples of ceramics from some of the sites discussed need to be analyzed compositionally to clarify the situation. Specifically, Q-Ranch and Kinishba are critical to an evaluation of the circulation of decorated ceramics in the east-central Arizona mountains. A systematic analysis of Kinishba ceramics, for instance, might reveal that it had a role similar to Grasshopper during the fourteenth century and that it supplied the eastern portion of the

reservation with ceramics in the Fourmile stylistic tradition. Kinishba Polychrome, however, was not produced at Kinishba; it came from the same source as some of the imported White Mountain Red Ware and was assigned to Compositional Group 1.

DISCUSSION

White Mountain Red Ware was imported into the east-central Arizona mountains from at least two distinct sources. Imported vessels at Grasshopper Pueblo and at surrounding contemporary settlements may have come predominantly from an area north of the Mogollon Rim. This source is associated with Compositional Group 1 and analyzed ceramics from Pinedale Ruin and Showlow Ruin seem also to have come from this source.

Imported White Mountain Red Ware at sites to the south and east of Grasshopper Pueblo may have come predominantly from the second source, represented by Compositional Group 2. This source may be located northeast of the Mogollon Rim, perhaps in the Springerville area. Vessels found at sites between these two areas apparently came from both sources. Clearly, two different sources of imported White Mountain Red Ware are documented in the east-central Arizona mountains, which probably correspond to two different distribution spheres.

People from Grasshopper Pueblo may have provided Fourmile style ceramics throughout the Grasshopper region after substantial local production of these vessels started. Polychrome ceramics seem to have moved from Grasshopper Pueblo into the contemporary communities and do not appear to have been produced at those settlements. It is likely that local vessels did not circulate far beyond the Grasshopper region, however, except to the Q-Ranch area west of Grasshopper Pueblo.

To reiterate, the settlement aggregation south of the Mogollon Rim during the early A.D. 1300s coincides with high quantities of imported White Mountain Red Ware in these southern sites. This observation suggests that a large portion of these polychrome pots were brought in by people immigrating into the area, rather than predominantly by trade and exchange. The compositional evidence for substantial local production of Fourmile-style ceramics that were used and discarded later than most of the imported ceramics suggests that people settled in these southern areas and produced polychrome ceramics with local materials. The abandonment of a series of sites north of the Mogollon Rim (Haury and Hargrave 1931: 73–74; Martin and others 1961: 112–122, 1964, 1967; Mills, in press) parallels the settlement aggregation south of the Mogollon Rim and supports this interpretation.

The differential regional distribution of imported White Mountain Red Ware may indicate that people from different areas or villages north of the Mogollon Rim moved into the mountains of east-central Arizona. People predominantly from the Pinedale–Showlow area may have migrated into the Grasshopper region, settled at Grasshopper Pueblo, among other places, and eventually produced pottery decorated in Fourmile style. The latest construction date for Pinedale Ruin is A.D. 1286, and Haury and Hargrave (1931: 73–74) estimated that the pueblo was abandoned around A.D. 1330. Concurrent with this date, the decorated ceramic assemblage of Pinedale Ruin contained predominantly Pinedale Black-on-red or Pinedale Polychrome and Cedar Creek Poly-

chrome ceramics. Fourmile Polychrome occurred only in limited quantities (Haury and Hargrave 1931: 67–68).

In contrast, at Grasshopper Pueblo the majority of White Mountain Red Ware is Fourmile Polychrome, the latest type; the earlier Cedar Creek Polychrome occurs only in small amounts. Moreover, a rare "Salmon" variety of Roosevelt Red Ware that has been documented in considerable quantities at Grasshopper Pueblo (Mayro and others 1976: 86) also occurs at Pinedale Ruin. At Bailey Ruin, a large masonry pueblo situated about 20 km (12.4 miles) west of Pinedale (Haury and Hargrave 1931: 8, Fig. 1) that is currently being excavated by the University of Arizona Archaeological Field School under the direction of Barbara Mills (Mills, in press), the decorated ceramic assemblage is similar to that of Pinedale Ruin. White Mountain Red Ware occurs predominantly as Pinedale Black-on-red or Pinedale Polychrome and Cedar Creek Polychrome; almost no Fourmile Polychrome is present (Mills, in press). Mills projects that Bailey Ruin was abandoned between A.D. 1325 to 1330. Thus, both Pinedale Ruin and Bailey Ruin may have been points of departure for people who eventually settled at Grasshopper Pueblo and in the surrounding contemporary settlements. The presence of low quantities of Grasshopper-produced White Mountain Red Ware at Showlow Ruin, which was occupied until the end of the fourteenth century (latest cutting dates are A.D. 1378–1382; Haury and Hargrave 1931: 14–15), may indicate that reciprocal relationships with the homeland were maintained throughout the occupation of both pueblos.

People associated with the source of Compositional Group 2 ceramics may have moved into the eastern areas of the mountains, into Kinishba and surrounding communities. The large pueblo of Kinishba undoubtedly was a regional center in the fourteenth century. It is thus conceivable that, as at Grasshopper Pueblo, northerners started to produce White Mountain Red Ware at Kinishba and that it supplied the eastern portion of the reservation with Fourmile style ceramics. (To clarify this proposition, I am undertaking NAA on more than 130 samples from Kinishba, the results of which will be contrasted with the established compositional reference groups.) People from both source areas may have settled in the Cibecue, Carrizo, and Forestdale valleys.

CHAPTER SIX

Commodities and Common Containers: White Mountain Red Ware Reevaluated

Archaeologists have used White Mountain Red Ware frequently for modeling sociopolitical and socio-economic organization of the northern Southwest. It was most commonly interpreted as a highly regarded trade ware and used to trace prehistoric trade routes and exchange patterns (Carlson 1970; Graves 1982). Others analyzed White Mountain Red Ware to reconstruct pueblo sociopolitical organization, which led to a model of intercommunity alliances (Upham 1982; Upham and others 1981). According to this model, White Mountain Red Ware was a status symbol to which access was controlled by managerial elites (Cordell and Plog 1979; Lightfoot and Jewett 1984; Upham 1982; Upham and others 1981).

In those studies a circumscribed area on the southern Colorado Plateau, more specifically the Silver Creek drainage, was projected as the production zone of White Mountain Red Ware (Graves 1982: 322, 335). Interpretations that White Mountain Red Ware was widely distributed through long-distance trade networks or formal exchange between political alliances were based on an inferred locus of production and the subsequent distribution of ceramics from this production zone. However, most of the studies were based on stylistic analyses and relied almost exclusively on the criterion of abundance to establish provenance rather than on compositional analysis.

Large-scale compositional and petrographic analyses and a thorough investigation of archaeological contexts at Grasshopper Pueblo and at contemporary sites in the mountains of east-central Arizona resulted in a reevaluation of the production, distribution, and function of White Mountain Red Ware during the fourteenth century. The analyses described in the foregoing chapters demonstrate unambiguously that White Mountain Red Ware was also manufactured outside the Silver Creek area. Considerable quantities of Fourmile style ceramics, in varying degrees of quality, were produced at

Grasshopper Pueblo, starting most likely around A.D. 1320.

Parallel to the local production of polychrome ceramics with complex designs, a dramatic shift in the preference of decorated ceramics occurred in the Grasshopper region and elsewhere in the mountains. Ceramic assemblages of late Pueblo III period sites in the Grasshopper region are characterized by black-on-white pottery, predominantly Cibola White Ware that was almost exclusively produced outside the region (Zedeño 1991, 1994a). A rapid change from black-on-white to polychrome ceramics occurred at Chodistaas Pueblo toward the end of its occupation in the A.D. 1290s (Montgomery and Reid 1990), and some of the newly introduced polychrome ceramics were probably locally produced (Zedeño 1991: 209, 1994a: 95–99).

Decorated ceramics in Pueblo IV period sites are predominantly polychrome. Even decorated brown mountain ceramics such as McDonald Plain and McDonald Corrugated followed this trend and became Cibicue Polychrome (see Mauer 1970). Black-on-white ceramics occur only in minor quantities, mostly as *ollas* or water jars. Accompanying this shift in decorated ceramic assemblages from the late Pueblo III to the early Pueblo IV period was an increase in variability and local production of these ceramics (Zedeño and Triadan, in press).

During the late A.D. 1200s, most of the decorated ceramics were imported into the Grasshopper region, probably from the southern Colorado Plateau. The predominance of imported white wares at late Pueblo III period sites supports either substantial long-distance trade or exchange, or a periodic (perhaps seasonal) movement of northern people into the area (Reid 1984: 62–63; see also Zedeño 1991, 1994a for a detailed discussion). The presence of imported Cibola White Ware in different design styles and the identification of different compositional groups for this ware at Chodistaas Pueblo (Zedeño 1991: 163–168, 181–202, 1994a: 73–77, 83–92) may indicate an episodic, even joint use of the area by different northern groups (Reid 1989: 75; Zedeño 1994b). During the final phase of the occupation of Chodistaas Pueblo, people who knew how to make polychrome ceramics started to migrate into the area and probably settled there long enough to manufacture decorated pottery.

At Grasshopper Pueblo more than 50 percent of all Fourmile style polychrome ceramics were produced locally. It is not coincidental that increased local production of decorated ceramics paralleled major aggregation in the region. Large quantities of imported White Mountain Red Ware and the subsequent local production of these ceramics support a hypothesis of significant migrations of people into the area, most likely from the southern Colorado Plateau. The construction sequence at Grasshopper Pueblo shows that the settlement grew through the offspring of resident kin groups as well as by a series of movements of people into the pueblo until it reached its peak occupation between A.D. 1320 and 1340.

Grasshopper Pueblo became a large, complex community that probably incorporated people from different areas of the northern Southwest. Large quantities of Roosevelt Red Ware (Salado Polychrome) suggest that people from the north as well as people from other areas, for example, the Tonto Basin, moved into Grasshopper Pueblo (Reid 1989: 81). The analysis of the spatial distribution of White Mountain Red Ware and Grasshopper Polychrome, however, did not show any association with residential units or specific groups of burials. The even distribution and co-occurrence of these ceramics throughout the site indicate that all households had access to these wares. If different groups resided at Grasshopper Pueblo, the village was either already remarkably integrated or the decorated ceramics were not restricted to respective groups.

White Mountain Red Ware and its local variants were an integral part of the household assemblage and frequently ended up as funerary goods. This interpretation is not only supported by high quantities of these ceramics in household and mortuary contexts at Grasshopper Pueblo, but also by the high quantities of White Mountain Red Ware on the surface of contemporary sites in the region. (Even small sites such as field houses have large quantities of White Mountain Red Ware on the surface). These data contradict the hypothesis of Upham and others (Lightfoot and Jewett 1984; Upham 1982; Upham and others 1981) that White Mountain Red Ware was an elite or high-status good

restricted to the large sites (see also Adams 1991b, Adams and others 1993, and Crown 1995 for similar findings regarding Hopi yellow wares and Salado Polychrome).

On the other hand, it is interesting that more than half of all decorated ceramics recovered from Grasshopper Pueblo are decorated in the bold new design concept of the Fourmile style. This predominance of Fourmile style vessels suggests a strong northern orientation. Adams (1991a: 21–77, 96–101, 118–121, 132, 140–141) proposes that Fourmile style on ceramics indicates the presence of the katsina cult, which, following his argument, originated on the southern Colorado Plateau in the Silver Creek area. He argues that the katsina cult served as a strong integrative mechanism in the heterogeneous, highly aggregated fourteenth-century pueblos in east-central Arizona (Adams 1991a: 149–160, 185–191). A symbolic function for White Mountain Red Ware may be one explanation for the predominance of Fourmile style ceramics at Grasshopper Pueblo. (See Crown 1994: 198–225 for an ideological interpretation of design on Salado Polychrome.)

The limitations of compositional and artifactual analysis of ceramic assemblages become apparent on the intrasite level. It is clear that imported White Mountain Red Ware at Grasshopper Pueblo is generally earlier than the local variants. However, more specific questions with regard to the organization of local ceramic production, who produced White Mountain Red Ware and Grasshopper Polychrome and when, could only be answered tentatively. The main occupation at Grasshopper Pueblo lasted probably not more than 75 years, little more than three generations. The ceramic types used in the analyses indicate that they occur for at least 50 years and, because they overlap considerably in time, the types are not sensitive enough to answer these specific questions.

Scott Van Keuren is currently working on the systematic analysis of patterns of design structure and execution on White Mountain Red Ware to further investigate community interaction at Grasshopper Pueblo. (See Van Keuren 1994 for a detailed discussion of design structure.) Arnold (1981) stresses the importance of design structure as follows:

> The similarity of pottery within an interacting group, however, is not in the motifs or design elements but rather in the underlying structure of the design (Arnold 1981: 40).

conscious aspects of design, such as elements and their configuration, can diffuse through the community rapidly, even without interaction, and it is the *design structure* that reflects the face-to-face contact of the community of potters (Arnold 1981: 40, following Hardin 1970; emphasis added).

Thus, stylistic analysis of White Mountain Red Ware within this framework, in conjunction with the results of the compositional analysis, may provide a more detailed reconstruction of the organization of ceramic production and technological transfer at Grasshopper Pueblo.

Contrary to traditional assumptions (Carlson 1970; Graves 1982), the results of the compositional analysis point to at least two regional production zones for White Mountain Red Ware in the fourteenth century: one in the east-central Arizona mountains and one probably on the southern edge of the Colorado Plateau. Light-paste White Mountain Red Ware was imported into the Grasshopper region and adjacent areas from two different sources north of the Mogollon Rim. Subsequently, White Mountain Red Ware and Grasshopper Polychrome were produced at Grasshopper Pueblo using two different paste recipes.

Spatial analysis of imported ceramics from sites of the Grasshopper region and adjacent areas revealed a distinct pattern of distribution, analogous to the two different production sources. This pattern suggests that two different distributional systems existed within the mountains. White Mountain Red Ware at Grasshopper Pueblo and surrounding sites, including the northern part of the Canyon Creek drainage and the Q-Ranch area, may have come predominantly from a source directly to the north or northeast. (Both Pinedale Ruin and Showlow Ruin were only associated with Compositional Group 1.) In contrast, eastern sites around Kinishba may be connected to a source farther to the east of Showlow, perhaps the Springerville area. Pots could have moved along the north fork of the White River and then farther west along the Salt River. Settlements in the intermediate area, for instance in the Cibecue, Carrizo, and Forestdale valleys, seemed to have access to both sources of ceramics.

The differential distribution of imported White Mountain Red Ware suggests that people from at least two different areas or communities north of the Mogollon Rim moved into the mountains at the beginning of the fourteenth century. The Cibola White Ware imported into the Grasshopper region during the late A.D. 1200s came from yet a different source (Chapter 3), and a third area north of the Mogollon Rim may have played an early role in the migrations into the mountains.

It is likely that people from the area around Showlow and Pinedale moved into the Grasshopper region, settled, among other places, at Grasshopper Pueblo, and eventually began to produce their polychrome ceramics with local resources. After local production set in, Grasshopper Pueblo provided Fourmile style ceramics to the surrounding Grasshopper region. Pots probably did not move much beyond the Grasshopper region, except for the Q-Ranch area to the west of Grasshopper.

People associated with the second source of imported White Mountain Red Ware moved into the eastern part of the reservation, perhaps even into the Point of Pines region. It is conceivable that in addition to Grasshopper Pueblo and the Grasshopper region, other mountain production zones existed. Kinishba and Point of Pines Pueblo (Fig. 1.1), southeast of Grasshopper Pueblo, are both large aggregated pueblos that could have functioned as regional distribution centers for locally produced polychrome ceramics. At Point of Pines, a brown paste variety of Fourmile Polychrome, named Point of Pines Polychrome, is interpreted as a late local copy of Fourmile; it has been found at 18 sites in the Point of Pines region (Carlson 1970: 77–81; Wendorf 1950: 49).

The compositional analyses presented in this study demonstrate that an important factor in the wide distribution of White Mountain Red Ware during the fourteenth century was the movement of people. These results support the assumptions that the beginning of the fourteenth century in the east-central Arizona mountains was characterized by high mobility (Reid 1984: 62–63) that led to aggregation and subsequent changes in community and household organization (Lowell 1991; Montgomery 1992; Reid 1989; Reid and Whittlesey 1982) and coresidence of different groups (Reid 1989; Reid and Whittlesey 1982).

Because this study concentrated on Grasshopper Pueblo and the Grasshopper region, not all questions pertaining to the production and distribution of White Mountain Red Ware could be answered. Especially, the reconstruction of the regional circulation throughout the mountains should be viewed tentatively. However, one major achievement of this research is the establishment of well-defined compositional *ceramic reference groups* for White Mountain Red Ware and Grasshopper Polychrome. As neutron activation data can be calibrated between different laboratories if they use the same reference material, these reference groups provide a basis for subsequent compositional analysis of White Mountain Red Ware. It can now be readily determined if ceramics belong to the respective reference groups or if they belong to additional compositional groups that indicate other production loci for White Mountain Red Ware.

To evaluate the regional distribution of White Mountain Red Ware and to clarify the question of localized mountain production zones other than the Grasshopper region, future research should incorporate compositional analysis of substantial samples of ceramics from the largest sites in the mountains outside the Grasshopper region, such as Q-Ranch, Kinishba, and Point of Pines. White Mountain Red Ware from Q-Ranch should be analyzed systematically to determine if it was part of a Grasshopper distribution system or if its inhabitants produced their own local White Mountain Red Ware and to determine if imported White Mountain Red Ware belongs to Compositional Group 1.

Nieves Zedeño and I are currently analyzing ceramics from Point of Pines and Kinishba to determine the provenance of the imported ceramics and to investigate the possibility of local production at these two pueblos. Additional samples from surrounding contemporary sites are included in the analysis to establish the circulation of the local ceramics.

In the case of Kinishba and Point of Pines, petrographic analysis should provide valuable preliminary results and facilitate sampling for subsequent compositional analysis. The geology of the central Arizona mountains is exceptionally diverse (Chapter 3). Grasshopper Pueblo was built on alluvium overlying marine sediments and its inhabitants had access to igneous diabase about 5 km (3 miles) to the west in the Oak Creek-Canyon Creek drainage (Plate 2); it was used as temper for local White Mountain Red Ware and Grasshopper Polychrome pottery. Kinishba is located on recent alluvium, overlying marine sediments of the Supai formation. The nearest igneous rocks are basaltic flows, quite distinct from the diabase (Plate 2). Thus, local White Mountain Red Ware from Kinishba should be petrographically different from the ceramics produced at Grasshopper Pueblo. Point of Pines, in turn, is situated on silicic to mafic flows. Point of Pines Polychrome, the late local copy of Fourmile Polychrome (Wendorf 1950: 49), has a brown paste and is tempered with leucite tuff (Carlson 1970: 77-81), again, a temper distinct from the diabase.

The heterogeneity in the mountain geology also facilitates the compositional analysis. Source clays should be quite distinct for these areas, and thus the chemical profiles of local ceramics from Kinishba and Point of Pines should be distinct from those of vessels produced at Grasshopper Pueblo. Ultimately the results of the chemical characterization of ceramics from Point of Pines and Kinishba will be compared to the compositional data from Grasshopper Pueblo.

In addition to these mountain regions, ceramics from sites north of the Mogollon Rim need to be compositionally analyzed and compared with the established reference groups to investigate where the imported White Mountain Red Ware was produced. Barbara Mills and Andrew Duff recently submitted samples of White Mountain Red Ware from Bailey Ruin, located about 20 km (12.4 miles) west of Pinedale, and from the Upper Little Colorado drainage to the University of Missouri Research Reactor Facility (MURR) for NAA. Additionally, in 1990 James Woodman submitted ceramics from Fourmile Ruin for NAA at the Conservation Analytical Laboratory (CAL) of the Smithsonian Institution. The results of these analyses will be incorporated into an exceptional compositional data base that will provide a supraregional reconstruction of late prehistoric ceramic production and circulation and will clarify our current interpretations.

To further evaluate the organization of ceramic production within fourteenth-century mountain communities, additional compositional analysis should also be undertaken on material from Grasshopper Pueblo. Utilitarian brown wares and Cibicue Polychrome should be systematically analyzed to determine if they were manufactured with the same pastes as were used for the polychrome ceramics. Large scale analysis of Roosevelt Red Ware from Grasshopper Pueblo should clarify if this ware was also produced at the settlement. This information, combined with the data on White Mountain Red Ware production and Scott Van Keuren's ongoing design structure analysis, may provide a detailed reconstruction of the processes of aggregation, community interaction and integration, and abandonment at Grasshopper Pueblo.

To summarize, contrary to traditional assumptions, production of White Mountain Red Ware in east-central Arizona was localized during the fourteenth century. A major factor for its wide distribution and manufacture during this time was migration into the mountains that resulted in massive population aggregation. White Mountain Red Ware was a readily accessible household ware and may have had some socially integrative function. Inferences that White Mountain Red Ware was a restricted elite good or status symbol were not supported by this research. On the other hand, the systematic investigation of the sources of White Mountain Red Ware provided an independent line of evidence for the reconstruction of the sociodemographic processes that took place in east-central Arizona during the fourteenth century.

As mentioned at the beginning of this monograph, the reconstruction of prehistoric sociopolitical and socioeconomic organization is often based on the circulation of goods. However, meaningful inferences cannot be drawn before locally produced artifacts (for instance, ceramics) are distinguished from nonlocally produced ones. To determine the provenance of artifacts is essential in evaluating the behavioral inferences of their (archaeological) provenience. This analysis of the sources of a prominent Southwestern painted pottery ware, as well as Zedeño's (1991, 1994a) and Crown's (1994) studies of Cibola White Ware and Salado Polychrome, demonstrate that technological and compositional analyses, when integrated in archaeological research concepts, make critical contributions to the reconstruction of prehistoric societies.

Schematic Overview of White Mountain Red Ware Types at Grasshopper Pueblo

Date	Type	Decorative Style	Interior Design	Exterior Design
A.D. 1325 to 1400	Fourmile Polychrome	Fourmile	Fourmile style, centered design, black band along rim, space between center design and rim	Black bands with white outline, F-design
A.D. 1300 to 1350–1375	Cedar Creek Polychrome	Pinedale	Same as Pinedale Polychrome and Pinedale Black-on-red	Same as Fourmile

Date	Type	Decorative Style	Interior Design	Exterior Design
	Pinedale Polychrome	Pinedale	Center not decorated, design goes all the way up to rim	Isolated black motifs, outlined in white
A.D. 1275 to 1320				
	Pinedale Black-on-Red	Pinedale	Center not decorated, design goes all the way up to rim	Isolated black motifs
A.D. 1275 to 1320				

Date	Type	Decorative Style	Interior Design	Exterior Design
	St. Johns Polychrome	Tularosa	Center not decorated, design goes all the way up to rim, finer hatch and more repetitive motifs than Pinedale style	Isolated motifs or parallel lines executed in broad white lines
A.D. 1175 to 1280				
	St. Johns Black-on-Red	Tularosa	Center not decorated, design goes all the way up to rim, finer hatch and more repetitive motifs than Pinedale style	None
A.D. 1175 to 1280				

Provenience and Source Identification of Analyzed Ceramics

All the ceramic and raw material samples that were analyzed by NAA are listed by their laboratory identification number (NAA No.) and those additionally analyzed include their respective ICP (ICP No.) and petrography sample numbers (Petr. No.). Under descriptions of the material and pottery type (Descr., Type), the designations local or nonlocal reflect initial visual inspection. Catalogue numbers (Cat. No.) are those listed in the Arizona State Museum artifact catalogue and they identify reconstructible vessels. Provenience information is given by site, sample location, and geological formation for raw materials and by excavation unit for reconstructible vessels. NAA Group and Subgroup and Temper Group identifications of the samples are provided.

Ceramic ware and type abbreviations
WMR = White Mountain Red Ware
FM = Fourmile Polychrome
SL = Showlow Polychrome
CK = Cedar Creek Polychrome
PDB/R = Pinedale Black-on-red
PDP = Pinedale Polychrome
GH = Grasshopper Polychrome
K = Kinishba Polychrome

Site designations
Arizona State Museum Site Survey:
AZ P:, AZ V:
GFS = Grasshopper Field School number
BW = Banning Wash Pueblo
K = Kinishba Ruin
PD = Pinedale Ruin
Q = Q–Ranch site
SL = Showlow Ruin
TDT = Tundastusa Ruin

Provenience designations
Bur. = Burial
cl = cluster
FN = field number
G = geological level
GK = Great Kiva
L = level
Q = quadrant
RB = Room Block
RV = reconstructible vessel
TT = test trench
V = vessel

(Core) Color
mic. = micaceous

NAA No.	ICP No.	Petr. No.	Descr., Type	Cat. No.	Site	Provenience	(Core) Color	NAA Group	NAA Subgroup	Temper Group
DTC001		1	clay		K	alluvial, underlying site	light orange-beige			
DTC002		2	clay		K	alluvial, underlying site	light orange-beige			
DTC003		3	clay				Road 011, NW of 3 Way Tank, Martin Form.	red			
DTC004		4	clay				3 Way Tank, Road 011, Redwall Limestone	dark gray-brown			
DTC005		5	clay				S-peak of Spotted Mtn., Mafic–Younger Gravel	dark brown			
DTC006		6	clay				N-peak of Spotted Mtn., Mafic–Younger Gravel	dark brown			
DTC007		7	clay				N Spring Creek, Coconino–Upper Rim Gravel	yellowish brown			
DTC008		8	clay				N Spring Creek, Coconino–Upper Rim Gravel	yellowish brown			
DTC009		9	clay		P:14:1	about 50 m SE of RB 11, Supai (alluvial)	brown			
DTC010		10	clay			Grasshopper Tank No. 2, Naco (alluvial)	dark olive-brown			
DTC011		11	clay			S of Mud Tank, Naco (stream bed)	gray			
DTC012		12	clay			1 Mile Tank, Supai (alluvial)	dark olive-brown			
DTC013		13	clay		P:14:1	Rm. 414, NEQ, FN154	gray			
DTC014		14	clay		P:14:1	Rm. 420, SEQ, FN206	brown			
DTC015		15	clay		P:14:24	Rm. 18, NEQ	orange-brown			
DTC016		16	clay		P:14:1	Rm. 113, FN 621	yellow			
DTS017			sand		K	stream bed between room blocks	brown			
DTS018		21	sand			NW of 3 Way Tank, stream bed	dark brown			
DTS019		22	sand			Oak Creek, stream bed, spec. hematite-quartz	almost black			
DTS020		23	sand			Oak Creek, stream bed, mostly quartz	beige			
DTS021		24	sand		P:14:1	Rm. 107	white grains in brown soil matrix			
DTF022			FM	?	P:14:1	Rm. 21, NWQ, L3	gray	1	b	
DTF023			FM	?	P:14:1	?	dark gray	1	a	
DTF024			FM	?	P:14:1	GK, Bur. 111, Sec. 2, L4	light buff	1	b	
DTF025			FM	?	P:14:1	Rm. 146	white	1	b	
DTF026			FM	?	P:14:1	Rm. 100, L2, NW, cluster J	cream-buff			
DTF027			FM	?	P:14:1	Rm. 280, FN1230	buff			
DTF028			FM	438/610	P:14:1	?	cream, light gray core	1	b	
DTF029			SL	438/634	P:14:1	Rm. 438, NEQ, subfloor, L6	white	1	b	
DTF030			FM	74-13-112	P:14:1	Rm. 279, SWQ, G3, FN71-1	buff	1	b	
DTF031			FM	75-11-75	P:14:1	Plaza 1, Bur. 588, TT75-1, Sec. 3+4, subfloor	white	1	b	
DTF032			FM	75-11-76	P:14:1	Plaza 1, Bur. 588, TT75-1, Sec. 3+4, subfloor	cream, gray core	1	b	
DTF033			FM	A23, 606	P:14:1	Rm. 1, L3?	buff	1	b	
DTF034			FM	A23, 726	P:14:1	Rm. 11, L3, floor	cream-buff	1	b	
DTF035			FM/SL	A23, 768	P:14:1	Rm. 12, Bur. 45, subfloor	white	1	b	
DTF036			FM	A23, 849	P:14:1	Rm. 11, floor	buff-light gray	1	b	
DTF037			FM	A23, 961	P:14:1	Rm. 10, fill	light gray	1	b	
DTF038			FM	A28, 066	P:14:1	GK, Bur. 140?, Sec. 7, subfloor	dark gray	1	b	
DTF039			FM	A28, 241	P:14:1	Rm. 20, subfloor, same pit as Bur. 116	white	1	b	
DTF040			FM	A28, 244	P:14:1	Bur. 81, TT35, Sec. 3, V5	white	1	b	
DTF041			FM	A28, 514	P:14:1	Rm. 21, SWQ, L3	buff	1	b	
DTF042			FM	A29, 474	P:14:1	Rm. 26, SWQ, L1	white	1	b	
DTF043			FM	A29, 532	P:14:1	Bur. 202, TT44, VC	white	1	b	
DTF044			FM	A29, 599	P:14:1	Rm. 23, Bur. 211, subfloor, next to Bur. 210	buff, gray core	1	b	
DTF045			FM	A29, 634	P:14:1	TT73, Bur. 257, Sec. B	light gray-buff	1	b	
DTF046			FM	A29, 650	P:14:1	TT74, Bur. 274, Sec. B? (Sec. 3, 4?), FN2	dark gray	1	b	
DTF047			FM	A29, 958	P:14:1	Rm. 153, NWQ, L3	cream	1	b	

NAA No.	ICP No.	Petr. No.	Descr., Type	Cat. No.	Site	Provenience	(Core) Color	NAA Group	NAA Subgroup	Temper Group
DTF048			CK?	A34, 599	P:14:1	Rm. 33, Bur. 344, SE–SW, subfloor, pit 3, FN95	light gray	1	b	
DTF049			FM	A34, 979	P:14:1	Rm. 44, SWQ, floor, FN190	buff	1	b	
DTF050			FM	A35, 996	P:14:1	Rm. 183, SEQ, trash, LA4, FN29	buff, gray core	1	b	
DTF051			FM	A41, 166	P:14:1	Rm. 211, Bur. 437, SWQ,TT4, sbfl. L2, RV117,FN75	white	1	b	
DTF052			FM	A41, 175	P:14:1	Rm. 47, TT1N, fill, L6	buff, gray core	1	a	
DTF053			FM	A41, 181	P:14:1	Rm. 23, Bur. 211?, VB	cream	1	b	
DTF054			FM/SL	A41, 187	P:14:1	Rm. 116, NWQ, trash on floor, L3a	white	1	b	
DTB055			WMR	74-13-659	P:14:1	Bur. 579, Plaza?	orange, very dark gray-black core			
DTB056			GH/FM	74-13-660	P:14:1	Plaza 2, Bur. 584, Sec. 633, subfloor, G13, FN62	very dark brown-gray	4	a	
DTB057			CK/FM	74-13-722	P:14:1	?	orange-brown			
DTB058			?	75-11-1074	P:14:1	Rm. 279, Bur. 631, NEQ, TT12, sbfl., G12, FN900	dark gray	4	b	
DTB059			FM	75-11-1009	P:14:1	Rm. 438, SEQ, subfloor, G10	orange, gray core	2	a	
DTB060			FM	75-11-1011	P:14:1	?	dark brown, gray core	4	a	
DTB061			FM	A23, 600	P:14:1	Rm. 8, floor	dark gray	3	a	
DTB062			FM	A23, 604	P:14:1	Rm. 7, floor-trash	dark gray	1	a	
DTB063			FM	A28, 499	P:14:1	Rm. 21, L3	gray	3	a	
DTB064			FM	A29, 122	P:14:1	Rm. 23, SEQ, L4	very dark gray	3	c	
DTB065			FM	A29, 589	P:14:1	Rm. 23, Bur. 209, subfloor	very dark gray	3	a	
DTB066			FM	A29, 590	P:14:1	Rm. 23, Bur. 208, NEQ, subfloor, VD	gray	1		
DTB067			FM	A34, 963	P:14:1	Rm. 43, SWQ, L4, FN146	brown	4	a	
DTB068			FM	A35, 298	P:14:1	Rm. 40, Bur. 391, W1–2, subfloor, V1	orange	1	a	
DTB069			FM	A41, 177	P:14:1	Rm. 47, Bur. 453, TT2N, subfloor, RV101	dark brown-very dark gray	4	a	
DTB070			FM	A41, 497	P:14:1	Rm. 274, SEQ, floor, LA5	orange	2	b	
DTZ071			CK	A28, 381	P:14:1	TT35, Bur. 83, Sec. 5, V1>backhoe	buff-light gray	3	a	
DTZ072			CK	A34, 983	P:14:1	Rm. 21, NE–SE	cream, dark gray core	1		
DTZ073			CK	A35, 367	P:14:1	Rm. 44, Bur. 414, NWQ, subfloor, VA	orange-buff	1	a	
DTZ074			CK	A41, 179	P:14:1	Rm. 211, Bur. 458, NEQ, subfloor, RV119, FN170	gray	1	b	
DTL075			CK	75-11-741	P:14:1	Rm. 280, Bur. 648, NEQ, subfloor, FN1367	orange-brown	3	b	
DTL076			CK	75-11-1010	P:14:1	Rm. 438, Bur. 637?, SEQ, subfloor, G10	orange	2	b	
DTL077			CK?	77-27-74	P:14:1	Rm. 41, Bur. 374, subfloor	orange, dark gray core	3		
DTL078			CK	A28, 063	P:14:1	GK, Bur. 74, Sec. 5, floor	orange-brown	3		
DTL079			CK	A29, 155	P:14:1	Rm. 19, SE–SW, subfloor, L2	brown-gray	3	b	
DTL080			CK	A41, 170	P:14:1	Rm. 211, Bur. 458, NEQ, subfloor, RV121, FN172	orange, light gray core			
DTL081			CK?	A43, 571	P:14:1	Rm. 62, Bur. 568?, G8, trpit subplaza, NE, FN490	gray	3	a	
DTW082			PDB/R	74-13-721	P:14:1	Rm. 438, NWQ, floor 2, G8, FN602	buff-orange			
DTW083			SL	A28, 552	P:14:1	Rm. 13, N1–2, floor, V38	dark gray			
DTW084			PDP	A29, 040	P:14:1	GK, Bur. 188, Sec. 13, subfloor, L3, VD	gray			
DTG085			GH	RV72-50	P:14:1	?	very dark gray	3	c	
DTG086			GH	319/30	P:14:1	?	very dark gray	4	b	
DTG087			GH	74-13-108	P:14:1	Rm. 246, NWQ, roof, G3, FN99–1	dark brown-very dark gray	4	a	
DTG088			GH	74-13-198	P:14:1	Rm. 296, SWQ, roof, G4A3, F3, FN 210	very dark gray-black	3	a	
DTG089			GH	74-13-204	P:14:1	?	gray	3	a	
DTG090			GH	A23, 443	P:14:1	Lawson's TT	very dark gray	3	a	
DTG091			GH	A23, 448	P:14:1	Rm. 3, floor	very dark gray	4	a	
DTG092			GH/FM	A23, 617	P:14:1	Rm. 8, floor	very dark gray	3	a	
DTG093			GH	A23, 685	P:14:1	Rm. 11, L3, 90 cm below datum	very dark gray	4	a	
DTG094			GH	A23, 727	P:14:1	Rm. 11, L2	very dark gray	4	b	

NAA No.	ICP No.	Petr. No.	Descr., Type	Cat. No.	Site	Provenience	(Core) Color	NAA Group	NAA Subgroup	Temper Group
DTG095			GH	A23,789	P:14:1	Rm. 11, floor	very dark gray	3	c	
DTG096			GH	A23,884	P:14:1	Rm. 5, Bur. 58, subfloor, L4, 1.20 m below datum	very dark gray	3	c	
DTG097			GH	A23,913	P:14:1	Rm. 10, fill	dark gray-buff	3	a	
DTG098			GH	A23,958	P:14:1	Rm. 13, floor	dark gray	3	a	
DTG099			GH	A28,081	P:14:1	Rm. 19, SWQ, L3	very dark gray	3	b	
DTG100			GH	A28,548	P:14:1	Rm. 21, L2	very dark gray	3	a	
DTG101			GH	A29,085	P:14:1	GK, Bur. 175, Sec. 6, subfloor, L2, VF	dark gray	3	b	
DTG102			GH	A29,530	P:14:1	Rm. 37, NEQ, subfloor, L4,	very dark gray	3	b	
DTG103			GH	A29,534	P:14:1	Rm. 26, Bur. 226, NE–NW, subfloor, L4	very dark gray	4	b	
DTG104			GH	A29,535	P:14:1	Rm. 37, NWQ, floor, L3	very dark gray	4	b	
DTG105			GH	A29,600-X1	P:14:1	Rm. 23, Bur. 210, subfloor, next to Bur. 210	very dark gray	3	c	
DTG106			GH	A29,613	P:14:1	Rm. 23, Bur. 208, NEQ, subfloor, VI	very dark gray	3	a	
DTG107			GH		P:14:1	Rm. 175, fill	very dark gray-black	3	a	
DTG108			GH	A29,683	P:14:1	Rm. 153, NW–SW, TT, L3, FN26	very dark gray	3	a	
DTG109			GH	A29,851	P:14:1	Rm. 114, L2, NW	very dark gray-black	3	c	
DTG110			GH	A29,963	P:14:1	Rm. 23, Bur. 208, NEQ, subfloor, VE	very dark gray-black	4	a	
DTG111			GH?	A34,183	P:14:1	Rm. 45, SWQ, L3, FN65	dark gray	3	b	
DTG112			GH	A34,957	P:14:1	Rm. 35, NEQ, L1, FN21	orange, gray core	3	a	
DTG113			GH	A35,487	P:14:1	Rm. 44, Bur. 412, TT3–4, subfloor, VB	very dark gray gray-black	4	b	
DTG114			GH	A35,773	P:14:1	Rm. 26, NEQ, L2, FN128	very dark gray	3	a	
DTG115			GH	A35,905	P:14:1	Rm. 231, TT1, LA2, FN4	very dark gray	3	a	
DTG116			GH	A38,895	P:14:1	Rm. 100, L2, NW	very dark gray gray-black	3	c	
DTG117			GH–FM	A39,030	P:14:1	Rm. 44, floor	gray	3	a	
DTG118			GH	A39,092	P:14:1	Rm. 205, L5, floor, SE, 1.37 m below datum, FN26	brown-dark gray	3	c	
DTG119			GH	A41,182	P:14:1	Rm. 23, L4, NE	very dark gray	4	a	
DTG120			GH	A41,251	P:14:1	Rm. 274, NWQ, TT1, LA4, FN13	brown, gray core	4	b	
DTG121			GH	A41,454	P:14:1	Rm. 216, Bur. 497, NEQ, subfloor, L6, FN152	dark gray	1	a	
DTK122			K	?	P:14:1	Rm. 100, L2, NW, cluster T	buff, dark gray core	1	b	
DTK123			K	A23,769	P:14:1	Rm. 12, Bur. 63?	buff	1	a	
DTK124			K	A23,807	P:14:1	Rm. 10, fill, Rm. 16?	orange-buff, light gray core	1	b	
DTK125			K	A35,912	P:14:1	Rm. 183, L2, NE	buff	1	b	
DTK126			K	A41,180	P:14:1	Rm. 215, SEQ, L6, RV21, FN66	buff	1	b	
DTK127			K	A41,277	P:14:1	Rm. 359, SEO, floor, LA2, FN16	white	3	b	
DTB128	GH2	31	local FM				brown	3	b	1
DTB129	GH5	34	local FM				brown	4	c	3
DTB130	GH6	35	local FM				brown	4	a	3
DTB131	GH9	38	local FM				brown	4		3?
DTB132	GH10	39	local FM				brown	4	c	3
DTB133	GH11	40	imported FM?				gray	3	b	2
DTF134	GH14	42	imported FM				white	1		1
DTF135	GH15	43	imported FM				white-buff	1	b	1
DTF136	GH16	44	imported FM				light gray	1	b	1
DTF137	GH17	45	imported FM				white	1	b	1
DTF138	GH21	49	imported FM				yellow-white, coarse	1		1
DTG139	GH25	51	GH				dark gray	4	b	3
DTG140	GH28	54	GH				dark gray, coarse			2
DTG141	GH29	55	GH				dark gray	3	b	2

NAA No.	ICP No.	Petr. No.	Descr., Type	Cat. No.	Site	Provenience	(Core) Color	NAA Group	NAA Subgroup	Temper Group
DTG142	GH30	56	GH		P:14:1		brown, mic.			3
DTG143	GH33	58	GH		P:14:1		gray	3	a	2
DTR144	13		local FM?		GFS 82-1		dark orange-brown, mic., specular hematite		a	
DTR145	14		local FM?		GFS 82-1		dark brown-gray	4	c	
DTR146	16		local FM?		GFS 82-1		dark brown-gray	3		
DTR147	17		local FM?		GFS 82-1		brown	3	c	
DTR148	21		CK		GFS 82-1		gray, brown edges	3	a	
DTR149	24		GH? local CK?		GFS 82-1		very dark gray to black	3	a	
DTR150	25		local FM?		GFS 82-1		brown, dark gray core	4	a	
DTR151	62		indet.local WMR		V:2:7		orange	2	a	
DTR152	63		indet.local WMR		V:2:7		orange			
DTR153	64		indet.local WMR		V:2:7		very dark gray to black			
DTR154	65		local FM		V:2:7		orange, very dark gray core	2	a	
DTR155	68		local WMR (CK?)		V:2:7		orange, gray core	2	a	
DTR156	70		local FM		V:2:7		orange	2	b	
DTR157	73		local WMR (CK?)		V:2:7		orange			
DTR158	74		local FM		V:2:7		orange–brown-gray	2	a	
DTR159	76		local FM		V:2:7		brown, light gray core	2	a	
DTK160	108		K		P:14:25		very dark gray	1	b	
DTR161	111		local WMR		P:14:25		brown-gray, calcite	3	b	
DTR162	114		local FM		P:14:25		very dark gray	1	b	
DTR163	116		local WMR		P:14:25		brown, very dark gray core, mic.	3	c	
DTR164	117		local FM		P:14:25		dark gray	1	b	
DTR165	130		local FM		V:2:62		very dark gray to black	4	a	
DTR166	131		local WMR		V:2:62		very dark gray to black, mic.	4	a	
DTR167	147		local FM?		V:2:62		orange, gray core	3	b	
DTR168	148		local FM		V:2:62		very dark gray to black	1	b	
DTR169	149		local FM		V:2:62		very dark gray to dark brown	4	a	
DTR170	151		local WMR		V:2:62		brown, very dark gray core			
DTR171	176		local FM		P:14:281		dark brown, gray core, mic.	4	a	
DTR172	184		imported FM?		P:14:281		olive-brown, light gray core, same as 185?	2	a	
DTR173	189		local FM		P:14:281		dark brown, mic.	4	a	
DTR174	193		local FM		P:14:281		brown, mic.	4	d	
DTR175	194		local WMR		P:14:281		brown, mic.	4	d	
DTR176	196		local FM		P:14:281		gray	4	c	
DTR177	197		local WMR		P:14:281		orange, olive-gray core	2	a	
DTR178	210		local WMR		V:2:13		very dark gray	1	a	
DTR179	211		local WMR		V:2:13		gray, mic., thick	4	b	
DTR180	212		local FM		V:2:13		orange brown, gray core	4	b	
DTR181	219		local WMR (PD?)		V:2:13		orange, light olive-brown core	2	a	
DTR182	221		local WMR		V:2:13		orange, olive-brown core	2	a	
DTR183	222		local WMR		V:2:13		brown, mic.	3	a	
DTR184	235		local FM		V:2:79		dark brown, mic.	4	d	
DTR185	242		local WMR (jar)		V:2:79		brown to gray			
DTR186	243		local FM		P:14:15		dark gray, brown edges, mic.	3	a	

NAA No.	ICP No.	Petr. No.	Descr., Type	Cat. No.	Site	Provenience	(Core) Color	NAA Group	NAA Subgroup	Temper Group
DTR187	248		imported FM		P:14:15		gray, fine			
DTR188	251		local FM		P:14:15		very dark gray, fine	1	b	
DTK189	252		K		P:14:15		pink, light buff core	1	b	
DTR190	254		imported FM		P:14:71		orange-buff, dark gray core	1	a	
DTR191	255		imported FM?		P:14:71		very dark gray, white edges	1	b	
DTR192	259		local WMR		P:14:71		brown, dark gray core			
DTR193	261		local WMR?		P:14:71		very dark gray, black core	3	a	
DTR194	263		local FM?		P:14:71		dark gray (hard)	1	b	
DTR195	270		local WMR (GH?)		GFS 88-9		very dark gray	1	a	
DTR196	271		local FM		GFS 88-9		orange	1	a	
DTR197	272		local WMR?		GFS 88-9		brown, dark gray core			
DTR198	273		local WMR		GFS 88-9		orange			
DTR199	277		local FM		GFS 88-9		orange	2	a	
DTR200	288		imported FM		GFS 88-10		very dark gray, white edges	1	b	
DTR201	290		local FM		GFS 88-10		orange	2	b	
DTR202	292		local PD B/R?		GFS 88-10		very dark gray	1	a	
DTR203	293		local FM		GFS 88-10		dark gray, thick; same vessel as DTR205			
DTR205	296		local FM		GFS 88-10		dark gray; same vessel as DTR203			
DTR206	303		imp. FM? CK?		GFS 85-3		light gray, orange edges			
DTR207	305		local WMR		GFS 85-3		orange-brown, mic.			
DTR208	306		local WMR		GFS 85-3		orange	2	b	
DTR209	309		local FM		GFS 85-3		orange, brown core, same paste as 304?			
DTR210	310		imported FM		GFS 85-3		gray, thick			
DTR211	317		imported FM?		Cibecue		light gray, orange edges	1	a	
DTR212	319		imported FM?		Cibecue		orange, gray core	2	b	
DTR213	324		local FM		Cibecue		brown, gray core	2	a	
DTR214	325		local FM		Cibecue		brown			
DTR215	326		local WMR		Cibecue		orange	2	a	
DTR216	334	59	imported FM?		TDT		dark gray, coarse	1	a	1
DTP217	336	60	PD (burned)		TDT		very dark gray to black			1
DTP218	337	61	GH?		TDT		very dark gray to black, some mic.			1
DTP219	338		local WMR		TDT		orange			
DTP220	339		local FM		TDT		orange	2	b	
DTP221	345		local FM?		BW		orange-brown, light gray core	2	a	
DTP222	346	62	local WMR		BW		orange, gray core	2	b	1
DTP223	347	63	PD? local?		BW		very dark gray to black	1	a	1
DTP224	354		imported FM		PD		dark gray, buff edges	1	b	
DTP225	355		imported FM		PD		very light gray			
DTP226	356		imported FM		PD		very light buff	1	b	
DTP227	357		imported FM		PD		pink, dark gray core, thick buff			
DTP228	358		imported FM		PD		very dark gray to black, brown edges			1
DTP229	363	64	local WMR?		PD		very dark gray			
DTP230	364		local WMR?		PD		very dark gray			
DTP231	365		local WMR?		PD		very dark gray	1	a	
DTP232	366		local WMR?		PD		very dark gray			

NAA No.	ICP No.	Petr. No.	Descr., Type	Cat. No.	Site	Provenience	(Core) Color	NAA Group	NAA Subgroup	Temper Group
DTF233	367		imported FM		SL		buff, dark gray core	1		
DTF234	368		imported FM		SL		buff to light gray	1	b	
DTF235	369		SL (local?)		SL		buff to light brown	1	b	
DTF236	370		local WMR?		SL		brown to gray	1	b	
DTF237	371	65	local WMR?		SL		very dark gray to black, brown edges			
DTP238	382	66	local FM		K		brown	3	b	2
DTP239	383	67	local FM?		K		very dark gray to black	2	b	1
DTP240	386		local FM?		K		gray-brown, coarse	2	a	
DTP241	387		local FM?		K		orange-brown	2	a	
DTP242	388		local FM?		K		orange, dark gray core	2	b	
DTP243	389		local FM?		K		gray-brown, orange edges	2	b	
DTP244	390		local FM?		K		gray-brown, orange edges			
DTP245	394	68	local FM?		Q		very dark gray to black, mic.	3	a	2/3
DTP246	397		local FM?		Q		very dark gray to black, mic.	4	c	
DTP247	399		local FM?		Q		very dark gray to black, fine, mic.	3	a	
DTP248	400		local FM? (jar)		Q		brown	4	a	
DTP249	404	69	local FM?		Q		brown, very dark gray to black core, mic.	4	a	
DTP250	405	70	local FM?		Q		brown, gray core, mic.	4	a	3
DTR251	411		local FM?		V:2:3		orange	3	b	3
DTR252	412		local WMR		V:2:3		orange	3	a	
DTR253	413		local FM		V:2:3		brown-orange, dark gray core	3	a	
DTR254	414		local FM		V:2:3		very dark olive-gray, fine	1	b	
DTR255	416		local FM		V:2:3		very dark gray to black	4	c	
DTR256	425		local FM?		V:2:3		orange-brown, dark gray core, mic.			
DTR257	426		local FM?		V:2:3		very dark brown-gray, orange edges, fine			
DTK258	440		K		P:14:13		buff, dark gray core	3	a	
DTK259	444		K		P:14:13		dark olive-gray	1	a	
DTR260	448		local WMR?		P:14:13		orange	1	a	
DTR261	450		local WMR?		P:14:13		brown, gray core, mic.	2	b	
DTR262	452		local WMR?		P:14:13		brown	3	a	
DTR263	453		local FM?		P:14:13		orange-brown	2	b	
DTR264	454		local CK?		P:14:13		brown, light gray core, thick	2		
DTR265	456		local FM?		P:14:13		gray, orange edges	3	b	
DTR266	457		local WMR?		P:14:13		dark orange, mic.	4	a	
DTK267	476		K		V:2:1		very dark gray to black, pink edges	1	a	
DTG268	480		GH		V:2:1		brown	4	a	
DTR269	483		local FM?		V:2:1		orange, gray core	4	d	
DTR270	484		local FM?		V:2:1		dark brown, very dark gray core, mic.	2	b	
DTR271	485		local FM?		V:2:1		very dark gray to black	4	d	
DTR272	486		local WMR?		V:2:1		very dark gray to black, mic., quartz	4	b	
DTM273	489		Maverick Mtn.?		V:2:1		very dark gray to black, mic.?	4	b	
DTR274	495		imp. FM (local?)		P:14:12		gray, dark brown edges, mic.	4	a	

NAA No.	ICP No.	Petr. No.	Descr., Type	Cat. No.	Site	Provenience	(Core) Color	NAA Group	NAA Subgroup	Temper Group
DTR275	496		local WMR?		P:14:12		very dark gray to black, brown edges, mic.	4	a	
DTR276	497		local FM?		P:14:12		very dark gray to black			
DTR277	498		local FM?		P:14:12		brown, very dark gray to black core, mic.			
DTG278	499		GH		P:14:12		brown, mic.	4	a	
DTR279	508		local FM?		P:14:12		olive to very dark brown, mic.	1	b	
DTR280	509		local FM?		P:14:12		olive (brown-beige)	3	a	
DTR281	510		local FM?		P:14:12		very dark gray to black, mic.	4	a	
DTR282	520		imp. FM (local?)		GFS 86-3		very dark gray, fine	1	b	
DTR283	527		local SL? (jar)		GFS 86-3		dark gray, mic.			
DTR284	528		local FM?		GFS 86-3		orange, light gray core	2	b	
DTR285	529		local FM?		GFS 86-3		orange, brown core	2	b	
DTR286	530		local FM?		GFS 86-3		orange-brown, brown core	2	b	
DTR287	531		local WMR?		GFS 86-3		orange	2	b	
DTR288	532		local FM?		GFS 86-3		orange, gray core	2	b	
DTR289	533		local FM?		GFS 86-3		orange, gray core	2	a	
DTR290	538		local FM?		V:2:49		brown-gray	2	b	
DTR291	539		local FM?		V:2:49		orange, light gray core	2	a	
DTR292	542		local FM?		V:2:49		orange	2	a	
DTR293	543		local WMR?		V:2:49		gray, orange edges	2	a	
DTR294	546		local FM?		V:2:49		orange, olive core	2	a	
DTR295	551		imp. FM (local?)		V:2:49		very dark gray	1	b	
DTP296	556	72	local FM?		V:2:87		orange, gray core, mic.	4	c	3
DTP297	558	73	local WMR?		V:2:87		orange, medium brown core	2	a	1
DTP298	559		local FM?		V:2:87		dark gray, white edges	1	b	
DTP299	560		local FM?		V:2:87		orange, gray core			
DTG300	561	74	GH		V:2:87		very dark gray, fine	3	b	2
DTG301	562		GH		V:2:87		olive-brown, fine	3	b	
DTG302	563		GH		V:2:87		olive-gray	3	a	
DTR303	567		imported FM		GFS 81-79		buff-orange			
DTR304	570		imported FM		GFS 81-79		very light gray, orange-brown edges	2	a	
DTR305	571		local WMR?		GFS 81-79		dark orange to brown	4	d	
DTR306	572		local FM?		GFS 81-79		dark orange, brown core	4	a	
DTR307	573		local FM?		GFS 81-79		very dark gray	1	b	
DTR308	583		local FM?		V:2:23		orange	2	a	
DTR309	584		local FM?		V:2:23		orange, dark gray core	2	b	
DTR310	588		local WMR?		V:2:23		dark gray, orange edges			
DTR311	591		imported WMR?		V:2:23		brown, dark gray core			
DTP312	593		imported WMR?		V:2:5		buff, light gray core	1	a	
DTP313	594		local FM		V:2:5		orange	1	a	
DTP314	595	75	imported FM		V:2:5		buff to dark olive			1
DTP315	596		local WMR?		V:2:83		orange			
DTP316	599	76	local WMR?		V:2:83		orange, brown core	2	a	1
DTP317	600	77	imported WMR?		V:2:83		buff, very dark gray core; large inclusions, Fe?			1
DTG318	601		GH		V:2:83		very dark gray to black	3	a	

NAA No.	ICP No.	Petr. No.	Descr., Type	Cat. No.	Site	Provenience	(Core) Color	NAA Group	NAA Subgroup	Temper Group
DTG319	602	78	GH		V:2:83		very dark gray to brown, mic.	3	c	1
DTP320	604		local CK?		V:2:83		orange to light olive, dark gray core	2	a	
DTP321	605	79	local WMR?		GFS 89-6		orange	2	a	3
DTP322	606		imported FM?		P:13:2		orange, light gray core	1		
DTP323	607	80	imported FM		P:13:2		buff, gray core	1	b	1
DTP324	609		local FM?		P:13:2		orange, dark brown core	3	a	
DTR325	614		local FM?		P:14:14		orange, very dark brown to black core, mic	4	c	
DTR326	615		local FM?		P:14:14		orange, mic.	4	a	
DTR327	619		local FM?		P:14:14		dark gray, brown edges, mic.?, diabase?	4	a	
DTR328	620		local FM?		P:14:14		dark olive-brown, fine	3	a	
DTR329	621		local FM?		P:14:14		very dark gray to black, mic.	4	c	
DTR330	622		local FM?		P:14:14		orange, dark brown to gray core	4	c	
DTP331			diabase			about 60 m S of Oak Creek Ranch	gray			
DTP332			diabase			about 60 m S of Oak Creek Ranch	yellowish gray			

Group Membership Probabilities

Samples Belonging to Compositional Group 1
(Probabilities Expressed in %)

Samp. No.	1	2	3	4	Sub-group	Samp. No.	1	2	3	4	Sub-group
DTF022	56.910	0	0	0	b	DTK126	39.743	0	0	0	b
DTF023	11.477	0.131	0.074	0	a	DTK127	5.409	0	0	0	b
DTF024	31.451	0	0	0	b·	DTF134	13.969	0	0	0	b
DTF025	83.043	0.010	0	0	b	DTF135	79.020	0.001	0	0	b
DTF026	62.658	0	0	0	b	DTF136	16.858	0	0	0	b
DTF028	88.110	0	0	0	b	DTF137	96.044	0	0	0	b
DTF029	99.972	0.002	0	0	b	DTK160	45.095	0	0	0	b
DTF030	95.360	0	0	0	b	DTR162	46.602	0	0	0	b
DTF031	3.978	0	0	0	b	DTR164	82.668	0	0	0	b
DTF032	16.911	0	0	0	b	DTR168	49.896	0	0	0	b
DTF033	61.844	0	0	0	b	DTR178	27.300	0	0	0	a
DTF034	78.585	0	0	0	b	DTR188	40.578	0.005	0	0	b
DTF035	95.793	0	0	0	b	DTK189	28.667	0	0	0	b
DTF036	41.260	0	0	0	b	DTR190	10.099	0	0	0	a
DTF037	48.055	0	0	0	b	DTR191	93.935	0	0	0	b
DTF038	91.408	0	0	0	b	DTR194	33.648	0	0	0	b
DTF040	76.386	0	0	0	b	DTR196	3.690	0	0	0	a
DTF041	85.917	0.005	0	0	b	DTR200	35.202	0	0	0	b
DTF042	96.446	0	0	0	b	DTR202	78.386	0.010	0	0	a
DTF043	65.295	0	0	0	b	DTR211	38.215	0	0.110	0	a
DTF044	89.760	0	0	0	b	DTP216	1.217	0	0	0	a
DTF045	67.412	0.011	0	0	b	DTP223	24.097	0.010	0	0	a
DTF046	65.351	0	0	0	b	DTF224	87.871	0	0	0	b
DTF047	90.693	0	0	0	b	DTF226	37.551	0	0	0	b
DTF048	13.682	0	0	0	b	DTP231	8.598	0.012	0	0	a
DTF049	14.136	0	0	0	b	DTF234	96.221	0.004	0	0	b
DTF050	52.480	0	0	0	b	DTP235	19.278	0	0	0	b
DTF051	50.478	0	0	0	b	DTP236	50.921	0	0	0	b
DTF052	91.434	0	0	0	a	DTR255	54.082	0	0	0	b
DTF053	91.345	0	0	0	b	DTK258	49.804	0.001	0·	0	a
DTF054	1.606	0	0	0	b	DTK259	90.130	0	0	0	a
DTB062	31.163	0	0	0	a	DTK267	84.801	0.005	0	0	a
DTB065	2.625	0	0	0	a	DTR279	30.397	0	0	0	b
DTB068	50.958	0.380	0	0	a	DTR282	42.547	0	0	0	b
DTZ072	20.322	0	0	0	a	DTR295	29.909	0	0.005	0	b
DTZ073	7.245	0	0	0	a	DTP298	29.562	0	0	0	b
DTZ074	8.160	0	0	0	a	DTR307	28.353	0	0	0	b
DTK122	97.821	0	0	0	b	DTP312	13.994	0.009	0.003	0	a
DTK123	32.268	0	0	0	a	DTP313	9.332	0.052	0	0	a
DTK124	8.719	0	0	0	a	DTP323	79.419	0	0	0	b
DTK125	90.555	0	0	0	b						

NOTE: Mahalanobis distance calculations based on base log 10 concentrations of 31 elements.

Samples Belonging to Compositional Group 2
(Probabilities Expressed in %)

Samp. No.	Group 1	2	3	4	Sub-group	Samp. No.	Group 1	2	3	4	Sub-group
DTB059	0.014	77.155	0	0	a	DTP242	0.005	92.180	0.035	0	b
DTB070	0.003	97.729	0	0	a	DTP243	0	8.680	0	0	b
DTL076	1.607	49.331	0	0	a	DTR260	0	10.906	0	0	a
DTR151	0	42.257	0	0	a	DTR262	0	17.980	0.001	0	a
DTR154	0.005	42.296	0	0	a	DTR263	0	6.002	0	0	b
DTR155	0.029	25.802	0.001	0	a	DTR269	0.187	65.234	0	0	a
DTR156	0.749	23.912	0.366	0	b	DTR284	0	10.025	0	0	b
DTR158	0.121	70.984	0.002	0	a	DTR285	0	5.925	0.004	0	b
DTR159	0.013	45.291	0	0	a	DTR286	0	84.425	0.207	0	b
DTR172	0	64.446	0	0	a	DTR287	0.061	65.010	0.808	0	b
DTR177	0	62.576	0	0	a	DTR288	0.020	56.763	0.002	0	b
DTR181	0.003	43.769	0.001	0	a	DTR289	0.245	52.817	0	0	a
DTR182	0.630	98.017	0	0	a	DTR290	0.004	97.556	0.053	0	b
DTR199	3.075	42.467	0.014	0	a	DTR291	0.019	58.504	0	0	a
DTR201	0.654	19.181	0.624	0	b	DTR292	0.038	79.402	0	0	a
DTR208	0.020	97.932	0.107	0	b	DTR293	0.796	23.584	0	0	a
DTR212	0.313	77.768	0.392	0	b	DTR294	0.106	93.914	0.007	0	a
DTR213	0.041	17.735	0	0	a	DTP297	13.187	33.264	0.413	0	a
DTR215	0.364	96.002	0	0	a	DTR304	0.003	66.533	0	0	a
DTP220	0	19.136	0.252	0	b	DTR308	0.894	23.230	0.234	0	a
DTP221	0.167	32.321	0.002	0	a	DTR309	1.359	40.274	0.117	0	b
DTP222	1.907	50.563	0.100	0	b	DTP316	0.056	1.818	0	0	a
DTP238	0	86.347	0.076	0	b	DTP320	3.604	33.648	0.124	0	a
DTP240	0	32.541	0	0	a	DTP321	0.227	26.581	0.022	0	a
DTP241	8.389	14.800	0	0	a						

NOTE: Mahalanobis distance calculations based on base log 10 concentrations of 31 elements.

Samples Belonging to Compositional Group 3
(Probabilities Expressed in %)

Samp. No.	Group 1	2	3	4	Sub-group	Samp. No.	Group 1	2	3	4	Sub-group
DTB061	0	0	95.026	0	a	DTG108	0	0	68.338	0	a
DTB063	0	0	6.843	0	a	DTG109	0	0	70.188	0.002	c
DTB064	0	0	2.884	0	c	DTG112	0	0	60.452	0	a
DTZ071	0	0	51.774	0	b	DTG113	0	0	85.298	0	b
DTL075	0	0	4.548	0	b	DTG115	0	0	88.386	0	a
DTL077	0	0	63.171	0	b	DTG116	0	0	8.861	0.108	c
DTL079	0	0	1.032	0	b	DTG117	0	0	92.112	0	a
DTL081	0	0	91.754	0.022	a	DTG118	0	0	15.852	0.013	c
DTG085	0	0	45.845	3.904	c	DTG119	0	0	97.344	0 ·	a
DTG088	0	0	98.875	0.002	a	DTB128	0	0	20.722	0	b
DTG089	0	0	74.787	0	a	DTB133	0	0	31.679	0	b
DTG090	0	0	38.280	0	a	DTG141	0	0	98.869	0	b
DTG092	0	0	26.729	0	a	DTG143	0	0	74.233	0	a
DTG095	0	0	7.475	0.006	c	DTR145	0	0	61.789	0.002	c
DTG096	0	0	36.761	0.017	c	DTR147	0	0	63.407	0.003	c
DTG098	0	0	89.072	0	a	DTR148	0	0	31.453	0	a
DTG099	0	0	68.139	0	a	DTR149	0	0	9.356	0	a
DTG100	0	0	16.331	0	b	DTR161	0	0	8.070	0	b
DTG101	0	0	2.052	0	a	DTR163	0	0	12.508	0.089	c
DTG102	0	0	36.033	0	b	DTR167	0	0	2.513	0	b
DTG105	0	0	3.410	0	c	DTR183	0	0	71.651	0.004	a
DTG106	0	0	36.456	0	a	DTR186	0	0	95.708	0	a
DTG107	0	0	61.476	0	a	DTR193	0	0	19.477	0	a

Compositional Group 3 (continued)

Samp. No.	Group 1	2	3	4	Sub-group	Samp. No.	Group 1	2	3	4	Sub-group
DTP237	0.001	0	4.890	0	b	DTR280	0	0	30.558	0	a
DTP245	0	0	90.242	0	a	DTG300	0	0	86.590	0	b
DTP247	0	0	54.407	0	a	DTG301	0	0	7.705	0	b
DTR251	0	0	65.632	0	b	DTG302	0	0	72.480	0	a
DTR252	0	0	54.872	0.014	a	DTG318	0	0	33.232	0	a
DTR254	0	0	97.234	0	a	DTG319	0	0	1.806	0.006	c
DTR257	0	0	96.263	0	a	DTP324	0	0	94.093	0	a
DTR261	0	0	22.746	0	b	DTR328	0	0	94.581	0	a
DTR265	0	0	96.694	0	b						

NOTE: Mahalanobis distance calculations based on base log 10 concentrations of 31 elements.

Samples Belonging to Compositional Group 4
(Probabilities Expressed in %)

Samp. No.	Group 1	2	3	4	Sub-group	Samp. No.	Group 1	2	3	4	Sub-group
DTB056	0	0	0.571	21.344	a	DTR175	0	0	0	11.806	d
DTB058	0.	0	0.003	27.558	b	DTR176	0	0	4.667	23.401	c
DTB060	0	0	0.003	20.804	a	DTR179	0	0	0.126	87.576	b
DTB067	0	0	0	87.594	a	DTR180	0	0	0.002	39.892	b
DTB069	0	0	0.010	12.761	a	DTR184	0	0	0	88.531	d
DTG086	0	0	12.492	89.494	b	DTP246	0	0	0	62.909	c
DTG087	0	0	0.002	39.374	a	DTP248	0	0	0.006	37.730	a
DTG091	0	0	1.250	95.684	a	DTP249	0	0	0.056	25.002	a
DTG093	0	0	4.361	10.337	a	DTR256	0	0	1.743	56.274	c
DTG094	0	0	0.068	68.235	b	DTR266	0	0	0.002	15.814	a
DTG103	0	0	3.630	63.677	b	DTG268	0	0	0.289	59.775	a
DTG104	0	0	0.009	55.377	b	DTR270	0	0	0	11.589	d
DTG111	0	0	0.220	97.417	b	DTR271	0	0	1.362	40.143	b
DTG114	0	0	0.017	13.456	a	DTR272	0	0	2.221	40.607	b
DTG120	0	0	13.019	53.265	b	DTR274	0	0	0.002	19.523	a
DTG121	0	0	0	37.115	a	DTR275	0	0	0.002	82.138	a
DTB129	0	0	0.006	99.714	c	DTR277	0	0	0.004	3.867	a
DTB130	0	0	0.004	89.402	a	DTG278	0	0	0	16.946	a
DTB132	0	0	7.225	44.786	c	DTR281	0	0	0.211	76.245	a
DTG139	0	0	0.064	22.146	b	DTP296	0	0	0.008	3.545	c
DTR144	0	0	0	22.330	a	DTR305	0	0	0	2.842	d
DTR150	0	0	0	64.140	a	DTR306	0	0	0.084	99.907	a
DTR165	0	0	0	17.205	a	DTR325	0	0	0.006	92.828	c
DTR166	0	0	0	81.012	a	DTR326	0	0	0.032	30.234	a
DTR169	0	0.	0	95.466	a	DTR327	0	0	0.002	2.057	a
DTR171	0	0	0	77.267	a	DTR329	0	0	0	44.036	c
DTR173	0	0	0	63.893	a	DTR330	0	0	0	43.633	c
DTR174	0	0	0	70.914	d						

NOTE: Mahalanobis distance calculations based on base log 10 concentrations of 31 elements.

Unassigned Samples
(Probabilities Expressed in %)

Samp. No.	Group 1	2	3	4	Sub-group	Samp. No.	Group 1	2	3	4	Sub-group
DTF027	0.011	0.008	0	0		DTR210	0	0	0.252	0	
DTF039	0.782	0	0	0		DTR214	5.869	6.030	0.262	0	
DTB055	0	0	0	0		DTP217	0.003	0.003	0	0	
DTB057	0	0	0.652	0.030		DTP218	0	0	0	0	
DTB066	0	0	0	0		DTP219	0	0.003	0	0	
DTL078	0	0	0.001	0		DTF225	0	0	0	0	
DTL080	0.132	0	0	0		DTF227	0.008	0	0	0	
DTW082	0.575	0	0	0		DTF228	0	0	0	0	
DTW083	0	0	0	0.218		DTP229	0.002	0.153	0.047	0	
DTW084	0.657	0.010	0	0		DTP230	0	0	0.008	0	
DTG097	0	0	0	0.012		DTP232	0.057	0	0	0	
DTG110	0	0	0.079	0		DTF233	0.112	0	0	0	
DTB131	0	0	1.961	0.803		DTP239	0	0	0	0	
DTF138	0	0	0	0		DTP244	0	0	0	0	
DTG140	0	0	0.224	0		DTP250	0	0	0	0.004	
DTG142	0	0	0.522	0.018		DTR253	0	0	0	0.010	
DTR146	0	0	0.002	0.145		DTR264	0	0	0.026	0	
DTR152	0	0.019	0	0		DTM273	0	0	0.215	0.006	
DTR153	0	0	0.098	0		DTR276	1.030	0.002	0	0	
DTR157	0	0	0	0		DTR283	0	0	0.042	1.559	
DTR185	0	0	0	0		DTP299	0	0.057	0	0	
DTR187	0.177	0	0.002	0		DTR303	0.133	0	0	0	
DTR192	0	0	0.015	0		DTR310	0.017	0.031	0.047	0	
DTR195	0	0	0.016	0		DTR311	0	0	0	0.229	
DTR198	0.688	0.160	0010	0		DTP314	0.285	0.044	0	0	
DTR203	0	0	0	0		DTP315	0.020	0	0	0	
DTR205	0	0	0	0		DTP317	0	0	0	0	
DTR206	0	0	0	0		DTP322	0.076	0.149	0.001	0	
DTR209	0.001	0.026	1.059	0							

NOTE: Mahalanobis distance calculations based on base log 10 concentrations of 31 elements.

References

ADAMS, E. CHARLES
  1991a *The Origin and Development of the Pueblo Katsina Cult.* Tucson: University of Arizona Press.
  1991b Homol'ovi II in the 14th Century. In "Homol'ovi II: Archaeology of an Ancestral Hopi Village," edited by E. Charles Adams and Kelley Ann Hays. *Anthropological Papers of the University of Arizona* 55: 116–122. Tucson: University of Arizona Press.

ADAMS, E. CHARLES, MIRIAM T. STARK, AND DEBORAH S. DOSH
  1993 Ceramic Distribution and Exchange: Jeddito Yellow Ware and Implications for Social Complexity. *Journal of Field Archaeology* 20(1): 3–21.

ADLER, MICHAEL A., EDITOR
  1996 *The Prehistoric Pueblo World, A.D. 1150–1350.* Tucson: University of Arizona Press.

ALFASSI, ZEEV B.
  1990 *Activation Analysis.* Vol. 2. Boca Raton, Florida: CRC Press.

ANTHONY, DAVID W.
  1990 Migration in Archaeology: The Baby and the Bathwater. *American Anthropologist* 92(4): 895–914.

ARNOLD, DEAN E.
  1981 A Model for the Identification of Nonlocal Ceramic Distribution: A View from the Present. In "Production and Distribution: A Ceramic Viewpoint," edited by Hilary Howard and Elaine L. Morris. *BAR International Series* 120: 31–44. Oxford: British Archaeological Reports.
  1985 *Ceramic Theory and Cultural Process.* Cambridge: Cambridge University Press.

BALDWIN, GORDON C.
  1937 The Pottery of Kinishba. *The Kiva* 3(1): 1–4.
  1938a A New Pottery Type from Eastern Arizona. *Southwestern Lore* 4(2): 21–26.
  1938b Excavations at Kinishba Pueblo, Arizona. *American Antiquity* 4(1): 11–21.
  1939 The Material Culture of Kinishba. *American Antiquity* 4(4): 314–327.

BERRY, DAVID R.
  1985 Dental Paleopathology of Grasshopper Pueblo, Arizona. In "Health and Disease in the Prehistoric Southwest," edited by Charles F. Merbs and Robert J. Miller. *Anthropological Research Papers* 34: 253–274. Tempe: Arizona State University.

BIRKBY, WALTER H.
  1973 Discontinuous Morphological Traits of the Skull as Population Markers in the Prehistoric Southwest. MS, Doctoral dissertation, University of Arizona, Tucson.
  1982 Biosocial Interpretations from Cranial Nonmetric Traits of Grasshopper Pueblo Skeletal Remains. In "Multidisciplinary Research at Grasshopper Pueblo, Arizona," edited by William A. Longacre, Sally J. Holbrook, and Michael W. Graves. *Anthropological Papers of the University of Arizona* 40: 36–41. Tucson: University of Arizona Press.

BISHOP, RONALD L.
  1980 Aspects of Ceramic Compositional Modeling. In "Models and Methods in Regional Exchange," edited by Robert E. Fry. *Society for American Archaeology Papers* 1: 47–66. Washington.
  1994 Pre-Columbian Pottery: Research in the Maya Region. In *Archaeometry of Pre-Columbian Sites and Artifacts*, edited by David A. Scott and Pieter Meyers, pp. 15–65. Los Angeles: The Getty Conservation Institute.

BISHOP, RONALD L., AND HECTOR NEFF
  1989 Compositional Data Analysis in Archaeology. In "Archaeological Chemistry IV," edited by Ralph O. Allen. *Advances in Chemistry Series* 220: 57–86. Washington: American Chemical Society.

BISHOP, RONALD L., ROBERT L. RANDS, AND GEORGE R. HOLLEY
  1982 Ceramic Compositional Analysis in Archaeological Perspective. In *Advances in Archaeological Method and Theory.* Vol. 5, edited by Michael B. Schiffer, pp. 275–330. New York: Academic Press.

BISHOP, RONALD L., VELETTA CANOUTS, SUZANNE P. DE ATLEY, ALFRED QÖYAWAYMA, AND C. W. AIKINS
  1988 The Formation of Ceramic Analytical Groups: Hopi Pottery Production and Exchange, A.D. 1300–1600. *Journal of Field Archaeology* 15(3): 317–337.

BLINMAN, ERIC, AND C. DEAN WILSON
1988   Overview of A.D 600–800 Ceramic Production and Exchange in the Dolores Project Area. In *Dolores Archaeological Program Supporting Studies: Additive and Reductive Technologies*, compiled by Eric Blinman, Carl J. Phagan, and Richard H. Wilshusen, pp. 395–423. Denver: U.S. Bureau of Reclamation, Engineering and Research Center.

BOHRER, VORSILA L.
1982   Plant Remains from Rooms at Grasshopper Pueblo. In "Multidisciplinary Research at Grasshopper Pueblo, Arizona," edited by William A. Longacre, Sally J. Holbrook, and Michael W. Graves. *Anthropological Papers of the University of Arizona* 40: 97–105. Tucson: University of Arizona Press.

BRONITSKY, GORDON
1986   Compressive Testing of Ceramics: A Southwestern Example. *The Kiva* 51(2): 85–98.

BURTON, JAMES H., AND ARLEYN W. SIMON
1993   Acid Extraction as a Simple and Inexpensive Method for Compositional Characterization of Archaeological Ceramics. *American Antiquity* 58(1): 45–59.

CAMERON, CATHERINE M.
1995   Migration and the Movement of Southwestern Peoples. In "Migration and the Movement of Southwestern Peoples," edited by Catherine M. Cameron. *Journal of Anthropological Archaeology* 14(2): 104–124.

CARLSON, ROY L.
1970   White Mountain Redware: A Pottery Tradition of East-central Arizona and Western New Mexico. *Anthropological Papers of the University of Arizona* 19. Tucson: University of Arizona Press.
1982   The Polychrome Complexes. In "Southwestern Ceramics: A Comparative View," edited by Albert H. Schroeder. *The Arizona Archaeologist* 15: 201–234. Phoenix: Arizona Archaeological Society.

CIOLEK-TORRELLO, RICHARD S.
1978   A Statistical Analysis of Activity Organization: Grasshopper Pueblo, Arizona. MS, Doctoral dissertation, University of Arizona, Tucson.
1984   An Alternative Model of Room Function from Grasshopper Pueblo, Arizona. In *Intrasite Spatial Analysis in Archaeology*, edited by Harold J. Hietala, pp. 127–153. Cambridge: Cambridge University Press.
1985   A Typology of Room Function at Grasshopper Pueblo, Arizona. *Journal of Field Archaeology* 12(1): 41–63.
1986   Room Function and Households at Grasshopper Pueblo. In "Mogollon Variability," edited by Charlotte Benson and Steadman Upham. *New Mexico State University Occasional Papers* 15: 107–119. Las Cruces: New Mexico State University.

CIOLEK-TORRELLO, RICHARD S., AND J. JEFFERSON REID
1974   Change in Household Size at Grasshopper. In "Behavioral Archaeology at the Grasshopper Ruin," edited by J. Jefferson Reid. *The Kiva* 40(1–2): 39–47.

CLEMMER, RICHARD O.
1979   Hopi History, 1940–1974. In *Handbook of North American Indians*, Vol. 9, *Southwest*, edited by Alfonso Ortiz, pp. 533–553. William C. Sturtevant, general editor. Washington: Smithsonian Institution.

COLTON, HAROLD S.
1941   Prehistoric Trade in the Southwest. *The Scientific Monthly* 52: 308–319.
1953   Potsherds: An Introduction to the Study of Prehistoric Southwestern Ceramics and Their Use in Historical Reconstruction. *Museum of Northern Arizona Bulletin* 25. Flagstaff: Northern Arizona Society of Science and Art.
1956   [Editor] Pottery Types of the Southwest. *Museum of Northern Arizona Ceramic Series* 3C. Flagstaff: Northern Arizona Society of Science and Art.

COLTON, HAROLD S., AND LYNDON L. HARGRAVE
1937   Handbook of Northern Arizona Pottery Wares. *Museum of Northern Arizona Bulletin* 11. Flagstaff: Northern Arizona Society of Science and Art.

CORDELL, LINDA S., AND FRED PLOG
1979   Escaping the Confines of Normative Thought: A Reevaluation of Pueblo Prehistory. *American Antiquity* 44(3): 405–429.

CORDELL, LINDA S., DAVID E. DOYEL, AND KEITH W. KINTIGH
1994   Processes of Aggregation in the Prehistoric Southwest. In *Themes in Southwestern Prehistory*, edited by George J. Gumerman, pp. 109–134. Advanced Seminar Series. Santa Fe: School of American Research.

COSTIN, CATHY L.
1991   Craft Specialization: Issues in Defining, Documenting, and Explaining the Organization of Production. In *Archaeological Method and Theory*, Vol. 3, edited by Michael B. Schiffer, pp. 1–56. Tucson: University of Arizona Press.

CROWN, PATRICIA L.
1981   *Variability in Ceramic Manufacture at the Chodistaas Site, East-Central Arizona*. Doctoral dissertation, University of Arizona, Tucson. Ann Arbor: University Microfilms.

1994   *Ceramics and Ideology: Salado Polychrome Pottery*. Albuquerque: University of New Mexico Press.

1995   The Production of Salado Polychromes in the American Southwest. In *Ceramic Production in the American Southwest*, edited by Barbara J. Mills and Patricia L. Crown, pp. 142–166. Tucson: University of Arizona Press.

CUMMINGS, BYRON

1940   *Kinishba, A Prehistoric Pueblo of the Great Pueblo Period*. Tucson: Hohokam Museums Association and The University of Arizona.

CUSHING, FRANK H.

1979   Origins of Pueblo Pottery. In *Zuñi: Selected Writings of Frank Hamilton Cushing*, edited by Jesse Green, pp. 227–245. Lincoln: University of Nebraska Press.

DAMOUR, ALFRED

1865   Sur la composition des haches en pierre trouvée dans les monuments celtique et chez les tribus sauvage. Comptes rendus 61: 313–321, 357–368. Paris: Academie de Sciences.

1866   Sur la composition des haches en pierre trouvée dans les monuments celtique et chez les tribus sauvage. Comptes rendus 63: 1038–1050. Paris: Academie de Sciences.

DAVIS, JOHN C.

1986   *Statistics and Data Analysis in Geology*. 2nd ed. New York: John Wiley.

DEAN, JEFFREY S.

1969   Chronological Analysis of Tsegi Phase Sites in North-Eastern Arizona. *Papers of the Laboratory of Tree-Ring Research* 3. Tucson: University of Arizona.

1970   Aspects of Tsegi Phase Social Organization: A Trial Reconstruction. In *Reconstructing Prehistoric Pueblo Societies*, edited by William A. Longacre, pp. 140–174. School of American Research Advanced Seminar Series. Albuquerque: University of New Mexico Press.

DEAN, JEFFREY S., AND WILLIAM J. ROBINSON

1982   Dendrochronology of Grasshopper Pueblo. In "Multidisciplinary Research at Grasshopper Pueblo, Arizona," edited by William A. Longacre, Sally J. Holbrook, and Michael W. Graves. *Anthropological Papers of the University of Arizona* 40: 46–60. Tucson: University of Arizona Press.

DEAN, JEFFREY S., WILLIAM H. DOELLE, AND JANET D. ORCUTT

1994   Adaptive Stress, Environment, and Demography. In *Themes in Southwestern Prehistory*, edited by George J. Gumerman, pp. 53–86. Advanced Seminar Series. Santa Fe: School of American Research Press.

DE ATLEY, SUZANNE P.

1986   Mix and Match: Traditions of Glaze Paint Preparation at Four Mile Ruin, Arizona. In "Technology and Style," edited by W. David Kingery and Esther Lense. *Ceramics and Civilization* 2: 297–329. Columbus, Ohio: American Ceramic Society.

DEUTCHMAN, HAREE L.

1980   Chemical Evidence of Ceramic Exchange on Black Mesa. In "Models and Methods in Regional Exchange," edited by Robert E. Fry. *Society for American Archaeology Papers* 1: 119–134.

DOUGLASS, AMY A.

1991   *Prehistoric Exchange and Sociopolitical Development in the Plateau Southwest*. New York: Garland Publishing.

DOYEL, DAVID E.

1991   Hohokam Exchange and Interaction. In *Chaco and Hohokam: Prehistoric Systems in the American Southwest*, edited by Patricia L. Crown and W. James Judge, pp. 225–252. Santa Fe: School of American Research Press.

DRENNAN, ROBERT D.

1984   Long-distance Movement of Goods in the Mesoamerican Formative and Classic. *American Antiquity* 49(1): 27–43.

DUFF, ANDREW I.

In press   The Process of Migration in the Late Prehistoric Southwest. In "Migration and Reorganization: The Pueblo IV Period in the American Southwest," edited by Katherine A. Spielmann. *Anthropological Research Papers* 50. Tempe: Arizona State University.

EARLE, TIMOTHY K., AND JONATHON E. ERICSON, EDITORS

1977   *Exchange Systems in Prehistory*. New York: Academic Press.

EHMANN, WILLIAM D., AND DIANE E. VANCE

1991   *Radiochemistry and Nuclear Methods of Analysis*. New York: John Wiley and Sons.

ELAM, J. MICHAEL, CHRISTOPHER CARR, MICHAEL D. GLASCOCK, AND HECTOR NEFF

1992   Ultrasonic Disaggregation and INAA of Textural Fractions of Tucson Basin and Ohio Valley Ceramics. In "Chemical Characterization of Ceramic Pastes in Archaeology," edited by Hector Neff. *Monographs in World Archaeology* 7: 93–112. Madison: Prehistory Press.

EULER, ROBERT C.

1988   Demography and Cultural Dynamics on the Colorado Plateaus. In *The Anasazi in a Changing Environment*, edited by George J. Gumerman, pp. 192–229. School of American Research Book. Cambridge: Cambridge University Press.

EZZO, JOSEPH A., JR.

1991   *Dietary Change at Grasshopper Pueblo, Arizona: The Evidence from Bone Chemistry Analysis*. Doctoral dissertation, University of Arizona, Tucson. Ann Arbor: University Microfilms.

1992   Dietary Change and Variability at Grasshopper Pueblo, Arizona. *Journal of Anthropological Archaeology* 11(3): 219–289.

1993   Human Adaptation at Grasshopper Pueblo, Arizona: Social and Ecological Perspectives. *International Monographs in Prehistory, Archaeological Series* 4. Ann Arbor: University of Michigan.

1994   Paleonutrition at Grasshopper Pueblo, Arizona. In "The Diet and Health of Prehistoric Americans," edited by Kristin D. Sobolik. *Occasional Papers* 22: 265–279. Carbondale: Center for Archaeological Investigations, Southern Illinois University.

FISH, PAUL R., SUZANNE K. FISH, GEORGE J. GUMERMAN, AND J. JEFFERSON REID

1994   Toward an Explanation for Southwestern "Abandonments." In *Themes in Southwestern Prehistory*, edited by George J. Gumerman, pp. 135–164. Advanced Seminar Series. Santa Fe: School of American Research Press.

FORTES, MEYER

1971   Introduction. In "The Developmental Cycle in Domestic Groups," edited by Jack Goody. *Cambridge Papers in Social Anthropology* 1: 1–14. Cambridge: Cambridge University.

FRY, ROBERT E., EDITOR

1980   Models and Methods in Regional Exchange. *Society for American Archaeology Papers* 1.

FULGINITI, LAURA CARR

1993   *Discontinuous Morphological Variation at Grasshopper Pueblo, Arizona*. Doctoral dissertation, University of Arizona, Tucson. Ann Arbor: University Microfilms.

GLADWIN, WINIFRED, AND HAROLD S. GLADWIN

1930   Some Southwestern Pottery Types, Series I. *Medallion Papers* 8. Globe, Arizona: Gila Pueblo.

1934   A Method for the Designation of Cultures and Their Variations. *Medallion Papers* 15. Globe, Arizona: Gila Pueblo.

GLASCOCK, MICHAEL D.

1992   Characterization of Archaeological Ceramics at MURR by Neutron Activation Analysis and Multivariate Statistics. In "Chemical Characterization of Ceramic Pastes in Archaeology," edited by Hector Neff. *Monographs in World Archaeology* 7: 11–26. Madison: Prehistory Press.

GÖBEL, FRIEDMANN

1842   Über den Einfluß der Chemie auf die Ermittlung der Völker der Vorzeit oder Resultate der chemischen Untersuchung metallischer Alterthümer, insbesondere der in den Ostseegouvernements vorkommenden, behufs der Ermittlung der Völker, von welchen sie abstammen. Erlangen.

GOLES, GORDON G.

1977   Instrumental Methods of Neutron Activation Analysis. In *Physical Methods in Determinative Mineralogy*, edited by Jack Zussman, pp. 343–369. London: Academic Press. 2nd Edition.

GRAVES, MICHAEL W.

1982   Breaking Down Ceramic Variation: Testing Models of White Mountain Redware Design Style Development. *Journal of Anthropological Archaeology* 1(4): 305–354.

1991   Estimating Tree-Ring Specimens from East-Central Arizona: Implications for Prehistoric Pueblo Growth at Grasshopper Ruin. *Journal of Quantitative Anthropology* 3: 83–115.

1994   Community Boundaries in Late Prehistoric Puebloan Society: Kalinga Ethnoarchaeology as a Model for the Southwestern Production and Exchange of Pottery. In *The Ancient Southwestern Community: Models and Methods for the Study of Prehistoric Social Organization*, edited by W. H. Wills and Robert D. Leonard, pp. 146–169. Albuquerque: University of New Mexico Press.

GRAVES, WILLIAM, AND SUZANNE L. ECKERT

In press   Decorated Ceramic Distributions and Ideological Developments in the Northern and Central Rio Grande Valley, New Mexico. In "Migration and Reorganization: The Pueblo IV Period in the American Southwest," edited by Katherine A. Spielmann. *Anthropological Research Papers* 50. Tempe: Arizona State University.

HANTMAN, JEFFREY L., AND STEPHEN PLOG

1982   The Relationship of Stylistic Similarity to Patterns of Material Exchange. In *Contexts for Prehistoric Exchange*, edited by Jonathon E. Ericson and Timothy K. Earle, pp. 237–263. New York: Academic Press.

HARBOTTLE, GARMON

1976   Activation Analysis in Archaeology. *Radiochemistry, Specialist Periodical Reports* 3: 33–72, edited by G. W. A. Newton. London: The Chemical Society.

HARDIN FRIEDRICH, MARGARET

1970   Design Structure and Social Interaction: Archaeological Implications of an Ethnographic Analysis. *American Antiquity* 35(3): 332–343.

HAURY, EMIL W.
1934   The Canyon Creek Ruin and the Cliff Dwellings of the Sierra Ancha. *Medallion Papers* 14. Globe, Arizona: Gila Pueblo.
1958   Evidence at Point of Pines for a Prehistoric Migration from Northern Arizona. In "Migrations in New World Culture History," edited by Raymond H. Thompson. *University of Arizona Bulletin* 29(2), *Social Science Bulletin* 27: 1–6. Tucson: University of Arizona.

HAURY, EMIL W., AND LYNDON L. HARGRAVE
1931   Recently Dated Pueblo Ruins in Arizona. *Smithsonian Miscellaneous Collections* 81(11): 1–73. Washington: Smithsonian Institution.

HAWLEY, FLORENCE M., AND FRED G. HAWLEY
1938   Classification of Black Pottery Pigments and Paint Areas. *University of New Mexico Bulletin* 321, *Anthropological Series* 2(4): 3–14. Albuquerque: University of New Mexico.

HAWLEY, FRED G.
1938   The Chemical Analysis of Prehistoric Southwestern Glaze-Paint, with Components. *University of New Mexico Bulletin* 321, *Anthropological Series* 2(4): 15–26. Albuquerque: University of New Mexico Press.

HAYS, KELLEY ANN
1991   Ceramics. In "Homol'ovi II: Archaeology of an Ancestral Hopi Village," edited by E. Charles Adams and Kelley Ann Hays. *Anthropological Papers of the University of Arizona* 55: 23–48. Tucson: University of Arizona Press.

HEGMON, MICHELLE, WINSTON HURST, AND JAMES R. ALLISON
1995   Production for Local Consumption and Exchange: Comparisons of Early Red and White Ware Ceramics in the San Juan Region. In *Ceramic Production in the American Southwest*, edited by Barbara J. Mills and Patricia L. Crown, pp. 30–62. Tucson: University of Arizona Press.

HILL, JAMES N.
1970   Broken K Pueblo: Prehistoric Social Organization in the American Southwest. *Anthropological Papers of the University of Arizona* 18. Tucson: University of Arizona Press.

HINKES, MADELINE J.
1983   *Skeletal Evidence of Stress in Subadults: Trying to Come of Age at Grasshopper Pueblo.* Doctoral dissertation, University of Arizona, Tucson. Ann Arbor: University Microfilms.

HODGES, HENRY W.
1981   *Artifacts: An Introduction to Early Materials and Technology.* Originally published in 1964 (London: John Baker). Reprinted, New Jersey: Humanities Press, and London: John Baker.

HOLBROOK, SALLY J.
1982a   The Prehistoric Local Environment of Grasshopper Pueblo. *Journal of Field Archaeology* 9(2): 207–215.
1982b   Prehistoric Environmental Reconstruction by Mammalian Microfaunal Analysis, Grasshopper Pueblo. In "Multidisciplinary Research at Grasshopper Pueblo, Arizona," edited by William A. Longacre, Sally J. Holbrook, and Michael W. Graves. *Anthropological Papers of the University of Arizona* 40: 73–86. Tucson: University of Arizona Press.
1983   Paleoecology of Grasshopper Pueblo, Arizona. *National Geographic Research Reports, 1974 Projects.* Washington: National Geographic Society.

HOLBROOK, SALLY J., AND MICHAEL W. GRAVES
1982   Modern Environment of the Grasshopper Region. In "Multidisciplinary Research at Grasshopper Pueblo, Arizona," edited by William A. Longacre, Sally J. Holbrook, and Michael W. Graves. *Anthropological Papers of the University of Arizona* 40: 5–11. Tucson: University of Arizona Press.

HOUGH, WALTER
1920   Archaeological Excavations in Arizona. *Smithsonian Miscellaneous Collections* 72(1): 6–64. Washington: Smithsonian Institution.
1930   Exploration of Ruins in the White Mountain Apache Indian Reservation, Arizona. *Proceedings of the U.S. National Museum* 78(2856): 1–21. Washington.

JARVIS, K. E., ALAN L. GRAY, AND R. S. HOUK
1992   *Handbook of Inductively-coupled Plasma Mass Spectrometry.* New York: Chapman and Hall.

JOHNSON, ALFRED E.
1965   The Development of Western Pueblo Culture. MS, Doctoral dissertation, University of Arizona, Tucson.

KELSO, GERALD K.
1982   Two Pollen Profiles from Grasshopper Pueblo. In "Multidisciplinary Research at Grasshopper Pueblo, Arizona," edited by William A. Longacre, Sally J. Holbrook, and Michael W. Graves. *Anthropological Papers of the University of Arizona* 40: 106–109. Tucson: University of Arizona Press.

KENDALL, DAVID G.
1971   Seriation from Abundance Matrices. In "Mathematics in the Archaeological and Historical Sciences," edited by F. Roy Hodson, David G. Kendall, and Petre Tăutu, pp. 215–252. *Proceedings of the Anglo-Romanian Conference, Mamaia 1970.* Edinburgh: University of Edinburgh Press.

KINTIGH, KEITH W.
1985   Settlement, Subsistence, and Society in Late Zuñi Prehistory. *Anthropological Papers of the University of Arizona* 44. Tucson, University of Arizona Press.
1996   The Cibola Region in the Post-Chacoan Era. In *The Prehistoric Pueblo World, A.D. 1150–1350*, edited by Michael A. Adler, pp. 131–144. Tucson: University of Arizona Press.

KRUGER, PAUL
1971   *Principles of Activation Analysis*. New York: John Wiley.

KRUSKAL, JOSEPH B.
1971   Multidimensional Scaling in Archaeology: Time is not the Only Dimension. In "Mathematics in the Archaeological and Historical Sciences," edited by F. Roy Hodson, David G. Kendall, and Petre Tăutu, pp. 119–137. *Proceedings of the Anglo-Romanian Conference, Mamaia* 1970. Edinburgh: University of Edinburgh Press.

KRUSKAL, JOSEPH B., AND MYRON WISH
1978   *Multidimensional Scaling*. Beverly Hills, California: Sage Publications.

LIGHTFOOT, KENT G., AND ROBERTA A. JEWETT
1984   Late Prehistoric Ceramic Distributions in East-Central Arizona: An Examination of Cibola Whiteware, White Mountain Redware and Salado Redware. In "Regional Analysis of Prehistoric Ceramic Variation: Contemporary Studies of the Cibola Whitewares," edited by Alan P. Sullivan III and Jeffrey L. Hantman. *Anthropological Research Papers* 31: 36–73. Tempe: Arizona State University.

LINDSAY, ALEXANDER J., JR.
1987   Anasazi Population Movements to Southeastern Arizona. *American Archeology* 6(3): 190–198.

LIPE, WILLIAM D.
1995   The Depopulation of the Northern San Juan: Conditions in the Turbulent 1200s. In "Migration and Movement of Southwestern Peoples," edited by Catherine M. Cameron. *Journal of Anthropological Archaeology* 14(2): 143–169.

LONGACRE, WILLIAM A.
1970   Archaeology as Anthropology: A Case Study. *Anthropological Papers of the University of Arizona* 17. Tucson: University of Arizona Press.
1975   Population Dynamics at the Grasshopper Pueblo, Arizona. In "Population Studies in Archaeology and Biological Anthropology: A Symposium," edited by Alan C. Swedlund. *Society for American Archaeology Memoirs* 30. *American Antiquity* 40(2, Part 2): 71–74.
1976   Population Dynamics at the Grasshopper Pueblo, Arizona. In *Demographic Anthropology: Quantitative Approaches*, edited by Ezra B. W. Zubrow, pp. 169–184. Albuquerque: University of New Mexico Press.

LONGACRE, WILLIAM A., AND J. JEFFERSON REID
1974   The University of Arizona Archaeological Field School at Grasshopper: Eleven Years of Multi-disciplinary Research and Teaching. In "Behavioral Archaeology at the Grasshopper Ruin," edited by J. Jefferson Reid. *The Kiva* 40(1–2): 3–38.

LONGACRE, WILLIAM A., SALLY J. HOLBROOK, AND MICHAEL W. GRAVES, EDITORS
1982   Multidisciplinary Research at Grasshopper Pueblo, Arizona. *Anthropological Papers of the University of Arizona* 40. Tucson: University of Arizona Press.

LORENTZEN, LEON H.
1993   From Atlatl to Bow: The Impact of Improved Weapons on Wildlife in the Grasshopper Region. MS, Master's report, Department of Anthropology, University of Arizona, Tucson.

LOWELL, JULIE C.
1991   Prehistoric Households at Turkey Creek Pueblo, Arizona. *Anthropological Papers of the University of Arizona* 54. Tucson: University of Arizona Press.

MARTIN, PAUL SIDNEY, WILLIAM A. LONGACRE, AND JAMES N. HILL
1967   Chapters in the Prehistory of Eastern Arizona, III. *Fieldiana: Anthropology* 57. Chicago: Natural History Museum.

MARTIN, PAUL SIDNEY, JOHN B. RINALDO, AND WILLIAM A. LONGACRE
1961   Mineral Creek Site and Hooper Ranch Pueblo, Eastern Arizona. *Fieldiana: Anthropology* 52. Chicago: Natural History Museum.

MARTIN, PAUL SIDNEY, JOHN B. RINALDO, WILLIAM A. LONGACRE, LESLIE G. FREEMAN, JR., JAMES A. BROWN, RICHARD H. HEVLY, AND M. E. COOLEY
1964   Chapters in the Prehistory of Eastern Arizona, II. *Fieldiana: Anthropology* 55. Chicago: Natural History Museum.

MAUER, MICHAEL D.
1970   Cibecue Polychrome: A Fourteenth Century Ceramic Type from East-Central Arizona. MS, Master's thesis, Department of Anthropology, University of Arizona, Tucson.

MAYRO, LINDA L., STEPHANIE M. WHITTLESEY, AND J. JEFFERSON REID
1976   Observations on the Salado Presence at Grasshopper Pueblo. *The Kiva* 42(1): 85–94.

McGUIRE, RANDALL H., E. CHARLES ADAMS, BEN A. NELSON, AND KATHERINE A. SPIELMANN
1994   Drawing the Southwest to Scale: Perspectives on Macroregional Relations. In *Themes in Southwestern Prehistory*, edited by George J.

Gumerman, pp. 239–265. Advanced Seminar Series. Santa Fe: School of American Research Press.

MCKUSICK, CHARMION P.
1982   Avifauna from Grasshopper Pueblo. In "Multidisciplinary Research at Grasshopper Pueblo, Arizona," edited by William A. Longacre, Sally J. Holbrook, and Michael W. Graves. *Anthropological Papers of the University of Arizona* 40: 87–96. Tucson: University of Arizona Press.

MILLS, BARBARA J.
In press   Migration and Pueblo IV Community Reorganization in the Silver Creek Area, East-Central Arizona. In "Migration and Reorganization: The Pueblo IV Period in the American Southwest," edited by Katherine A. Spielmann. *Anthropological Research Papers* 50. Tempe: Arizona State University.

MOHOLY-NAGY, HATTULA, FRANK ASARO,
AND FRED H. STROSS
1984   Tikal Obsidian: Sources and Typology. *American Antiquity* 47(1): 104–117.

MONTGOMERY, BARBARA K.
1992   *Understanding the Formation of the Archaeological Record: Ceramic Variability at Chodistaas Pueblo, Arizona.* Doctoral dissertation, University of Arizona, Tucson. Ann Arbor: University Microfilms.
1993   Ceramic Analysis as a Tool for Discovering Processes of Pueblo Abandonment. In *Abandonment of Settlements and Regions: Ethnoarchaeological and Archaeological Approaches*, edited by Catherine M. Cameron and Steve A. Tomka, pp. 157–164. Cambridge: Cambridge University Press.

MONTGOMERY, BARBARA K., AND J. JEFFERSON REID
1990   An Instance of Rapid Ceramic Change in the American Southwest. *American Antiquity* 55(1): 88–97.
1994   The Brown and the Gray: People, Pots, and Population Movement in East-Central Arizona. Paper presented at the 59th Annual Meeting of the Society for American Archaeology, Anaheim.

MOORE, RICHARD T.
1968   Mineral Deposits of the Fort Apache Indian Reservation. *Arizona Bureau of Mines Bulletin* 177. Tucson: University of Arizona.

MUNSELL COLOR COMPANY
1975   *Munsell Soil Color Charts.* Baltimore: Munsell Color Company.

NEFF, HECTOR, RONALD L. BISHOP,
AND EDWARD V. SAYRE
1988   A Simulation Approach to the Problem of Tempering in Compositional Studies of Archaeological Ceramics. *Journal of Archaeological Science* 15(2): 159–172.
1989   More Observations on the Problem of Tempering in Compositional Studies of Archaeological Ceramics. *Journal of Archaeological Science* 16(1): 57–69.

NEFF, HECTOR, MICHAEL D. GLASCOCK, RONALD L.
BISHOP, AND M. JAMES BLACKMAN
1996   An Assessment of the Acid-extraction Approach to Compositional Characterization of Archaeological Ceramics. *American Antiquity* 61(2): 389–404.

NELSON, GLENN C.
1984   *Ceramics: A Potter's Handbook.* 5th Edition. New York: CBS College Publishers.

OLSEN, JOHN W.
1980   *A Zooarchaeological Analysis of Vertebrate Faunal Remains from the Grasshopper Pueblo, Arizona.* Doctoral dissertation, University of California, Berkeley. Ann Arbor: University Microfilms.
1982   Prehistoric Environmental Reconstruction by Vertebrate Faunal Analysis, Grasshopper Pueblo. In "Multidisciplinary Research at Grasshopper Pueblo, Arizona," edited by William A. Longacre, Sally J. Holbrook, and Michael W. Graves. *Anthropological Papers of the University of Arizona* 40: 63–72. Tucson: University of Arizona Press.
1990   Vertebrate Faunal Remains from Grasshopper Pueblo, Arizona. *Museum of Anthropology Anthropological Papers* 83. Ann Arbor: University of Michigan.

OLSEN, STANLEY J.
1968   Canid Remains from Grasshopper Ruin. *The Kiva* 34(1): 33–40.
1982   Water Resources and Aquatic Fauna at Grasshopper Pueblo. In "Multidisciplinary Research at Grasshopper Pueblo, Arizona," edited by William A. Longacre, Sally J. Holbrook, and Michael W. Graves. *Anthropological Papers of the University of Arizona* 40: 61–62. Tucson: University of Arizona Press.

OLSEN, STANELY J., AND JOHN W. OLSEN
1970   A Preliminary Report on the Fish and Herpetofauna of Grasshopper Ruin. *The Kiva* 36(2): 40–43.
1974   The Macaws of Grasshopper Ruin. In "Behavioral Archaeology at the Grasshopper Ruin," edited by J. Jefferson Reid. *The Kiva* 40(1–2): 67–70.

PARRY, SUSAN J.
1991   *Activation Spectrometry in Chemical Analysis.* New York: John Wiley and Sons.

PEIRCE, H. WESLEY
1985   Arizona's Backbone: The Transition Zone. *Fieldnotes of the Arizona Bureau of Geology and Mineral Technology* 15(3): 1–6.

PIRES-FERREIRA, JANE W., AND KENT V. FLANNERY
1976   Ethnographic Models for Formative Exchange. In *The Early Mesoamerica Village*, edited by Kent V. Flannery, pp. 286–292. New York: Academic Press.

PLOG, STEPHEN
1989   The Sociopolitics of Exchange (and Archaeological Research) in the Northern Southwest. In *The Sociopolitical Structure of Prehistoric Southwestern Societies*, edited by Steadman Upham, Kent G. Lightfoot, and Roberta Jewett, pp. 129–148. Boulder: Westview Press.

PRICE, T. DOUGLAS, CLARK M. JOHNSON, JOSEPH A. EZZO, JONATHON ERICSON, AND JAMES H. BURTON
1994   Residential Mobility in the Prehistoric Southwest United States: A Preliminary Study Using Strontium Isotope Analysis. *Journal of Archaeological Science* 21(3): 315–330.

RANDS, ROBERT L., AND RONALD L. BISHOP
1980   Resource Procurement Zones and Patterns of Ceramic Exchange in the Palenque Region, Mexico. In "Models and Methods in Regional Exchange," edited by Robert E. Fry. *Society for American Archaeology Papers* 1: 19–46.

RATHJE, WILLIAM L.
1972   Praise the Gods and Pass the Metates: A Hypothesis of the Development of Lowland Rainforest Civilization. In *Contemporary Archaeology: A Guide to Theory and Contributions*, edited by Mark P. Leone, pp. 365–392. Carbondale: Southern Illinois University Press.

REID, J. JEFFERSON
1973   *Growth and Response to Stress at Grasshopper Pueblo, Arizona.* Doctoral dissertation, University of Arizona, Tucson. Ann Arbor: University Microfilms.
1974   [Editor] Behavioral Archaeology at the Grasshopper Ruin. *The Kiva* 40(1–2).
1984   Implications of Mogollon Settlement Variability in Grasshopper and Adjacent Regions. In "Recent Research in Mogollon Archaeology," edited by Steadman Upham, Fred Plog, David G. Batcho, and Barbara E. Kauffman. *New Mexico State University Occasional Papers* 10: 59–67. Las Cruces: New Mexico State University.
1985   Measuring Social Complexity in the American Southwest. In *Status, Structure, and Stratification: Current Archaeological Reconstructions*, edited by Marc Thompson, Maria T. Garcia, and Françoise Kense, pp. 167–173. Calgary: University of Alberta Press.

1989   A Grasshopper Perspective on the Mogollon of the Arizona Mountains. In *Dynamics of Southwest Prehistory*, edited by Linda S. Cordell and George J. Gumerman, pp. 65–97. Washington: Smithsonian Institution Press.

REID, J. JEFFERSON, AND IZUMI SHIMADA
1982   Pueblo Growth at Grasshopper: Methods and Models. In "Multidisciplinary Research at Grasshopper Pueblo, Arizona," edited by William A. Longacre, Sally J. Holbrook, and Michael W. Graves. *Anthropological Papers of the University of Arizona* 40: 12–18. Tucson: University of Arizona Press.

REID, J. JEFFERSON, AND STEPHANIE M. WHITTLESEY
1982   Households at Grasshopper Pueblo. *American Behavioral Scientist* 25(6): 687–703.
1990   The Complicated and the Complex: Observations on the Archaeological Record of Large Pueblos. In *Perspectives on Southwestern Prehistory*, edited by Paul E. Minnis and Charles L. Redman, pp. 184–195. Boulder: Westview Press.

REID, J. JEFFERSON, JOHN R. WELCH, BARBARA K. MONTGOMERY, AND M. NIEVES ZEDEÑO
1996   A Demographic Overview of the Late Pueblo III Period in the Mountains of East-central Arizona. In *The Prehistoric Pueblo World, A.D. 1150–1350*, edited by Michael A. Adler, pp. 73–85. Tucson: University of Arizona Press.

RICE, PRUDENCE M.
1987   *Pottery Analysis: A Sourcebook.* Chicago: University of Chicago Press.

RICHARDS, THEODORE W.
1895   The Composition of Athenian Pottery. *American Chemical Journal* 17(3): 152–154.

RIES, HEINRICH
1927   *Clays, Their Occurrence, Properties, and Uses, with Special Reference to Those of the United States of Canada.* 3rd Edition. New York: John Wiley.

RIGGS, CHARLES R., JR.
1994   Dating Construction Events at Grasshopper Pueblo: New Techniques for Architectural Analysis. MS, Master's thesis, Department of Anthropology, University of Arizona, Tucson.

ROCK, JAMES. T.
1974   The Use of Social Models in Archaeological Interpretation. In "Behavioral Archaeology at the Grasshopper Ruin," edited by J. Jefferson Reid. *The Kiva* 40(1–2): 81–91.

ROHN, ARTHUR H.
1989   Northern San Juan Prehistory. In *Dynamics of Southwest Prehistory*, edited by Linda S. Cordell and George J. Gumerman, pp. 149–177. Washington: Smithsonian Institution Press.

RONEY, JOHN R.
1995 Mesa Verdean Manifestations of the San Juan River. In "Migration and the Movement of Southwestern Peoples," edited by Catherine M. Cameron. *Journal of Anthropological Archaeology* 14(2): 171–183.

RYE, OWEN
1981 Pottery Technology: Principles and Reconstruction. *Manuals on Archaeology* 4. Washington: Taraxacum Press.

SAYRE, EDWARD V.
1975 Brookhaven Procedures for Statistical Analyses of Multivariate Archaeometric Data. Unpublished Brookhaven National Laboratory Report BNL–23128. Brookhaven National Laboratory, New York.

SCHNEIDER, GERWULF, BETTINA HOFFMANN, AND ERWIN WIRZ
1979 Significance and Dependability of Reference Groups for Chemical Determinations of Provenance of Ceramic Artifacts. In *Proceedings of the 18th International Symposium on Archaeometry and Archaeological Prospection*, pp. 269–285. Archäo-Physika 10. Bonn: Rheinisches Landesmuseum.

SHEPARD, ANNA O.
1936 The Technology of Pecos Pottery. In "The Pottery of Pecos," Vol. 2, by Alfred V. Kidder and Anna O. Shepard, pp. 389–587. *Papers of the Phillips Academy Southwestern Expedition* 7. New Haven: Yale University Press.

1939 Technology of La Plata Pottery. In "Archaeological Studies in the La Plata District, Southwestern Colorado and Northwestern New Mexico," by Earl H. Morris, pp. 249–287. *Carnegie Institution of Washington Publication* 519. Washington.

1942 Rio Grande Glaze Paint Ware: A Study Illustrating the Place of Ceramic Technological Analysis in Archaeological Research. *Contributions to American Anthropology and History* 7(39). *Carnegie Institution of Washington Publication* 528. Washington.

1965 Rio Grande Glaze-Paint Pottery: A Test of Petrographic Analysis. In "Ceramics and Man," edited by Frederick R. Matson, pp. 62–87. *Viking Fund Publications in Anthropology* 41. New York: Wenner-Gren Foundation for Anthropological Research.

1985 Ceramics for the Archaeologist. *Carnegie Institution of Washington Publication* 609. Washington. (12th printing.)

SHIPMAN, JEFFREY H.
1982 *Biological Relationships Among Prehistoric Western Pueblo Indian Groups Based on Metric and Disease Traits of the Skeleton*. Doctoral dissertation, University of Arizona, Tucson. Ann Arbor: University Microfilms.

SMITH, WATSON
1971 Painted Ceramics of the Western Mound at Awatovi. *Papers of the Peabody Museum of American Archaeology and Ethnology* 39(1). Cambridge: Harvard University.

SPIELMANN, KATHERINE A., EDITOR
In press Migration and Reorganization: The Pueblo IV Period in the American Southwest. *Anthropological Research Papers* 50. Tempe: Arizona State University.

SPIER, LESLIE
1918 Ruins in the White Mountains, Arizona. *Museum of Natural History Anthropological Paper* 18(5): 363–387. Washington.

SULLIVAN, ALAN P., III
1980 *Prehistoric Settlement Variability in the Grasshopper Area, East-Central Arizona*. Doctoral dissertation, University of Arizona, Tucson. Ann Arbor: University Microfilms.

1988 Prehistoric Southwestern Ceramic Manufacture: Limitations of Current Evidence. *American Antiquity* 53(1): 23–35.

SUMNER, DALE R.
1984 *Size, Shape, and Bone Mineral Content in the Human Femur in Growth and Aging*. Doctoral dissertation, University of Arizona, Tucson. Ann Arbor: University Microfilms.

THOMPSON, MICHAEL, AND J. NICHOLAS WALSH
1989 *Handbook of Inductively-coupled Plasma Spectrometry*. 2nd ed. New York: Chapman and Hall.

THOMPSON, RAYMOND H., AND WILLIAM A. LONGACRE
1966 The University of Arizona Archaeological Field School at Grasshopper, East Central Arizona. *The Kiva* 31(4): 255–275.

TOLL, H. WOLCOTT
1991 Material Distributions and Exchange in the Chaco System. In *Chaco and Hohokam: Prehistoric Systems in the American Southwest*, edited by Patricia L. Crown and W. James Judge, pp. 77–107. Santa Fe: School of American Research Press.

TRIADAN, DANIELA
1989 Defining Local Ceramic Production at Grasshopper Pueblo, Arizona. MS, Master's thesis, Lateinamerikainstitut, Freie Universität Berlin, Germany. (On file in the Arizona State Museum Library, University of Arizona, Tucson.)

1994 *White Mountain Redware: Expensive Trade Goods or Local Commodity? A Study of the Production, Distribution and Function of White Mountain Redware During the 14th Century in*

TRIADAN, DANIELA (*continued*)
    the Grasshopper Region, East-central Arizona.
    Doctoral dissertation, Freie Universität Berlin,
    Germany. Ann Arbor: University Microfilms.

TUGGLE, H. DAVID
1970   *Prehistoric Community Relationships in East-central Arizona.* Doctoral dissertation, University of Arizona, Tucson. Ann Arbor: University Microfilms.

UPHAM, STEADMAN
1982   *Polities and Power: An Economic and Political History of the Western Pueblo.* New York: Academic Press.

UPHAM, STEADMAN, KENT G. LIGHTFOOT, AND GARY M. FEINMAN
1981   Explaining Socially Determined Ceramic Distribution in the Prehistoric Plateau Southwest. *American Antiquity* 46(4): 822–833.

VAN KEUREN, SCOTT
1994   Design Structure Variation in Cibola White Ware Vessels from Grasshopper and Chodistaas Pueblos, Arizona. MS, Master's thesis, Department of Anthropology, University of Arizona, Tucson.

WEIGAND, PHIL C., GARMON HARBOTTLE, AND EDWARD V. SAYRE
1977   Turquoise Sources and Source Analysis: Mesoamerica and the Southwestern U.S.A. In *Exchange Systems in Prehistory*, edited by Timothy K. Earle and Jonathon E. Ericson, pp. 15–34. New York: Academic Press.

WELCH, JOHN R.
1991   From Horticulture to Agriculture in the Late Prehistory of the Grasshopper Region, Arizona. In *Mogollon V*, edited by Patrick H. Beckett, pp. 75–92. Las Cruces: COAS Publishing Co.

WENDORF, FRED
1950   A Report on the Excavation of a Small Ruin Near Point of Pines, East Central Arizona. *University of Arizona Bulletin* 21(3), *Social Science Bulletin* 19. Tucson: University of Arizona.

WHITTAKER, JOHN C.
1984   *Arrowheads and Artisans: Stone Tool Manufacture and Individual Variation at Grasshopper Pueblo.* Doctoral dissertation, University of Arizona, Tucson. Ann Arbor: University Microfilms.
1986   Projectile Points and the Question of Specialization at Grasshopper Pueblo, Arizona. In "Mogollon Variability," edited by Charlotte Benson and Steadman Upham. *New Mexico State University Occasional Papers* 15: 121–

140. Las Cruces: New Mexico State University.
1987   Individual Variation as an Approach to Economic Organization: Projectile Points at Grasshopper Pueblo, Arizona. *Journal of Field Archaeology* 14(4): 465–479.

WHITTLESEY, STEPHANIE M.
1974   Identification of Imported Ceramics Through Functional Analysis of Attributes. In "Behavioral Archaeology at the Grasshopper Ruin," edited by J. Jefferson Reid. *The Kiva* 40(1–2): 101–112.
1978   *Status and Death at Grasshopper Pueblo: Experiments Toward an Archaeological Theory of Correlates.* Doctoral dissertation, University of Arizona, Tucson. Ann Arbor: University Microfilms.
1984   Uses and Abuses of Mogollon Mortuary Data. In "Recent Research in Mogollon Archaeology," edited by Steadman Upham, Fred Plog, David G. Batcho, and Barbara E. Kauffman. *New Mexico State University Occasional Papers* 10: 276–284. Las Cruces: New Mexico State University.

ZEDEÑO, M. NIEVES
1991   *Refining Inferences of Ceramic Circulation: A Stylistic, Technological, and Compositional Analysis of Whole Vessels from Chodistaas, Arizona.* Doctoral dissertation, Southern Methodist University, Dallas. Ann Arbor: University Microfilms.
1994a   Sourcing Prehistoric Ceramics at Chodistaas Pueblo, Arizona: The Circulation of People and Pots in the Grasshopper Region. *Anthropological Papers of the University of Arizona* 58. Tucson: University of Arizona Press.
1994b   A Return to the Gift: Exploring Prehistoric Reciprocity in the Northern Southwest. Paper presented at the 59th Annual Meeting of the Society for American Archaeology, Anaheim.
1995   The Role of Population Movement and Technology Transfer in the Manufacture of Prehistoric Southwestern Ceramics. In *Ceramic Production in the American Southwest*, edited by Barbara J. Mills and Patricia L. Crown, pp. 115–141. Tucson: University of Arizona Press.

ZEDEÑO, M. NIEVES, AND DANIELA TRIADAN
In press   The Material Correlates of Ceramic Circulation: Ceramic Evidence for Community Reorganization and Change in East-Central Arizona. In *Proceedings of the 8th Mogollon Conference*, edited by David Carmichael. El Paso: University of Texas.

Index

Abandonment
  of Bailey Ruin, 104
  of Grasshopper Pueblo, 13
  of Grasshopper region, 13
  of northern Southwest, 5, 94, 104
  of Pinedale Ruin, 104
  See also Migrations; Population
    aggregation
Aggregation. *See* Population
  aggregation
Alliance systems (elite), controlling
  ceramic distribution, 2, 3, 5, 105,
  106, 108. *See also* Sociopolitical
    organization
Aluminum (Al), 28, 31, 33, 35, 41,
  43, 44, 45, 51
Anasazi, lambdoidal head deformation
  by, 81
Antimony (Sb), 28, 31
Archaeological site locations, 4, 14,
  26, 96, 99, 100, 102, 103
Archaeological sites (Arizona State
  Museum Site Survey)
  AZ P:13:2, 98, 102, 123
  AZ P:14:1. *See* Grasshopper Pueblo
  AZ P:14:8. *See* Grasshopper Springs
    site
  AZ P:14:12. *See* Hilltop Pueblo
  AZ P:14:13. *See* Brush Mountain
    Pueblo
  AZ P:14:14. *See* Red Rock House
  AZ P:14:15. *See* Oak Creek Pueblo
  AZ P:14:24. *See* Chodistaas Pueblo
  AZ P:14:25. *See* Red Canyon Tank
    Pueblo
  AZ P:14:71, 98
  AZ P:14:188: 10
  AZ P:14:197, 10
  AZ P:14:281, 96–101, 119
  AZ V:2:1. *See* Canyon Creek Cliff
    Dwelling
  AZ V:2:3. *See* Spotted Mountain
    Pueblo
  AZ V:2:5. *See* Hole Canyon Cliff
    Dwelling
  AZ V:2:7. *See* Ruin's Tank Pueblo
  AZ V:2:12, 10

AZ V:2:13. *See* Blue House
  Mountain Pueblo
AZ V:2:23, 98, 122
AZ V:2:49. *See* Canyon Butte
  Pueblo
AZ V:2:62, 96–101, 119
AZ V:2:79. *See* Double Springs
  Cliff Dwelling
AZ V:2:83, 96–101, 122–123
AZ V:2:87, 98, 103, 122
See also Bailey Ruin; Banning Wash
  Pueblo; Cibecue Pueblo; Fourmile
  Ruin; Kinishba Ruin; Pinedale
  Ruin; Point of Pines site; Q-Ranch
  site; Showlow Ruin; Tundastusa
  site
Archaeological sites, Grasshopper
  Field School survey
  GFS 81–79, 98, 122
  GFS 82–1. *See* Spring Creek Pueblo
  GFS 85–3. *See* Cedar Creek Pueblo
  GFS 86–3. *See* Black Mountain
    Pueblo
  GFS 88–9. *See* Carrizo Creek
    Pueblo
  GFS 88–10. *See* Blue Spring Pueblo
  GFS 89–6. *See* Sanrace Cliff
    Dwelling
Arsenic (As), 28, 31
Atomic absorption, in ceramic analysis,
  17

Bailey Ruin
  abandonment of, 104
  analysis of ceramics from, 108
  ceramic assemblage at, 104
  excavations at, 104
Banning Wash Pueblo, sherd samples
  from, 27, 41, 48, 98, 103, 120
Barium (Ba), 28, 31, 41
Basin-and-Range province, 7
Bear Butte, 19
Bergfeld, Deborah, 46
Black Mountain Pueblo (GFS 86–3)
  sherd samples from, 27, 41, 96–104,
  122

Black-on-white ceramics
  frequencies of, 58, 60, 61–64, 98
  distribution on room floors, 81, 87
  in burials, 65, 69, 71, 76
  in Pueblo III assemblages, 105
  in Pueblo IV assemblages, 105
  replaced by black-on-red and
    polychrome, 13
Blue House Mountain, 19
Blue House Mountain Pueblo
  (AZ V:2:13 ASM)
  sherd samples from, 27, 41, 96–104,
  119
Blue Spring Pueblo (GFS 88–10)
  sherd samples from, 27, 41, 120
Bonito Prairie physiographic
  subprovince, 18, 19
bowls, sizes of, 92–93, 94. *See also*
  "Nestability"
Brown wares
  in ceramic assemblages, 13
  local production of, 5, 35, 38, 39,
    40–46
  See also Utilitarian wares
Brush Mountain Pueblo
  (AZ P:14:13 ASM)
  sherd samples from, 27, 41, 96–104,
  121
Bulk chemical analyses, 17, 40, 46
Burials. *See* Grasshopper Pueblo,
  burials at
Burton, James H., 40

Calcium (Ca), 28, 31, 35, 41
Canyon Butte, source clays from, 22
Canyon Butte Pueblo
  (AZ V:2:49 ASM)
  sherd samples from, 27, 41, 96–104,
  122
Canyon Creek, sands from, 47
Canyon Creek Cliff Dwelling
  (AZ V:2:1 ASM)
  establishment of, 13
  sherd samples from, 27, 41, 96–104,
  121
Canyon Creek–Salt River Canyon
  physiographic subprovince, 18–19

Abstract

In the American Southwest, where ceramics are the focus of extensive archaeological research, the evaluation of provenance has proven indispensable for addressing anthropological problems of long-standing relevance, such as ethnic affiliation, population movement, craft specialization, trade and exchange, and ritual. The application of multiple analytical techniques to ceramic vessels from well-dated and controlled contexts is paramount for the development of middle-range principles linking archaeological variability to past behavior encoded in ceramic remains.

This monograph presents a large-scale compositional sourcing study of White Mountain Red Ware, a painted pottery that was widely distributed in the northern Southwest during the thirteenth and fourteenth centuries A.D. Ceramic assemblages from Grasshopper Pueblo and contemporary sites in east-central Arizona supplied the body of data for this research. They were complemented by a systematic raw material survey. These assemblages provided the basis to (1) define the source or sources of fourteenth-century White Mountain Red Ware, (2) investigate the organization of ceramic production and consumption within a large, aggregated late prehistoric community, and (3) evaluate the mechanisms of its circulation.

The analyses entailed chemical characterization and petrography on 106 reconstructible vessels from Grasshopper Pueblo, on more than 200 sherds from contemporary sites in the surrounding regions, and on sampled raw materials. In addition, physical properties of source clays and potential tempering agents were tested to assess the utility of the available raw materials for making pottery.

These analyses established multiple production zones for White Mountain Red Ware during Pueblo IV times, including one in the Grasshopper region, as well as compositional reference groups that provide a basis for future compositional analyses of decorated ceramics in a broader regional context. The compositional data combined with settlement information and a thorough analysis of archaeological contexts demonstrate that White Mountain Red Ware vessels were readily accessible and widely used household goods and that migration and subsequent local production in the destination areas were important factors for their wide distribution during the fourteenth century. The results of this study provide new insights into the organization of ceramic production and distribution in the northern Southwest and into the processes of social reorganization that took place during the A.D. 1300s and 1400s.

Resumen

En el suroeste norteamericano, donde la cerámica es foco de investigación arqueológica extensiva, la evaluación de procedencia es indispensable para resolver problemas antropológicos relevantes, tales como afiliación étnica, migración, especialización productiva, intercambio, y ritual. La aplicación de múltiples técnicas analíticas a vasijas cerámicas de fecha y contexto conocidos es crucial para el desarrollo de principios de rango medio que conectan la variabilidad arqueológica con la conducta pasada codificada en los restos cerámicos.

Esta monografía presenta un estudio a gran escala de composición y procedencia de la Cerámica Roja White Mountain, una vajilla pintada distribuida ampliamente en el suroeste septentrional durante los siglos XIII y XIV de nuestra era. Los conjuntos cerámicos de Grasshopper Pueblo y otros sitios contemporáneos en Arizona centro-este constituyeron el cuerpo de datos para esta investigación. Estos datos se complementaron con una prospección sistemática de materia prima. Los conjuntos cerámicos proveyeron una base para (1) definir la procedencia de Cerámica Roja White Mountain del siglo XIV, (2) investigar la organización de producción y consumo de esta cerámica en una extensa comunidad agregada, y (3) evaluar los mecanismos de su circulación.

El análisis envolvió la caracterización química y petrográfica de 106 vasijas reconstruibles recuperadas en Grasshopper Pueblo, más de 200 tiestos provenientes de sitios contemporáneos en las regiones vecinas, y muestras de materia prima. Además, las propiedades físicas de las arcillas y materiales antiplásticos se pusieron a prueba para investigar el potencial de la materia prima disponible para producir cerámica.

Estos análisis establecieron múltiples zonas de producción de Cerámica Roja White Mountain durante el período Pueblo IV, incluyendo una zona en la región de Grasshopper, así como grupos químicos de referencia que constituyen una base para estudios futuros en un contexto regional más amplio. Los datos de composición, junto con información detallada sobre asentamiento y contextos arqueológicos, demuestran que las vasijas de Cerámica Roja White Mountain fueron utensillos domésticos de acceso general y que la migración y subsiguiente producción local en las áreas de destino fueron factores importantes para su amplia distribución durante el siglo XIV. Los resultados de este estudio proveen nueva información sobre la organización de producción y distribución cerámica en el suroeste septentrional y sobre los procesos de reorganización social occuridos durante 1300 y 1400 d.C.

ANTHROPOLOGICAL PAPERS OF THE UNIVERSITY OF ARIZONA

Anthropological Papers listed as O.P., D are available as Docutech reproductions (high quality xerox) printed on demand. They are tape or spiral bound and nonreturnable.

THE UNIVERSITY OF ARIZONA PRESS

1230 North Park Avenue, Tucson, Arizona 85719